THE *Kellogg's*™ COOKBOOK

200 CLASSIC RECIPES FOR TODAY'S KITCHEN

THE *Kellogg's*™ COOKBOOK

Kellogg Kitchens™
Edited by Judith Choate

Food Photography by Ben Fink

BULFINCH PRESS
NEW YORK . BOSTON

Copyright © 2006 by Kellogg NA Co.
Food photography copyright © 2006 by Ben Fink

All trademarks, images of Kellogg products and characters are used under license and with permission of the Kellogg North America Co. © 2006 Kellogg NA Co.

We gratefully acknowledge the following for permission to reprint their recipes: "Crunchy Baked Chicken" by Jean-Georges Vongerichten; "Pan-Roasted Crisp Sea Bass" by '21' Club; "Shrimp with Black Pepper–Seasoned CORN POPS" by David Burke; "Vanilla-Scented Baked Winter Squash and Apples" by Charlie Palmer; "KELLOGG'S Summer Strawberry Delight" by John Doherty and Charlie Romano; "Karen's Sundae Cups" by Andrew Dornenburg; and "Milk Chocolate RICE KRISPIES Crunchies" by Kate Zuckerman.

Bulfinch Press
Time Warner Book Group
1271 Avenue of the Americas, New York, NY 10020
Visit our Web site at www.bulfinchpress.com

First Edition: February 2006

Library of Congress Cataloging-in-Publication Data

   The Kellogg's cookbook : 200 classic recipes for today's kitchen / Kellogg Kitchens ;
edited by Judith Choate.
     p. cm.
  ISBN 0-8212-5737-4 (hardcover)
   1. Cookery, American. 2. Brand name products. 3. Kellogg Company. I. Choate, Judith. II. Title.

TX715.K34 2005
641.5973—dc22   2005021626

Design by Joel Avirom, Jason Snyder, and Meghan Day Healey

PRINTED IN CHINA

eplace, but she's letting
Small boy is
g up that milk
ose golden flakes.
od to him—they
od in his mouth—
in. They taste
ind of flavor
ng up that spoon.
Flakes

years,
little people
and big people.

When Norman Rockwell painted this small boy for us, this
was the spirit he was trying to capture. Maybe it will give you
the idea to check up on your supply of Kellogg's Corn Flakes.

CONTENTS

A TRIP DOWN MEMORY LANE: 100 YEARS OF THE KELLOGG COMPANY

The seeds for the development of Kellogg Company, the company that would become the world's leading producer of ready-to-eat cereals, were sprouted in the pioneering notion of good health being relative to good eating habits. The revolution began in the relationship of two brothers, Dr. John Harvey Kellogg and Will Keith Kellogg, in the latter part of the nineteenth century at the Battle Creek Sanitarium in Battle Creek, Michigan. Dr. Kellogg was the physician-in-chief, and his much younger brother W. K. was his general factotum, running the business end of the internationally known Seventh-Day Adventist hospital and health-related spa. The San (as it was known) combined basic Adventist tenets, focusing on simple natural restorative methods and the use of hydrotherapy and vegetarianism for healing, with Dr. Kellogg's interest in the most modern achievements in diagnostic medicine.

When the first precooked flaked cereal became part of the San diet in 1894, the Kellogg brothers had no inkling that they were in the process of inventing a whole new style of breakfast food. They were simply looking for a substitute for bread that would be easier for their patients to digest. Up to this point at the San, precooked cereal-like foods were limited to "granula," leftover bread that had been oven dried and ground, and zwieback, a raised bread that was sliced and oven

Many recipes of lasting appeal have been developed in the KELLOGG KITCHENS.

dried. Both of these foods came from Dr. Kellogg's investigation of the effect of oven heat on starchy foods. He knew that when heat acted with the diastase in the cereal grain, the starch would be converted to dextrin. The conversion of raw starch into dextrin is the first step in human digestion, and therefore when the oven heat dextrinized a starchy food, this natural predigestion also occurred.

Granula was not fully dextrinized, and zwieback was extremely hard and difficult to chew. In fact, it was said that so many patients broke their false teeth on the hard biscuits and demanded restitution that it became a financial necessity to find a healthful alternative. Dr. Kellogg eventually developed a cereal-like food that he called Granola, made from a mix of wheat, oatmeal, and cornmeal that was formed into biscuits, baked until completely dextrinized, and then ground.

Although all of the food for the San was prepared as an important part of the patients' regimen, none of it was available to the general public, or even to the patients once they departed care. The demand for Sanitarium-made foods grew year by year, and eventually the Sanitas Food Company was formed. As work began in the new company, the idea for a more digestible cereal came through a patient who brought a shredded wheat food to the attention of Dr. Kellogg. When the inventor proved to be less than forthcoming with his innovative ideas, the Kellogg brothers worked to develop their own cereal food.

Experimenting late at night after his long hours at the Sanitarium, W. K. tried boiling different quantities of wheat for different periods of time, and then together the two brothers tried rolling the different wheats on the same rollers that were used to make Granola.

Dr. Kellogg fed the wheat into the hopper at the top of the rollers, while W. K. got down underneath the rolls and hand-scraped the clammy dough off the rolls with a chisel. This went on for a few nights with unacceptable results. In frustration, W. K. suggested that the scraping might be better done with a wide knife. He hooked two well-worn knives up so that they pressed against the rollers, thereby automatically scraping off the dough.

This experiment continued for many, many nights. One Thursday, W. K. boiled up a batch of wheat that he intended to process on the rollers that evening. However, work at the Sanitarium interfered, and it wasn't until Saturday night that he was able to get to his cereal project. At this point, the wheat had become a bit moldy and had thickened, but rather than waste the product the brothers decided to give it a trial run through the rollers. Unbelievably, as the moldy matter was pressed through the rollers it flew off in large, thin flakes. Unlike all other times, each little wheat berry had become one individual flake. And once baked, the flakes were crisp, despite a hint of moldiness. After months of further experimentation, W. K. learned that when the boiled wheat was allowed to rest in tin-lined bins for several hours, the moisture would equalize throughout the wheat berries, resulting in the flaking when rolled. The shorter resting period also, fortunately, eliminated the moldiness!

Kellogg developed wholesome recipes for children's camps, schools, and other institutions.

It would, however, be quite some time before these early flakes, which were quite tough and virtually tasteless, with just a bit of salt added, would even begin to resemble the light, fragrant, almost transparent flakes that we now know as KELLOGG'S CORN FLAKES. Yet they were so much better than what had been available that they quickly became immensely popular with the San population, with rapidly expanding sales.

Beginning in 1895, commercial production of the wheat flaked cereal began in a barn on the Sanitarium grounds, turning out 100,000 ten-ounce boxes by the end of that year. The cereal, which sold for 15 cents a box, was also being sold via mail order all across the United States. Corn flakes were born a few years later.

Although Dr. Kellogg had been the driving force behind the development of new foods, it was W. K.'s aggressive belief in the strength of marketing and advertising that was the deciding factor in the rapid expansion of their company. W. K. not only acted as business manager for the Sanitarium on a full-time basis, he was also managing the Sanitas Food Company, the Modern Medicine Publishing Company, *Good Health* magazine, and a half-dozen other companies that belonged to his brother. By the turn of the new century he had also taken over the experimental work in the food laboratory. Although cereal sales were primary, literally hundreds of other foods were developed under W. K.'s direction.

A consumer-friendly display introducing a new KELLOGG'S cereal, APPLE JACKS.

As one might suspect, after years of playing second fiddle to his demanding older brother, doing a great deal of the work and getting little financial remuneration and even less recognition, W. K. eventually had enough. In 1906 he parted with his brother and the Sanitarium and formed his own cereal company. On April 1, a week before his forty-sixth birthday, the Battle Creek Toasted Corn Flake Company began production.

Even before he had started his own company, W. K. Kellogg believed that cereals should be marketed not just as health food but as food that was simply good to eat. And because there was a burgeoning amount of competition, W. K. also thought there should be some distinguishing characteristic on the packaging that would indicate the quality of the unseen packaged goods. It is not clear why he chose to put his signature on the boxes, but in early 1903, while he was still at the Sanitas Company, the cereal boxes were red-inked with "Beware of imitations. None genuine without this signature, W. K. Kellogg." And when W. K. went on to form his company, this same notice would appear on his cereal boxes for many years to come.

Through the early years of the company, the growth was phenomenal, in spite of the factory's being destroyed by fire in 1907. W. K.'s determination had a new factory up and running in less than six months. Innovative sales promotions such as "Give the Grocer a Wink," which offered a free sample of cereal to every woman who winked at her grocer on Wednesday, had sales skyrocketing.

W. K. Kellogg's bold, pioneering ideas about marketing took the company through spectacular expansion. From a sign on the side of a boxcar reading "21 CAR LOADS—THE LARGEST SHIPMENT OF BREAKFAST FOOD EVER SENT TO ONE PERSON" (announcing a shipment of Toasted Corn Flakes to one food broker) to the "Fresher Than Ever Before" which heralded the new "weather proof wrap" that kept the boxed cereal crisp and flavorful, W. K. stood by everything he advertised. Kellogg was one of the first companies to use full-color magazine ads, test markets, premiums, and widespread product sampling to increase consumer awareness. Innovation in packaging also brought the products to the limelight, particularly when a waxed paper lining was used inside the box rather than the usual external wrap.

With the help of W. K.'s son, John L. Kellogg, who discovered a malting process that allowed cereal flakes to mimic the flavor of nuts, the product line rapidly expanded. Krumbles were introduced to the public in 1912, followed quickly by Bran Flakes and ALL-BRAN. The cereals were gaining attention outside the United States, and by 1924 Kellogg had plants in Canada and Australia and the introduction of RICE KRISPIES was just around the corner.

One of the most extraordinary offshoots of the Kellogg Company was W. K.'s formation, in 1930, of a foundation that would support agricultural, health, and educational programs. The W. K. Kellogg Foundation has grown to be one of America's most important, generous, and richest philanthropic institutions, granting hundreds of millions of dollars in support of Mr. Kellogg's stated directives.

Up to the time of his death in 1951 at age ninety-one, W. K. Kellogg was the guiding light for the foundation's giving as well as a major presence in the continuing success of his company. Although he had turned over the day-to-day activities of running the business to others, he took enormous satisfaction in watching the expansion and international reach of the company that he had started with just one health-related cereal.

The 1950s saw the introduction of many new cereals. Childhood favorites such as FROSTED FLAKES, SUGAR SMACKS, CORN POPS, and COCOA KRISPIES lined the supermarket shelves, and with the advent of television, cartoon characters such as TONY THE TIGER sparked increased sales.

During the 1960s three extremely important new products were introduced, FROOT LOOPS, SPECIAL K, and POP-TARTS, all three of which remain high in popularity today.

As consumers became increasingly aware of the importance of diet in the 1970s, the sales of sugared cereals fell, encouraging Kellogg Company to rework many of its cereals, eliminating sugars and finding even more healthful mixes to create adult-friendly breakfast foods. It was during this period that Kellogg also purchased other companies, such

One of Kellogg Company's most recognizable icons, TONY THE TIGER.

as Mrs. Smith Pie Company and Fearn International (which included the EGGO brand), adding many, many new products to its roster.

With the increased consumer awareness of the 1970s augmented by medical news of the importance of diet in the prevention of disease, the 1980s found many new KELLOGG'S cereals introduced to an ever more discerning marketplace. NUTRI-GRAIN became the first line of whole-grain flaked cereals, and it was quickly followed by CRISPIX, JUST RIGHT, and MUESLIX. To increase consumer awareness of the importance of fiber for good health, in 1984 Kellogg began printing messages from the National Cancer Institute on boxes of its ALL-BRAN cereal.

From the 1990s through the present, Kellogg has continued to expand its operations by purchasing complementary companies such as the vegetarian-based food group Worthington Foods (producers of MORNINGSTAR FARMS products) in 1999 and the organic-based food group Kashi Company in 2000. Kellogg also acquired Keebler Foods in 2001. As it has throughout its history, Kellogg Company has developed, tested, and introduced new products to the marketplace based on consumer tastes and government-recommended dietary requirements. It is now the world's leading producer of cereal and a leading producer of convenience foods, including cookies, crackers, toaster pastries, cereal bars, frozen waffles, meat alternatives, pie crusts, and ice cream cones. KELLOGG'S products are manufactured in 17 countries and available in more than 180 countries around the world.

An announcement introducing one of the health-conscious KELLOGG'S cereals developed for the adult market.

IN THE KITCHEN WITH *Kellogg's*™

W. K. Kellogg's goal was for Kellogg consumers to enjoy KELLOGG'S cereals throughout the day. To help homemakers use Kellogg products in creative ways, an experimental kitchen was established so on-the-box recipes could be developed using standardized measurements and ingredients, making the recipes easier to reproduce and enjoy in the home. This test kitchen, set up in the 1920s, was one of the first in the food industry.

Through the decades, the KELLOGG KITCHENS created many lasting recipes, taking cereal beyond the breakfast bowl and using Kellogg products in a wide range of dishes, many of which are found in the following pages. Over the years, thousands of recipes have been developed, including those for appetizers, main dishes, snacks, and desserts.

Just how did all of these recipes evolve? Originally, they came not only from the KELLOGG KITCHENS staff of home economists, but from home cooks through recipe contests, from special projects with newspaper and magazine food editors, and from store promotions with sales representatives and grocers.

Our recipe collection has evolved over many decades to meet a variety of criteria for taste, texture, nutrition, appearance, ease of preparation, and availability of ingredients so all of our consumers can enjoy our recipes.

This cookbook brings the best Kellogg recipes directly to your kitchen. Many of these recipes, including KELLOGG'S ALL-BRAN Muffins, Double-Coated Chicken, and, of course, the famous RICE KRISPIES TREATS, have been popular with Kellogg consumers for decades. Some of them might already be among your family favorites, while others are new and will, we hope, become family traditions in the years to come.

Throughout our company's history, the Kellogg emphasis on good health through good food was never more apparent than in its commitment to the work of the test kitchen. It is our hope that you will find the spirit of the hearts and hands of these dedicated cooks in every recipe.

COOKING HINTS—
BEYOND THE CEREAL BOWL

Shortly after Kellogg introduced ready-to-eat cereal flakes to the American breakfast table, other uses for these foods became apparent. To accustom the consumer to the notion that cereal could go beyond the cereal bowl, the KELLOGG KITCHENS began developing recipes to appear on cereal boxes and in free-to-the-public booklets.

The flavor and crispness of KELLOGG'S ready-to-eat cereals is often of great benefit to the texture, taste, and nutrition of many recipes. Virtually all KELLOGG'S cereals are fortified with anywhere from 10 percent to 25 percent of the United States Recommended Daily Allowances for many essential vitamins and minerals. KELLOGG'S bran-based cereals are also rich in dietary fiber. The cereals also contribute an attractive golden brown color to the finished dish.

To guarantee accurate amounts, KELLOGG'S ready-to-eat cereals should be measured using individual graduated measuring cups—those most commonly used to measure all dry ingredients. When measuring, pour the cereal into the cup and level with the straight edge of a knife or a spatula, taking care not to crush the cereal.

When combining the cereal with liquid, most recipes will require that the mixture be allowed to rest for a couple of minutes so that the cereal can soften. This is to insure that the cereal will be evenly distributed throughout the final product. In breads, this step helps to produce the desirable fine, even texture (or crumb) of the bread.

Many, many recipes call for the cereal to be crushed before incorporating it into a dish. The simplest way to crush cereal is to place it in a resealable plastic bag, seal the bag, and crush the cereal with a rolling pin. You can also crush the cereal using a blender or food processor; however, these electrical appliances do not allow as much control over the final texture as does hand rolling. *If the recipe specifies the amount of crumbs required, heed the direction.* If you have more than you are supposed to, the crumbs are not fine enough; if less than required, the crumbs are too fine. Either result will require further attention, as you must have the exact amount called for to properly execute the recipe. Generally with cereal flakes, 1 cup will yield 1/4 cup fine crumbs or 1/2 cup medium crumbs. If the recipe calls for crushed KELLOGG'S CORN FLAKES and you want to skip this step, Kellogg has premade crumbs, sold as KELLOGG'S Corn Flake Crumbs, which can be substituted.

To add a crisp, flavorful, and nutritious accent to vegetable or main dish casseroles, combine 1/2 cup of a favorite KELLOGG'S ready-to-eat cereal with 2 tablespoons melted butter (or margarine) or olive oil (the type of fat used is dependent upon the flavor of the dish) along with complementary herbs or spices. Sprinkle the mixture over the dish before baking to achieve a crisp, golden brown crust.

KELLOGG'S ready-to-eat cereals crushed to fine or medium crumbs make an excellent breading for poultry, meat, and fish. Season the crumbs as you please with salt, pepper, and other spices or herbs. Dip the item to be breaded into an egg-milk mixture, melted butter, margarine, or oil; then roll the item in the seasoned crumbs and, for better nutrition, bake rather than fry.

Crushed flakes or crunchy cereal bits can also be used to add interest to breads, rolls, and cookies. For breads and rolls, lightly coat the unbaked dough with melted butter or margarine or olive oil using a pastry brush, sprinkle with the cereal, and bake. The cereal will add both crunch and flavor. If you add herbs, spices, or grated cheese to the cereal, you will create an even more flavorful bread. For drop cookies, simply sprinkle the tops with cereal flakes, bits, or crumbs before baking.

Cereals can also be used to extend a dish, particularly those made with ground meat, tofu, or flaked fish. For recipes yielding 6 servings, about 1/2 cup of cereal added to the mix will be just enough to make it go a little bit further.

Most KELLOGG'S ready-to-eat cereals make delicious crusts for refrigerated or frozen desserts. Bring a mixture of 1/3 cup butter, 1/4 cup sugar, and 1/8 teaspoon ground spice and/or freshly grated orange or lemon zest to a boil, then add 1 cup of finely crushed cereal crumbs. Press the mixture into a 9-inch square baking dish or a 9-inch pie plate. Chill thoroughly before filling with puddings or frozen ices, creams, or yogurts. Freeze or refrigerate until ready to serve, garnished with fresh fruits. If serving frozen, allow the dessert to sit 15 minutes at room temperature for easier serving.

Throughout this book we often call for pans to be sprayed with nonstick cooking spray. You can also use nonstick cookware or any other fat that you would normally use to prevent an item from sticking to the pan when baked or cooked. It is your choice.

In keeping with contemporary cooking, we specified canola oil throughout this cookbook due to its heart-healthy properties and because it is flavorless. You may use whatever other vegetable oil you prefer.

If you want to reduce calories, fat, and cholesterol, you can replace full-fat products with reduced-fat or nonfat ingredients in many recipes. For instance, whole milk can be replaced with fat-free or low-fat milk; full-fat yogurt and sour cream can be replaced with reduced-fat or nonfat versions; and cream cheese can be replaced with Neufchâtel cheese. Two egg whites or 1/4 cup egg substitute can replace 1 large whole egg. Fresh herbs and spices add intense flavor to dishes without the addition of any calories or fat. Experiment as you would with any other recipe to find the right balance for your needs.

Cooking with ready-to-eat cereals is simply another marvelous way to enjoy the goodness of nutritious grains. Recipes incorporating KELLOGG'S ready-to-eat cereals are generally easy to prepare and delicious. Many of these recipes are already American traditions, and we hope that all of them will encourage you to expand the use of ready-to-eat cereals in your own treasury of recipes.

BREAKFAST

Master Breads Mix

4 cups all-purpose flour

3 1/4 cups KELLOGG'S ALL-BRAN

1 cup sugar

3 tablespoons baking powder

1 1/2 teaspoons salt

This is an extremely convenient mix to keep on hand at all times. In just a few minutes, the busy cook can whip up some pleasing pancakes or bake a batch of muffins or a crunchy, fragrant coffee cake. The bran cereal adds a dense, nutty flavor and fiber to the mix! MAKES 6 CUPS

1. Combine the flour, cereal, sugar, baking powder, and salt, stirring to blend well.

2. Transfer to an airtight container and store in a cool, dry place for up to 3 months.

To Make 14 Pancakes: In a large mixing bowl, beat 1 egg until foamy. Add 1 3/4 cups milk and 1/4 cup melted butter or margarine or canola oil. Beat well. Add 2 cups of the Master Breads Mix. Combine thoroughly. Let stand 1 to 2 minutes, or until cereal is softened. Use 1/4 cup batter for each pancake. Cook on greased and preheated griddle, turning once, until golden brown on both sides. Serve immediately.

To Make 12 Muffins: In a large mixing bowl, beat 1 egg slightly. Add 1 cup milk (whole or fat free) and 1/4 cup melted butter or margarine or canola oil. Beat well. Add 2 cups of the Master Breads Mix, stirring just to blend. Let stand 1 or 2 minutes, or until cereal is softened. Fill greased muffin cups evenly. Bake at 400°F for 25 minutes, or until lightly browned. Serve warm.

To Make One 9-inch Coffee Cake: Prepare batter as for muffins and pour it into a 9-inch square baking pan coated with nonstick cooking spray. Make a topping by combining 1/2 cup firmly packed brown sugar, 1/4 cup each chopped nuts and flaked coconut, 2 tablespoons all-purpose flour, and 2 teaspoons ground cinnamon. Work 2 tablespoons softened butter or margarine into the dry ingredients to

First introduced as KELLOGG'S BRAN in 1916, the cereal was changed from flakes to shreds in 1919 and renamed ALL-BRAN.

make coarse crumbs. Sprinkle the mixture on top of the batter, place pan in a preheated 350°F oven, and bake for about 45 minutes, or until a cake tester inserted in the center comes out clean. Serve warm.

Breakfast Quesadilla

Three 4-ounce cartoons MORNINGSTAR FARMS SCRAMBLERS, thawed

4 burrito-size flour tortillas, lightly browned

$^1/_2$ cup MORNINGSTAR FARMS Sausage Style RECIPE CRUMBLES

$^2/_3$ cup shredded Monterey Jack or sharp Cheddar cheese or other cheese of choice

$^1/_2$ cup finely chopped onion

$^1/_4$ cup chopped fresh cilantro

Low-fat sour cream, optional garnish

Bottled salsa, optional garnish

If you haven't tried vegetarian products made by MORNINGSTAR FARMS, this recipe will be a great introduction to their flavor and diversity. These fragrant quesadillas offer a special and not-too-spicy way to start the day. MAKES 2

1. Prepare the SCRAMBLERS according to package directions. Set aside.

2. Spoon one half of the SCRAMBLERS on each of 2 tortillas, spreading to evenly cover. Layer one half of the Crumbles, cheese, onions, and cilantro over each tortilla. Top each layered tortilla with one of the remaining tortillas.

3. Heat a heavy frying pan, preferably cast iron, over low heat. Add the quesadillas, one at a time, and cook, turning only if necessary to keep the bottom from getting too brown, for about 4 minutes, or until the cheese has melted and the filling is warm.

4. Remove from the pan, cut each quesadilla into 8 wedges, and serve, garnished with sour cream and salsa if desired.

Baked French Toast

2 large eggs

³/₄ cup milk

¹/₂ teaspoon pure vanilla extract

³/₄ cup KELLOGG'S Corn Flake Crumbs

6 slices day-old white or whole wheat bread

¹/₄ cup butter or margarine, melted

This recipe offers an easy way to serve French toast without standing over a hot stove. The crumbs provide a great crispy crunchiness that is hard to beat! SERVES 4

1. Preheat oven to 450°F.

2. Generously coat a large shallow baking pan with nonstick cooking spray. Set aside.

3. Place the eggs in a shallow dish and beat until foamy. Stir in milk and vanilla.

4. Place the crumbs in a second shallow dish.

5. Working with one piece at a time, dip the bread into the egg mixture, turning once to allow both sides to soak up some of the liquid.

6. Dip the soaked bread into the crumbs, turning to lightly coat both sides.

7. Place the coated bread in a single layer in the prepared pan. Drizzle with melted butter and place in the preheated oven. Bake for about 10 minutes, or until golden brown on both sides.

8. Remove from oven, cut slices into halves on the diagonal, and serve with butter, syrup, jelly, or honey.

Easy Four-Grain Pancakes

4 cups KELLOGG'S PRODUCT 19

1 cup Master Breads Mix (see page 2)

2 large eggs, beaten

2 cups fat-free milk

2 tablespoons butter or margarine, melted

PRODUCT 19 incorporates corn, oats, wheat, and rice for a new take on an old breakfast-time favorite—pancakes!

MAKES 12

1. Place the PRODUCT 19 in a resealable plastic bag. Seal the bag and, using a rolling pin, crush the cereal to fine crumbs. Open the bag and measure the crumbs; you should have 1 cup.

2. Combine the crumbs with the Master Breads Mix in a medium mixing bowl. Add the eggs, milk, and butter or oil, stirring until the batter is almost smooth. Batter will be thin. To thicken, allow to set for 5 minutes.

3. Preheat a griddle over medium heat. Lightly coat with nonstick cooking spray.

4. For each pancake, ladle about 1/4 cup of the batter into the hot griddle. Cook, turning once, for about 4 minutes, or until golden brown on both sides and cooked through.

5. Remove from the pan and serve with syrup, jelly, or honey.

Brancakes

1 cup KELLOGG'S ALL-BRAN

1 egg, lightly beaten

2 cups fat-free milk

2 tablespoons butter or margarine, melted

1 teaspoon freshly grated orange zest

1½ cups Master Breads Mix (see page 2)

These slightly sweet pancakes are fragrant with orange zest. The addition of bran cereal makes them a terrific breakfast option. For an extra-special breakfast, serve them with warm orange syrup, garnished with sautéed fresh orange segments. MAKES 14

1. Combine the ALL-BRAN with the egg, milk, butter, and orange zest, stirring to blend. Set aside for 2 minutes, or until the cereal has softened.

2. Add the Master Breads Mix and stir just enough to combine. The batter should be lumpy.

3. Preheat a griddle over medium heat. Lightly coat with nonstick cooking spray.

4. For each pancake, ladle about ¼ cup of the batter into the hot griddle. Cook, turning once, for about 4 minutes, or until golden brown on both sides and cooked through.

5. Remove from the pan and serve with syrup, jelly, or honey.

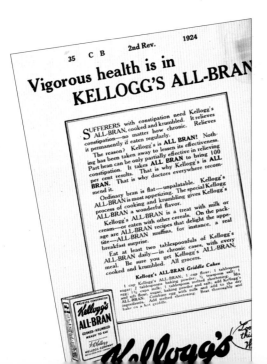

This early advertisement featured ALL-BRAN in cooking and as a ready-to-eat cereal.

Meatless Sausage-Spinach Quiche

Three 4-ounce cartons MORNINGSTAR FARMS BETTER'N EGGS

$1/2$ cup fat-free milk

$1/4$ teaspoon ground nutmeg

$1/2$ teaspoon salt

$1/8$ teaspoon ground pepper

One 9-inch prepared deep-dish pie crust, unbaked (thawed if frozen)

1 tablespoon butter or margarine or canola oil

$1/2$ cup diced onion

$1/2$ cup diced button (or other) mushrooms

One 10-ounce package frozen chopped spinach, thawed, well-drained

One 8-ounce package MORNINGSTAR FARMS Veggie Breakfast Sausage Patties, crumbled

1 cup shredded sharp Cheddar, Swiss, or other firm cheese of choice

Like an omelette in a crust, this morning quiche is a terrific way to add a little zest to the start of your day. MORNINGSTAR FARMS Sausage Style RECIPE CRUMBLES (or, for a nonvegetarian option, cooked pork breakfast sausage) can be used in place of the sausage patties.

SERVES 8

1. Preheat oven to 400°F.

2. Combine the BETTER'N EGGS, milk, nutmeg, salt, and pepper in a medium mixing bowl. Set aside.

3. Place the butter in a nonstick sauté pan over medium heat. When hot, add the onion and mushrooms and sauté for about 5 minutes, or until soft. Scrape the vegetables into the pie shell.

4. Add the spinach, crumbled patties, and cheese, spreading out in an even layer.

5. Pour the reserved BETTER'N EGGS mixture into the shell. Bake in the preheated oven for about 35 minutes, or until slightly puffed and golden brown.

6. Remove from oven, cut into wedges, and serve.

CHEEZ-IT® Soufflé

1 cup SUNSHINE CHEEZ-IT crackers

6 large eggs

1½ cups milk

¼ cup butter or margarine

1 teaspoon grated onion

Salt and freshly ground pepper to taste

This recipe takes CHEEZ-IT crackers from the snack box to make a light, flavorful soufflé that works as a breakfast or brunch dish or as a light lunch or supper. For lunch or supper, you might want to spoon a bit of cheese sauce or chili sauce over each serving to make a more elegant presentation. SERVES 6

1. Preheat oven to 300°F.

2. Place the CHEEZ-IT crackers in a resealable plastic bag. Seal the bag and, using a rolling pin, crush the crackers to a fine crumb. Set aside.

3. Separate the eggs. Place the yolks in a small, heatproof bowl and beat to blend. Set aside.

4. Place the egg whites in a large bowl. Set aside.

5. Combine the milk and butter in a small, heavy-bottomed saucepan over medium heat. Cook, stirring constantly, for about 2 minutes, or just until the butter has melted. Add half of the reserved crumbs along with the onion and salt and pepper to taste. Continue to cook, stirring constantly, for about 5 minutes, or until the mixture begins to thicken and boil. Immediately lower the heat and whisk a bit of the hot mixture into the egg yolks to temper them. Scrape the egg yolk mixture into the hot mixture. Cook, stirring constantly, for about 3 minutes, or until the mixture returns to a boil. Remove from heat.

6. Using a hand-held electric mixer, beat the reserved egg whites until stiff but not dry. Fold the egg whites into the hot CHEEZ-IT mixture to just incorporate. Fold in the remaining CHEEZ-IT crumbs to just blend.

7. Pour the mixture into an ungreased 1½-quart casserole. Bake in the preheated oven for about 1¼ hours, or until puffed and lightly browned.

8. Remove from oven and serve immediately.

CHEEZ-IT crackers were first introduced as a snack by the Sunshine Biscuit Company in 1921. Sunshine eventually became part of the Kellogg family.

Banana Drop Biscuits

1 tablespoon granulated sugar

1/4 teaspoon ground cinnamon

2 cups KELLOGG'S COMPLETE Wheat Bran Flakes

1 cup mashed very ripe bananas

1/3 cup fat-free milk

2 large egg whites

1 teaspoon pure vanilla extract

1 3/4 cups all-purpose flour

1 tablespoon baking powder

1/2 teaspoon salt

1/2 cup butter or margarine

GLAZE

1/2 cup confectioners' sugar

1 tablespoon fat-free milk

1/2 teaspoon pure vanilla extract

2 tablespoons sliced toasted almonds, optional garnish

Not your ordinary, everyday biscuit! These are delicious and rich and send wonderfully fragrant aromas throughout the house. What a great way to begin the day—cinnamon, bananas, bran cereal, and nuts! MAKES 10

1. Preheat oven to 400°F.

2. Lightly coat an 8-inch square baking pan with nonstick cooking spray. Set aside.

3. Combine the granulated sugar and cinnamon in a small bowl. Set aside.

4. Combine the cereal with the bananas and 1/3 cup fat-free milk, stirring to blend. Set aside for 2 minutes, or until the cereal has softened. Stir in the egg whites and 1 teaspoon vanilla, beating to completely incorporate.

5. Combine the flour, baking powder, and salt in a large mixing bowl. Add the butter and, using a pastry blender, cut the butter into the dry ingredients to make coarse crumbs. Add the flour mixture to the cereal mixture, stirring to just combine.

6. Using a 1/4-cup measure, drop the dough into the prepared pan, leaving about 1 inch between biscuits. Sprinkle with the reserved cinnamon sugar. Bake in the preheated oven for about 25 minutes, or until golden.

7. While the biscuits are baking, make the glaze.

8. Combine the confectioners' sugar with 1 tablespoon fat-free milk and 1/2 teaspoon vanilla, beating until smooth. Cover tightly with plastic film until ready to use.

9. Remove the biscuits from the oven. Drizzle the glaze over the top and sprinkle with almonds. Serve immediately.

Baked Banana Doughnuts

2 tablespoons granulated sugar

2 tablespoons finely chopped walnuts

3 cups KELLOGG'S RICE KRISPIES

2 cups all-purpose flour

2 teaspoons baking powder

1/2 teaspoon baking soda

1/4 teaspoon pumpkin pie spice

2 large egg whites

1 cup mashed very ripe bananas

1 cup firmly packed brown sugar

1 tablespoon canola oil

These baked, not fried, doughnuts are a banana twist on an old favorite. For variety, you can also sprinkle the finished doughnuts with cinnamon sugar or roll them in confectioners' sugar. The more ambitious cook might consider a chocolate glaze to make them *really* special.

MAKES ABOUT 15

1. Preheat oven to 400°F.

2. Lightly coat 2 baking sheets with nonstick cooking spray. Set aside.

3. Combine the granulated sugar and nuts in a small bowl. Set aside.

4. Combine RICE KRISPIES with the flour, baking powder, baking soda, and pumpkin pie spice in a mixing bowl. Set aside.

5. Combine the egg whites, bananas, brown sugar, and oil in the bowl of a standing electric mixer and beat to blend. Add the dry ingredients and beat on medium speed until incorporated.

6. Drop the dough, using a 1/4-cup measure, onto the prepared baking sheets, forming each piece into a slightly flat, neat circle with a spatula. Using a small rubber spatula coated with nonstick cooking spray, create a 1-inch hole in the center of each circle.

7. Sprinkle each "doughnut" with some of the reserved sugar-nut mixture. Bake in the preheated oven for 10 minutes, or until lightly browned around the edges.

8. Remove from oven and transfer to wire racks to cool. Serve warm or at room temperature.

The Original ALL-BRAN Muffins®

1¼ cups all-purpose flour
½ cup sugar
1 tablespoon baking powder
¼ teaspoon salt
2 cups KELLOGG'S ALL-BRAN
1¼ cups fat-free milk
1 large egg
¼ cup canola oil

This basic muffin has been one of our most requested recipes since it was first developed in the 1930s. Though this is the standard, other versions have included additions of dried fruit, fresh berries, and nuts. Whichever recipe you prefer, muffins made with ALL-BRAN are always a winner.
MAKES 12

1. Preheat oven to 400°F.

2. Lightly coat the 2½-inch-diameter cups of a 12-cup muffin pan with nonstick cooking spray. Set aside.

3. Stir together the flour, sugar, baking powder, and salt. Set aside.

4. Combine ALL-BRAN and milk in a large mixing bowl. Let stand for 2 minutes, or until cereal softens. Add egg and oil. Beat well. Add flour mixture, stirring until just combined.

5. Spoon the batter evenly into the prepared muffin cups. Bake in the preheated oven for about 20 minutes, or until golden brown.

6. Remove from oven and serve warm.

> NOTE: To further reduce calories, fat, and cholesterol, use 2 tablespoons sugar, 2 tablespoons oil, and replace the egg with 2 egg whites or the appropriate amount of egg substitute.

Glazed Peach Muffins

1 cup all-purpose flour

3 tablespoons sugar

2 teaspoons baking powder

$1/2$ teaspoon pumpkin pie spice

$1/2$ teaspoon salt

One 16-ounce can sliced cling peaches in light syrup

1 cup KELLOGG'S ALL-BRAN

$1/2$ cup fat-free milk

1 large egg white

2 tablespoons canola oil

Lemon Sauce (recipe follows)

Quite elegant with the peach decoration and the tart Lemon Sauce, these are very special muffins to be saved for a special breakfast or tea. MAKES 8

1. Preheat oven to 400°F.

2. Lightly coat the $2^{1}/2$-inch-diameter cups of an 8-cup muffin pan with nonstick cooking spray. Set aside.

3. Combine the flour, sugar, baking powder, pumpkin pie spice, and salt in a bowl. Set aside.

4. Drain the peaches, separately reserving 8 peach slices and $1/3$ cup of the syrup. Chop the remaining peaches and discard the remaining syrup.

5. Combine the cereal and milk with the $1/3$ cup syrup, stirring to combine. Let stand for about 2 minutes, or until the cereal has softened.

"Bran muffins are our specialty"

MANY restaurants are finding it profitable to feature a special —like bran muffins. ALL-BRAN muffins are delicious. They have won instant favor throughout America. More and more people every day are asking for bran muffins. They make a valued addition to every menu. In addition, they are healthful and nourishing. There are many other

delightful ways to serve ALL-BRAN. You can increase business by bringing them before your customers. Suggest sprinkling ALL-BRAN over other cereals. Kellogg's Corn Flakes and ALL-BRAN make a delightful combination—a real health treat? Suggest ALL-BRAN in soups. Or just served with cold milk or cream. Write us for recipes and other helps.

Kellogg's ALL-BRAN

Kellogg Company, Battle Creek, Mich.

6. Add the egg white and oil, beating well to blend. Stir in the chopped peaches. Add flour mixture, stirring until just combined.

7. Spoon the batter into the prepared muffin cups. Lay a peach slice across the center of each muffin.

8. Bake in the preheated oven for about 25 minutes, or until golden brown.

9. Remove the muffins from the oven and from the pan. Place the muffins on a wire rack and drizzle the Lemon Sauce over the top.

10. Serve warm.

LEMON SAUCE

1/3 cup sugar

2 tablespoons cornstarch

1 1/2 cups cold water

1 tablespoon fresh lemon juice

1 teaspoon freshly grated lemon zest

1. Combine the sugar and cornstarch in a medium heavy-bottomed pan. Add the water and place over medium heat. Cook, stirring constantly, for about 5 minutes, or until the mixture comes to a boil. Lower the heat and simmer, stirring constantly, for 3 minutes.

2. Remove from heat and stir in the lemon juice and zest.

3. Keep warm until ready to serve.

Blueberry Lover's Muffins

2 cups all-purpose flour

4 teaspoons baking powder

¹/₄ teaspoon salt

1¹/₂ teaspoons ground cinnamon

¹/₃ cup sugar

3¹/₂ cups KELLOGG'S COMPLETE Wheat Bran Flakes

1³/₄ cups fat-free milk

2 large egg whites

3 tablespoons canola oil

1¹/₂ cups fresh blueberries, well washed and dried

Although this recipe calls for blueberries, you can use raspberries or other fresh berries (except strawberries, which are a bit too juicy and will make the batter too wet) or chopped dried fruit or raisins. Chopped nuts can also be added—just a quarter cup will do nicely. However you make them, there is almost nothing more welcome at breakfast or snack time. MAKES 12

1. Preheat oven to 400°F.

2. Lightly coat the 2¹/₂-inch-diameter cups of a 12-cup muffin pan with nonstick cooking spray. Set aside.

3. Combine the flour, baking powder, salt, cinnamon, and sugar in a small mixing bowl. Set aside.

4. Combine the cereal and milk in a large mixing bowl. Set aside to soften for 2 minutes.

5. Stir the egg whites and oil into the softened cereal, beating well with a wooden spoon. Add the flour mixture, stirring to just combine. Fold in the blueberries, taking care not to break them.

6. Spoon the batter into the prepared muffin cups. Bake in the preheated oven for about 25 minutes, or until golden brown.

7. Remove from oven and serve warm with butter and jam on the side, if desired.

Onion-Dill Muffins

1 cup whole wheat flour
$^3/_4$ cup all-purpose flour
$^1/_4$ cup sugar
4 teaspoons baking powder
$1^1/_2$ teaspoons dried dill weed
$^1/_2$ teaspoon dry mustard
$^1/_2$ teaspoon salt
$1^1/_2$ cups KELLOGG'S ALL-BRAN
$1^1/_2$ cups fat-free milk
3 large egg whites
3 tablespoons canola oil
$^1/_2$ cup finely chopped onion

These savory muffins make a perfect accompaniment to a piping hot bowl of soup or a main course salad. ALL-BRAN cereal and whole wheat flour add fiber to these delicious muffins. MAKES 12

1. Preheat oven to 400°F.

2. Lightly coat the $2^1/_2$-inch-diameter cups of a 12-cup muffin pan with nonstick cooking spray. Set aside.

3. Combine the wheat and white flours, sugar, baking powder, dill weed, mustard, and salt in a bowl. Set aside.

4. Combine the ALL-BRAN and milk, stirring to combine. Let stand for about 2 minutes, or until the cereal has softened.

5. Add the egg whites and oil, beating well to blend. Stir in $^1/_4$ cup of the onions. Add flour mixture, stirring until just combined.

6. Spoon the batter into the prepared muffin cups. Sprinkle the top of each muffin with an equal portion of the remaining $^1/_4$ cup onions.

7. Bake in the preheated oven for about 18 minutes, or until golden brown.

8. Remove from oven and serve warm.

Cocoa-Banana Muffins

1 cup all-purpose flour

1/2 cup sugar

2 tablespoons unsweetened cocoa powder

2 teaspoons baking powder

1/2 teaspoon salt

1 1/2 cups KELLOGG'S ALL-BRAN

3/4 cup fat-free milk

2 large egg whites

2 tablespoons canola oil

1 cup sliced ripe bananas

These are great big wonderful muffins filled with great taste from the combination of cocoa and banana! Cocoa-Banana Muffins are a terrific, on-the-go breakfast muffin.

MAKES 6

1. Preheat oven to 400°F.

2. Lightly coat six 6-ounce custard cups with nonstick cooking spray. Set aside.

3. Combine the flour, sugar, cocoa powder, baking powder, and salt in a bowl. Set aside.

4. Combine the ALL-BRAN and milk, stirring to combine. Let stand for about 2 minutes, or until the cereal has softened.

5. Add the egg whites and oil, beating well to blend. Stir in the bananas. Add flour mixture, stirring until just combined.

6. Spoon the batter into the prepared custard cups. Bake in the preheated oven for about 30 minutes, or until lightly browned.

7. Remove from oven and serve warm.

NOTE: To make 12 regular-size muffins, use a 12-cup muffin pan with 2 1/2-inch-diameter cups lightly coated with cooking spray in place of larger custard cups. Reduce baking time to 25 minutes.

Applesauce-Raisin Muffins

3/4 cup all-purpose flour

1/2 cup whole wheat flour

1/2 cup sugar

1 tablespoon baking powder

1 teaspoon ground cinnamon

1/2 teaspoon baking soda

1/4 teaspoon salt

2 cups KELLOGG'S ALL-BRAN

1 1/2 cups unsweetened applesauce

1/4 cup fat-free milk

3 large egg whites

1/2 cup seedless raisins

Applesauce-Raisin Muffins are one of Kellogg Company's most requested recipes. There is no oil—the applesauce works to keep the muffins moist. ALL-BRAN cereal and whole wheat flour add fiber, and the raisins add their own special sweetness. MAKES 12

1. Preheat oven to 400°F.

2. Lightly coat the 2 1/2-inch-diameter cups of a 12-cup muffin pan with nonstick cooking spray. Set aside.

3. Combine the white and wheat flours, sugar, baking powder, cinnamon, baking soda, and salt in a bowl. Set aside.

4. Combine the ALL-BRAN, applesauce, and milk in a medium mixing bowl. Let stand for 5 minutes, or until the cereal has softened. Stir in the egg whites and raisins, mixing to blend. Add flour mixture, stirring until just combined.

5. Spoon the batter into the prepared muffin cups. Bake in the preheated oven for about 20 minutes, or until lightly browned.

6. Remove from oven and serve warm.

Corn Flake Muffins

1 1/2 cups all-purpose flour

1/4 cup sugar

1 tablespoon baking powder

1/4 teaspoon salt

1 cup KELLOGG'S Corn Flake Crumbs, or 2 cups KELLOGG'S CORN FLAKES, crushed to 1 cup

1 1/4 cups fat-free milk

1 large egg

3 tablespoons canola oil

Simple, easy-to-make, and perfect with a hot cup of coffee or a cold glass of milk, Corn Flake Muffins are a wonderful way to begin the day. MAKES 12

1. Preheat oven to 400°F.

2. Lightly coat the 2 1/2-inch-diameter cups of a 12-cup muffin pan with nonstick cooking spray. Set aside.

3. Combine the flour, sugar, baking powder, and salt in a bowl. Set aside.

4. Combine the KELLOGG'S Corn Flake Crumbs and milk in a medium mixing bowl. Let stand for 2 minutes, or until the cereal has softened. Stir in the egg and oil, mixing to blend. Add flour mixture, stirring to just combine.

5. Spoon the batter into the prepared muffin cups. Bake in the preheated oven for about 20 minutes, or until lightly browned.

6. Remove from oven and serve warm.

Surprise Muffins

1¹/₂ cups all-purpose flour

¹/₃ cup sugar

1 tablespoon baking powder

¹/₄ teaspoon salt

2 cups KELLOGG'S CORN FLAKES

1 cup fat-free milk

1 large egg

¹/₄ cup canola oil

¹/₄ cup pure fruit preserves or jam, any flavor

Whipped cream cheese, optional

Here's a Kellogg take on a kid favorite! Surprise Muffins are a sure thing every time. These are even better when served with a touch of cream cheese, which brings out the fruity sweetness of the jam. MAKES 12

1. Preheat oven to 400°F.

2. Lightly coat the 2¹/₂-inch-diameter cups of a 12-cup muffin pan with nonstick cooking spray. Set aside.

3. Combine the flour, sugar, baking powder, and salt in a bowl. Set aside.

4. Combine the Corn Flakes and milk in a medium mixing bowl. Let stand for 2 minutes, or until the cereal has softened. Stir in the egg and oil, mixing to blend. Add the flour mixture, stirring to just combine.

5. Spoon the batter into the prepared muffin cups. Using a teaspoon, make a deep indentation in each muffin. Fill each indentation with a teaspoon of preserves or jam. Bake in the preheated oven for about 20 minutes, or until lightly browned.

6. Remove from oven and serve warm with whipped cream cheese, if desired.

Cherry-Pear Muffins

1½ cups all-purpose flour

½ cup firmly packed brown sugar

1 tablespoon baking powder

1 teaspoon ground cinnamon

½ teaspoon baking soda

¼ teaspoon salt

One 16-ounce can sliced pears

4 cups KELLOGG'S CORN FLAKES

3 large egg whites

2 tablespoons canola oil

½ cup dried tart cherries

GLAZE

1 cup confectioners' sugar

½ teaspoon ground cinnamon

5 teaspoons reserved pear liquid

This is another great breakfast muffin with cereal and fruit. The cherries are used in honor of our home state of Michigan, where cherries are a key crop. The tartness they provide balances the sweetness of the pears for a wonderfully mellow muffin! MAKES 12

1. Preheat oven to 400°F.

2. Lightly coat the 2½-inch-diameter cups of a 12-cup muffin pan with nonstick cooking spray. Set aside.

3. Combine the flour, brown sugar, baking powder, 1 teaspoon cinnamon, baking soda, and salt in a mixing bowl. Set aside.

4. Drain the pears, separately reserving the liquid.

5. Combine the pears with the cereal, egg whites, and oil in the bowl of a food processor fitted with the metal blade. Add ³/4 cup of the pear syrup and process for about 30 seconds, or until smooth.

6. Add pear mixture and cherries to flour mixture and stir to just combine.

7. Spoon the batter into the prepared muffin cups. Bake in the preheated oven for about 20 minutes, or until golden brown.

8. While the muffins are baking, make the glaze.

9. Combine the confectioners' sugar and ½ teaspoon cinnamon with 5 teaspoons of the reserved pear liquid, beating until smooth.

10. Remove the muffins from the oven and from the pan. Place the muffins on a wire rack and drizzle the glaze over the top.

11. Serve warm or cold.

Cinnamon-Topped Dried Plum Muffins

TOPPING

1 tablespoon sugar

1/4 teaspoon ground cinnamon

1 1/4 cups all-purpose flour

1 tablespoon baking powder

1/2 teaspoon salt

1/3 cup sugar

2 cups KELLOGG'S PRODUCT 19

1 1/4 cups fat-free milk

1 large egg

1/4 cup canola oil

3/4 cup diced pitted dried plums (prunes)

These muffins are a great way to start the day. The dried plums (prunes) bring a sweet, mellow flavor to the breakfast table. MAKES 12

1. Preheat oven to 400°F.

2. Lightly coat the 2 1/2-inch-diameter cups of a 12-cup muffin pan with nonstick cooking spray. Set aside.

3. To make the topping, combine 1 tablespoon sugar with the cinnamon. Set aside.

4. Combine the flour, baking powder, and salt with 1/3 cup sugar in a bowl. Set aside.

5. Combine PRODUCT 19 with the milk in a medium mixing bowl. Let stand for 2 minutes, or until the milk has been absorbed. Stir in the egg and oil, beating to incorporate. Stir in the dried plums. Add flour mixture, stirring to just combine.

6. Spoon the batter into the prepared cups. Sprinkle with the reserved cinnamon-sugar mixture and place in the preheated oven. Bake for about 20 minutes, or until golden.

7. Remove from oven and serve warm.

Streusel Bran Muffins

CRUMB TOPPING

2 tablespoons firmly packed brown sugar

3 tablespoons all-purpose flour

1 tablespoon butter, cold

1¼ cups all-purpose flour

1 tablespoon baking powder

½ teaspoon ground cinnamon

½ teaspoon salt

¼ teaspoon ground nutmeg

1½ cups KELLOGG'S COMPLETE Wheat Bran Flakes

¾ cup fat-free milk

½ cup firmly packed brown sugar

2 large egg whites

¼ cup canola oil

½ teaspoon pure vanilla extract

½ cup seedless raisins

Streusel Bran Muffins are an excellent breakfast muffin. They have the nice touch of the streusel topping to begin the day in a special way. The smell of warm cinnamon and nutmeg is sure to make this a favorite at your house.

MAKES 12

1. Preheat oven to 400°F.

2. Lightly coat the 2½-inch-diameter cups of a 12-cup muffin pan with nonstick cooking spray. Set aside.

3. Combine 2 tablespoons brown sugar and 3 tablespoons flour in a small bowl. Using a pastry blender or fork, cut in butter until mixture resembles coarse crumbs. Set aside.

4. Combine 1¼ cups flour, baking powder, cinnamon, salt, and nutmeg in another bowl. Set aside.

5. Combine the COMPLETE Wheat Bran Flakes and milk in a medium mixing bowl. Let stand for 3 minutes, or until the cereal has softened. Stir in ½ cup brown sugar, egg whites, oil, and vanilla, mixing to blend. Stir in the raisins. Add the flour mixture, stirring to just combine.

6. Spoon the batter into the prepared muffin cups. Top each muffin with an equal portion of the crumb mixture.

7. Bake in the preheated oven for about 20 minutes, or until golden brown.

8. Remove from oven and serve warm.

Pineapple Upside-Down Muffins

1/4 cup firmly packed brown sugar

2 tablespoons butter, melted

6 maraschino cherries, well drained and cut in half lengthwise

1 1/4 cups all-purpose flour

1/3 cup granulated sugar

1 tablespoon baking powder

1 teaspoon salt

1 1/2 cups KELLOGG'S COMPLETE Wheat Bran Flakes

One 8-ounce can crushed pineapple in juice, undrained

1/4 cup fat-free milk

2 large egg whites

1/4 cup canola oil

Not just for breakfast, these muffins are almost like little cakes and could just as easily serve as a dessert or snack.

MAKES 12

1. Preheat oven to 400°F.

2. Lightly coat the 2 1/2-inch-diameter cups of a 12-cup muffin pan with nonstick vegetable spray.

3. Combine the brown sugar and melted butter in a small bowl. When blended, spoon an equal portion into the bottom of each muffin cup. Place a maraschino cherry half in the center of each cup and set pan aside.

4. Combine the flour, granulated sugar, baking powder, and salt in another bowl. Set aside.

5. Place the cereal in a medium mixing bowl. Stir in the pineapple and milk and let stand for 3 minutes, or until the cereal has softened slightly. Stir in the egg whites and oil, beating to incorporate. Add flour mixture, stirring to just combine. (The batter will be thick.)

6. Spoon the batter into the prepared muffin cups. Bake in the preheated oven for about 25 minutes, or until golden brown.

7. Remove from oven and immediately invert onto a serving plate. Serve warm.

APPETIZERS AND SNACKS

Baked Cheese Sticks

4 cups KELLOGG'S CORN FLAKES

1 teaspoon garlic salt

1/4 teaspoon dried oregano

1/4 cup all-purpose flour

2 large egg whites

2 tablespoons water

One 8-ounce piece mozzarella cheese

2 cups Spicy Tomato Sauce, warmed, optional (recipe follows)

Everybody is familiar with mozzarella sticks, a cheese snack usually deep-fried to crunchy crispness with the hot, melting cheese runny and delicious at the first bite. This redo of a snack-food classic produces an equally crusty and oozingly luscious snack or appetizer by creating a crust with egg white and crushed KELLOGG'S CORN FLAKES. No frying here! MAKES 12

1. Either lightly spray a baking sheet with nonstick cooking spray or line it with parchment paper. The latter will add even fewer calories to the finished dish.

2. Place KELLOGG'S CORN FLAKES in a resealable plastic bag. Seal the bag and, using a rolling pin, crush the flakes to a fine crumb. Open the bag and measure the crumbs; you should have 1 cup.

3. Place the crumbs in a shallow bowl, such as a soup bowl. Stir in the garlic salt and oregano. Set aside.

4. Place the flour in a second shallow bowl. Then whisk the egg whites and water together in a third shallow bowl.

5. Line the bowls up with the flour first, followed by the egg whites and then the crumb mixture.

6. Using a sharp knife, cut the cheese into 12 sticks approximately 2 3/4 inches long.

7. Working with one piece of cheese at a time, dip each stick into the flour, then the egg whites, and finally in the Corn Flake mixture, making sure that all sides are coated. Carefully repeat the dipping process to double-coat the cheese stick completely. As each stick is coated, place it on the prepared baking sheet, leaving about an inch between sticks.

8. Very lightly spray the sticks with nonstick cooking spray and set aside for 30 minutes.

9. Preheat oven to 400°F.

10. Bake the cheese sticks in the preheated oven for about 8 minutes, or until the cheese has softened and the outside is golden brown. Remove from oven and serve hot with Spicy Tomato Sauce for dipping on the side.

SPICY TOMATO SAUCE

1 tablespoon olive oil

2 cloves garlic, peeled and minced

2 cups canned tomato purée

1/2 tablespoon minced fresh basil leaves, or 1/2 teaspoon dried basil

1/2 teaspoon dried red pepper flakes, or to taste

Salt and freshly ground pepper to taste

1. Heat the olive oil in a medium saucepan over medium heat. Stir in the garlic and sauté for 2 minutes. Add the tomato purée, basil, red pepper flakes, and salt and pepper. Bring to a simmer and simmer for 10 minutes, or just until flavors are nicely blended.

2. Remove from heat and serve warm. Or transfer to a nonreactive container, cover, and refrigerate for up to 3 days or freeze for up to 3 months. Reheat before using.

NOTES: Rather than use nonstick cooking spray, you can fill a plastic misting bottle with olive oil and spray it on the pan and the cheese sticks for a more authentic Italian flavor.

The sticks can be given a different ethnic twist by changing the seasonings and the dipping sauce. For instance, you could add some taco seasoning to the crumbs and use a salsa as the dipping sauce or add a bit of ginger to the crumbs and soy sauce to the egg whites and prepare an Asian-flavored dipping sauce. You could even offer an assortment for a cocktail party or children's gathering.

Crunchy Zucchini Rings

4 cups KELLOGG'S CORN FLAKES

1 large egg white, lightly beaten

Salt and freshly ground pepper to taste

Pinch cayenne pepper, or to taste

1 large zucchini, well washed, dried, trimmed, and cut crosswise into ⅛-inch-thick slices

1 lemon, cut into small wedges, optional

Zucchini is often cut into sticks, breaded, and then deep-fat fried. This take on the old favorite is as delicious, but without the frying. The zucchini has a very delicate flavor, while the spicy, crunchy coating adds some zest. SERVES 6

1. Preheat oven to 400°F.

2. Either lightly spray a baking sheet with nonstick cooking spray or line it with parchment paper. The latter will add even fewer calories to the finished dish.

3. Place the KELLOGG'S CORN FLAKES in a resealable plastic bag. Seal the bag and, using a rolling pin, crush the flakes to a fine crumb. Open the bag and measure the crumbs; you should have 1 cup.

4. Place the egg white in a shallow soup bowl.

5. Place the cereal crumbs in another shallow bowl. Stir in the salt, pepper, and cayenne to taste. Set aside.

6. Working with a few pieces at a time, dip the zucchini slices into the egg white, shaking off excess, and then place the slices in the Corn Flake mixture, turning to coat well on both sides.

7. Place the coated zucchini slices on the prepared baking sheet.

8. When all of the zucchini has been coated, lightly spray each slice with nonstick vegetable spray.

9. Bake in the preheated oven for about 7 minutes, or until the zucchini is soft in the center and the coating is crisp and golden brown.

10. Remove from oven and season with salt and pepper. Serve immediately with lemon wedges, if desired.

Taco Bites

1/4 cup KELLOGG'S Corn Flake Crumbs

2 tablespoons grated Parmesan cheese

One 1 1/4-ounce package taco seasoning

Two 12-count packages KELLOGG'S EGGO Minis Homestyle Waffles

Red Tomato Salsa (recipe follows) or 1 cup bottled salsa

This is a pretty simple recipe to pull together and can easily be doubled or tripled or made in batches large enough to feed an army! To make it even simpler, you can replace the homemade salsa with bottled. SERVES 12

1. Combine the KELLOGG'S Corn Flake Crumbs, cheese, and taco seasoning in a resealable plastic bag. Seal and shake to combine.

2. Preheat oven to 375°F.

3. Break the waffles into individual pieces. Either spray each side with nonstick cooking spray or, using a pastry brush, very lightly coat with olive oil.

4. Working with a few at a time, place the coated waffles in the seasoned crumbs, seal the bag, and shake to coat.

5. Place the seasoned waffles on a nonstick baking sheet and bake in the preheated oven for about 10 minutes, or until crisp.

6. Remove from oven and transfer to a serving platter or tray. Serve hot with salsa on the side.

RED TOMATO SALSA

3 very ripe tomatoes, peeled, cored, seeded, and quartered

1 hot fresh chili, well washed, stemmed, seeded, membrane removed

1/2 cup chopped scallions

1/2 cup chopped red onion

1/4 cup fresh cilantro leaves

1 tablespoon fresh lime juice

Salt and freshly ground pepper to taste

1. Place the tomatoes, chili, scallions, onion, cilantro, and lime juice in the bowl of a food processor fitted with the metal blade. Process, using quick on and off turns, to a chunky mix.

2. Transfer to a serving bowl. Season with salt and pepper to taste and serve or store, covered and refrigerated, for up to 2 days.

Cheesy Ham Savories

6 cups KELLOGG'S CORN FLAKES

$^1/_4$ cup butter, softened

1 large egg white

$^1/_2$ cup all-purpose flour

1 cup grated reduced-fat Cheddar cheese

$^3/_4$ cup minced smoked ham

2 tablespoons grated onion

2 tablespoons minced button mushrooms

$^1/_2$ teaspoon Worcestershire sauce

Salt and cayenne pepper to taste

These very tasty little snacks make a perfect tidbit to serve before dinner or as an afternoon snack for the whole family. They have a hint of spice, a nice cheesy flavor, and just a touch of smoky ham. MAKES ABOUT 3 DOZEN

1. Place the KELLOGG'S CORN FLAKES in a resealable plastic bag. Seal the bag and, using a rolling pin, crush the flakes to a fine crumb. Open the bag and measure the crumbs; you should have 1$^1/_2$ cups. Pour the crumbs into a shallow soup bowl. Set aside.

2. Preheat the oven to 350°F.

3. Line a baking pan with parchment paper. Set aside.

4. Place the butter in a mixing bowl and, using a hand-held electric mixer, beat until creamy. Add the egg white and beat to incorporate. Add the flour and beat until well blended.

5. Using a wooden spoon, beat in the cheese, ham, onion, mushrooms, and Worcestershire sauce. Season with salt and cayenne to taste.

6. Shape the mixture into approximately thirty-six 1-inch round balls.

7. Working with one piece at a time, roll each ball in the crumbs, coating well.

8. Place the coated balls in the prepared baking pan. When all of the balls have been coated, place the pan in the preheated oven and bake, without turning, for about 20 minutes, or until balls are nicely browned and hot in the center.

9. Remove from oven and serve hot.

ALL-BRAN® Corn Cakes with Prosciutto

1 cup KELLOGG'S ALL-BRAN

1 cup hot water

2 cups all-purpose flour

1 tablespoon sugar

1 tablespoon baking powder

1 teaspoon baking soda

1 teaspoon salt

1 large egg

1½ cups milk

1 cup canned corn kernels, well drained

About 3 cups fresh arugula, well washed and dried

1 cup sliced sun-dried tomatoes packed in oil, well drained

18 thin slices prosciutto or other fine-quality smoked ham

Honey mustard

This is an example of how a simple, basic recipe can be made into a fancy, guest-pleasing dish. We have taken the old-fashioned ALL-BRAN griddle cake and turned it into a gourmet corn cake with a savory, Italian-inspired garnish of prosciutto, arugula, and sun-dried tomatoes. SERVES 6

1. Combine the ALL-BRAN and hot water in a large heatproof mixing bowl. Set aside to soften for 2 minutes.

2. Combine the flour, sugar, baking power, baking soda, and salt in a medium mixing bowl.

3. Stir the egg and milk into the softened cereal, beating well with a wooden spoon. Add the flour mixture, stirring to just combine. Fold in the corn.

4. Preheat a griddle over medium-high heat until very hot but not smoking. Spoon about ¼ cup of the batter onto the griddle, pushing out slightly with the back of a spoon to make a neat circle. Cook, turning once, for about 4 minutes, or until golden on both sides. You will need to make 12 small cakes.

5. Place one cake on each of 6 luncheon plates. Nestle a small handful of arugula on each cake, top with about 3 tablespoons of sun-dried tomatoes, and fold about 3 slices of prosciutto over each salad. Top with another corn cake and serve with honey mustard on the side.

Chicken Fingers

1/2 cup all-purpose flour

1/2 teaspoon poultry seasoning

1 teaspoon paprika

1/4 teaspoon garlic powder

1 large egg, beaten

1/2 cup water

Salt and freshly ground pepper to taste

1/4 cup olive oil (see note)

2 boneless, skinless chicken breasts, trimmed of all fat and cut into 1 x 1 1/2-inch strips

2 cups KELLOGG'S Corn Flake Crumbs

KELLOGG'S Corn Flake Crumbs and the oven make these chicken fingers a welcome alternative to the standard heavily breaded, deep-fat-fried version of the children's favorite. To achieve a more adult-appealing flavor, try using olive oil. You can use the Spicy Tomato Sauce (see page 27) as a dipping sauce, or sprinkle the hot chicken fingers with fresh lemon juice or cider vinegar. SERVES 6

1. Combine the flour with the poultry seasoning, paprika, and garlic powder in a mixing bowl. Add the egg and water, whisking with a fork to blend well. Season with salt and pepper to taste.

2. Set aside to rest for 15 minutes.

3. Place the olive oil in a spray bottle.

4. Preheat oven to 375°F.

5. Dip the chicken strips into the batter, shaking off any excess. Evenly coat with the crumbs.

6. Place the battered strips onto a nonstick baking sheet. When all the chicken has been coated, lightly spray with olive oil. Place the baking sheet in the oven and bake, turning once and spraying with olive oil, for about 15 minutes or until cooked through and golden brown.

7. Remove from oven and serve hot.

NOTES: You can, of course, use other oils, including nonstick cooking spray.

If desired, you can change the flavor of the Chicken Fingers by adding Italian, Mexican, or Asian seasonings to the batter in place of the poultry seasoning and paprika. Also, if you have picky eaters, you can skip the other seasonings entirely and add just salt and pepper to the batter.

Salmon and Lemon Pâté

3 cups KELLOGG'S SPECIAL K

7 ounces canned salmon

2 tablespoons fresh lemon juice

1 teaspoon freshly grated lemon zest

2 teaspoons minced fresh dill

¼ cup butter, softened

Salt and freshly ground pepper to taste

This pâté can be served as a spread for an hors d'oeuvre, or the recipe could be doubled and then formed into individual molds and served as an appetizer on a bed of salad greens, on a Corn Cake (see page 31), or on a toast round. If you wish to unmold the pâté, first line the dish or mold with plastic film, leaving an edge all around. When ready to unmold, simply invert the filled mold onto a serving plate, then remove the mold and peel off the plastic film. SERVES 6

1. Place the SPECIAL K in a resealable plastic bag. Seal the bag and, using a rolling pin, crush the cereal to a fine crumb.

2. Place the salmon in a mixing bowl and, using a dinner fork, thoroughly mash. Stir in the SPECIAL K along with the lemon juice, zest, and dill. Add the butter and again using the fork, mash the mixture together until very well blended. Season with salt and pepper to taste.

3. Pack the pâté into a small, attractive serving dish, smoothing the top with a rubber spatula. Cover with plastic film and refrigerate for about 1 hour, or until firm.

4. When ready to serve, uncover and serve with crackers, toast points, pita crisps, or other crisp breads.

Crab and Shrimp Appetizer Balls

In this recipe, RICE KRISPIES cereal adds a bit of crunch to an elegant cocktail nibble. Here again, the basic recipe is so terrific that with just a few changes, you can create a whole new taste. A bit of fresh ginger, hot fresh chilies, red bell pepper, a drop or two of sesame oil—any one of these would add an element of surprise. A spectacular hors d'oeuvre or appetizer served piping hot with a beautiful bowl of Cilantro Sauce in the center of the platter or tray. MAKES ABOUT 3 DOZEN

3 cups KELLOGG'S RICE KRISPIES

2 tablespoons grated Parmesan cheese

6 ounces crab meat, finely chopped

1/4 pound cleaned raw shrimp, finely chopped

1/4 cup finely chopped celery

2 tablespoons finely chopped scallions

1 tablespoon finely chopped fresh cilantro leaves

2 large egg whites

2 tablespoons reduced-calorie mayonnaise

1/2 teaspoon seasoned pepper

1/2 teaspoon dry mustard

1/4 teaspoon hot sauce, or to taste

Cilantro Sauce (recipe follows)

1. Measure out 1 cup RICE KRISPIES and place it in a resealable plastic bag. Seal the bag and, using a rolling pin, crush the cereal to a fine crumb. Add the grated cheese, seal the bag, and shake to combine. Pour the mixture into a shallow soup bowl and set aside.

2. Preheat oven to 350°F.

3. Place the crab meat, shrimp, celery, scallions, and cilantro in a mixing bowl. Add the egg whites, mayonnaise, seasoned pepper, mustard, and hot sauce and stir to combine well. Fold in the remaining 2 cups RICE KRISPIES.

4. Using a spoon or a small melon baller, form the mixture into balls 1 inch in diameter. Roll each ball in the cereal-cheese mixture, taking care that each one is evenly covered.

5. Place the balls in a nonstick baking pan or in a traditional baking pan lined with parchment paper. Bake in the preheated oven for about 10 minutes, or until cooked through and golden brown.

6. Remove from oven and serve immediately with Cilantro Sauce.

CILANTRO SAUCE

6 tablespoons reduced-calorie mayonnaise

3 tablespoons Dijon mustard

1 tablespoon minced fresh cilantro leaves

1 tablespoon minced scallions, including some green part

1/4 teaspoon hot sauce, or to taste

Combine the mayonnaise, mustard, cilantro, scallions, and hot sauce in a small mixing bowl. Cover and refrigerate until ready to use.

CRISPIX MIX® Original

7 cups KELLOGG'S CRISPIX

1 cup mixed nuts

1 cup pretzels

3 tablespoons butter or margarine, melted

¼ teaspoon garlic salt

¼ teaspoon onion salt

2 teaspoons lemon juice

4 teaspoons Worcestershire sauce

This is one of the Kellogg Kitchens' all-time favorite snack mixes. The tang of the lemon juice and the zip of the Worcestershire sauce work well with the toasted sweetness of the corn-and-rice cereal to make this a most-requested recipe! MAKES ABOUT 9 CUPS

1. Preheat oven to 250°F.

2. Combine KELLOGG'S CRISPIX, nuts, and pretzels in a 13 x 9 x 2-inch baking pan, tossing to blend well. Set aside.

3. Combine the butter with the garlic and onion salts, lemon juice, and Worcestershire sauce in a small mixing bowl. Pour over the cereal mixture. Stir until evenly coated.

4. Bake in the preheated oven, stirring every 15 minutes, for 45 minutes.

5. Remove from oven and spread on paper towels to cool.

6. Store in an airtight container.

NOTE: This mixture may be cooked in a microwave. Microwave the seasoned cereal mix on high for 4 minutes, stirring after 2 minutes. Spread on paper towels to cool.

In 1931 Kellogg established the Cottage Kitchen to house the test kitchen and entertain visitors to the Battle Creek plant.

Maple Praline Mix

5½ cups KELLOGG'S CRISPIX

½ cup pecans, broken into pieces

⅓ cup pure maple syrup

3 tablespoons butter, melted

2 teaspoons pure vanilla extract

¼ cup flaked coconut

1 tablespoon sesame seeds

This popular snack mix is a great party snack—blending the toasty corn-and-rice cereal with sweet coconut, butter, and maple syrup. Kids love it! MAKES ABOUT 5 CUPS

1. Preheat oven to 300°F.

2. Lightly coat a 15 x 10 x 1-inch jellyroll pan with nonstick cooking spray. Add CRISPIX and pecans, tossing to blend.

3. Combine the syrup, butter, and vanilla in a small mixing bowl. Add the coconut and sesame seeds, stirring well. Drizzle the syrup mixture over the cereal, tossing until evenly coated.

4. Bake in the preheated oven, stirring twice to keep the cereal from sticking and burning, for about 30 minutes, or until beginning to brown.

5. Remove from oven and set aside to cool, stirring occasionally.

6. Serve when cool, or store in an airtight container.

Cereal Scramble

2½ cups KELLOGG'S MINI-WHEATS Frosted Bite Size cereal

2½ cups KELLOGG'S CRACKLIN' OAT BRAN

1 cup dried banana chips

1 cup multicolored, fruit-flavored, bite-size candies

1 cup peanuts

This mix is easy to put together and makes a tasty after-school snack for hungry kids. Even grown-ups will enjoy the combination of crunchy cereal, nuts, and fruity sweetness. MAKES 8 CUPS

1. Combine the cereals with the banana chips, candies, and peanuts in an extra-large resealable plastic bag. Seal the bag and shake to blend well.

2. Serve immediately, or store in an airtight container.

Spicy Mix-Up

7 cups KELLOGG'S CRISPIX

2 cups corn chips

3 tablespoons butter or margarine, melted

2 teaspoons chili powder

1/4 teaspoon garlic salt

1/2 teaspoon onion salt

1/4 cup grated Parmesan cheese

This is a great snack to add to a Sunday-afternoon football buffet. It goes well with Mexican dishes, pizza, and other hearty foods. You can use traditional corn chips or substitute any of the more exotic tortilla chips now on supermarket shelves. MAKES 9 CUPS

1. Preheat oven to 250°F.

2. Combine CRISPIX and corn chips in a large mixing bowl.

3. Place the butter in a small bowl. Add the chili powder, along with the garlic and onion salts. Drizzle the butter mixture over the cereal mixture and gently toss to coat.

4. Place the mixture in a 13 x 9 x 2-inch baking pan. Bake in the preheated oven for 15 minutes. Remove from oven and sprinkle with the cheese.

5. Return to the oven and continue to bake, stirring occasionally, for about 30 minutes, or until lightly browned.

6. Remove from oven and transfer to a double layer of paper towel to cool.

7. Serve when cool, or store in an airtight container.

NOTE: This mixture may be cooked in a microwave. Microwave the seasoned cereal mix on high for 2 minutes, stirring once. Sprinkle on the cheese and continue cooking on high for an additional 2 minutes, stirring once.

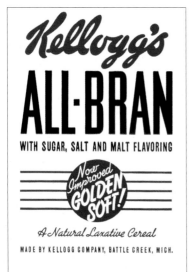

CORN POPS® Crunch Snack

1/4 cup butter or margarine, melted

1 teaspoon Worcestershire sauce

1 tablespoon sesame seeds (optional)

1/2 teaspoon onion salt

1/4 teaspoon dried oregano

1/8 teaspoon dried dill weed

3 cups KELLOGG'S CORN POPS

1/2 cup pecan halves

CORN POPS cereal makes a great snack mix because it has a great corn flavor and a terrific crunchy texture. Combined with herbs and nuts, it offers a nice change from plain mixed nuts. MAKES ABOUT 3 1/2 CUPS

1. Preheat oven to 350°F.

2. Pour the melted butter into a 12 x 9 x 2-inch baking pan. Add the Worcestershire sauce, along with the sesame seeds, onion salt, oregano, and dill weed, stirring to combine.

3. Add CORN POPS and pecans and gently toss to coat.

4. Bake in the preheated oven, stirring occasionally, for about 15 minutes.

5. Remove from oven and set aside to cool.

6. Serve when cool, or store in an airtight container.

Barbecued Corn Dogs

1 cup barbecue sauce of choice

1/2 cup grape jelly

1/4 cup prepared mustard

One 10-ounce package MORNINGSTAR FARMS Mini Corn Dogs

One 20-ounce can unsweetened pineapple chunks, well drained

2 tablespoons sliced scallions

This recipe is a bit of a take on the classic Chinese sweet-and-sour dishes. You can spice it up depending on the flavor of barbecue sauce that you choose. The corn dogs make terrific party snacks. SERVES 6

1. Combine barbecue sauce, jelly, and mustard in a medium saucepan over medium heat. Cook, stirring frequently, for about 4 minutes, or until the ingredients are blended and the mixture is smooth.

2. Add the Mini Corn Dogs and pineapple, lower the heat to a simmer, and cook, stirring occasionally, for about 10 minutes, or until the corn dogs are hot.

3. Remove from heat and pour into a bowl. Sprinkle with scallions and serve.

Spicy Bean Dip

One 15.5-ounce can pinto beans with their liquid

1 cup KELLOGG'S ALL-BRAN

³/₄ cup bottled salsa of choice

¹/₄ cup chopped onion

¹/₄ teaspoon garlic salt

¹/₄ teaspoon ground cumin

¹/₄ teaspoon hot sauce

1 tablespoon chopped fresh cilantro

2 tablespoons nonfat yogurt or sour cream

2 tablespoons finely chopped fresh tomato

2 tablespoons finely sliced scallions

Tasty and a little bit zesty, this is a microwavable dish, so preparation is a snap! MAKES 2¹/₂ CUPS

1. Drain beans, reserving liquid.

2. Combine the beans, ALL-BRAN, salsa, onion, garlic salt, cumin, hot sauce, and ¹/₂ cup of reserved bean liquid in the bowl of a food processor fitted with the metal blade. Process to a smooth purée.

3. Scrape the mixture into a 1-quart microwavable bowl and stir in cilantro. Cover loosely and place in the microwave. Microwave on high, stirring twice during the cooking, until thoroughly heated, 3–4 minutes.

4. Transfer to a serving dish. Garnish with a dollop of nonfat yogurt or sour cream. Sprinkle on the tomato and scallions and serve warm with tortilla chips or fresh vegetables.

A WEEK OF MEALS FOR THE KELLOGG KIDS

	BREAKFAST	NOON MEAL	EVENING MEAL
Sunday	Sliced Oranges Kellogg's Krumbles Omelet Toasted Muffins Milk Coffee (adults)	Roast Lamb Mashed Potatoes Buttered String Beans Vegetable Salad Ice Cream	Toasted Cheese Sandwiches Celery All-Bran Cookies Tea *Children's Supper* Kellogg's Corn Flakes Stewed Figs All-Bran Cookies Milk
Monday	Stewed Prunes Kellogg's New Oata Bacon Toast Milk Coffee (adults)	Potato Soup All-Bran Muffins Poached Eggs Braised Carrots Kellogg's Mock Apple Strudel	Sliced Lamb Currant Jelly Browned Potatoes Sauce Lettuce Salad Squash Caramel Custard *Children's Supper* Pep Milk Jelly Sandwiches Caramel Custard
Tuesday	Apple Sauce Kellogg's Corn Flakes Poached Eggs Rolls Milk Coffee (adults)	Creamed Eggs Shredded Lettuce (Adults—French Dressing) (Children—Fruit Juice) Sponge Cake Tea (adults) Whipped Cream Milk	Veal Cutlets Creamed Potatoes Spinach Baked Pears *Children's Supper* Creamed Potatoes Spinach Baked Pears Milk
Wednesday	Oranges Kellogg's New Oata Scrambled Eggs Toast Milk Coffee (adults)	Tomato Toast Baked Potatoes Milk Junket Tea (adults)	Pot Roast with Vegetables Cabbage Salad Prune Whip *Children's Supper* Kellogg's Corn Flakes Peanut Butter Sandwiches Prune Whip Milk

Crumble-Potato Wontons

2 cups MORNINGSTAR FARMS GRILLERS Burger Style Veggie RECIPE CRUMBLES

1 large potato, peeled and finely chopped

1 medium yellow onion, peeled and finely chopped

$1/2$ teaspoon minced garlic

1 cup vegetable broth

$1/2$ teaspoon ground cumin

$1/2$ teaspoon ground allspice

Salt and freshly ground pepper to taste

2 tablespoons chopped fresh cilantro

36 wonton wrappers

These are not your classic Chinese wontons, but they are certainly a tasty take on them. You can serve them plain or with any type of dipping sauce, even bottled salsa. If you like spicy food, add some fresh chili or hot sauce to the Crumbles mix. MAKES 3 DOZEN

1. Combine the CRUMBLES with the potato, onion, and garlic in a large saucepan. Place over medium heat and stir in the broth. Add the cumin and allspice and cook, stirring frequently, for about 10 minutes, or until the potatoes are cooked and the broth has evaporated.

2. Remove from heat and transfer to a mixing bowl. Season with salt and pepper to taste and stir in the cilantro. Cover with plastic film and refrigerate for about 1 hour or until well chilled.

3. When ready to bake, preheat oven to 400°F.

4. Fill a small bowl with cold water.

5. Working with one piece at a time, use a pastry brush to lightly coat the edge of the wonton wrapper with water. Place $1/2$ to $3/4$ tablespoon of the chilled Crumbles filling in the center of the wrapper and then fold the wrapper over the filling to make a triangle. Lightly press the edges together and then, using a dinner fork, crimp the edges together. Place the finished pastry on a nonstick baking sheet. Continue making pastries until all of the wonton wrappers have been used.

6. Lightly spray the finished wontons with nonstick cooking spray or with olive oil (see page 27).

7. Bake in the preheated oven, turning at least once, for about 9 minutes, or until crisp and golden brown.

Cheese Wafers

2 cups grated sharp Cheddar cheese

1/2 cup butter or margarine, softened

3/4 cup all-purpose flour

1/2 teaspoon salt

Cayenne pepper to taste

1 1/2 cups KELLOGG'S RICE KRISPIES, or 1 cup KELLOGG'S ALL-BRAN

These are terrific crackers to have on hand for snacks or to serve with a soup or salad. They also make a great gift from your kitchen during the holidays. You might want to make one batch with RICE KRISPIES and one with ALL-BRAN, as each cereal adds its special flavor. You can also sprinkle poppy or sesame seeds on the crackers before baking to add another dimension of taste. MAKES 5 DOZEN

1. Preheat oven to 350°F.

2. Combine the cheese and butter in the bowl of a standing electric mixer and beat until very light and fluffy.

3. Combine the flour, salt, and cayenne and add to the cheese mixture, beating to incorporate.

4. Remove the bowl from the mixer and, using a wooden spoon, stir in the RICE KRISPIES or ALL-BRAN.

5. Drop the mixture by the teaspoon onto ungreased cookie sheets, leaving about 1 inch between the mounds.

Using a table fork dipped in flour, flatten each piece to make an even, ridged round wafer.

6. Bake in the preheated oven for about 12 minutes, or until lightly browned around the edges.

7. Remove from oven and immediately transfer to wire racks to cool completely.

SOUPS AND SALADS

Fresh Tomato Gazpacho

5 cups peeled, seeded, and chopped very ripe tomatoes

One 6-ounce can tomato paste

1 clove garlic, peeled and finely chopped

1/4 cup chopped onion

1/4 cup white or red wine vinegar

Salt to taste

1/4 cup olive oil

2 cups KELLOGG'S Stuffing Mix

1 clove garlic, peeled and cut in half lengthwise

1 medium tomato, peeled and diced

1 medium green bell pepper, stemmed, seeded, and diced

1 medium cucumber, peeled and diced

1 hard-cooked egg, peeled and coarsely chopped

Who would have thought that this light, refreshing summertime soup could be made even tastier garnished with garlic-seasoned croutons made using KELLOGG'S Stuffing Mix, a perennial favorite among our consumers? This soup is the perfect beginning to a warm evening's supper; it also makes a delicious light lunch. SERVES 6

1. Measure out 2 cups of the chopped tomatoes. Place them in the container of a blender along with the tomato paste, garlic, onion, vinegar, and salt to taste. Process to a smooth purée. Pour the mixture into a mixing bowl.

2. Place the remaining 3 cups of chopped tomatoes in the blender container and process until smooth. Pour into the tomato-onion mixture, stirring to combine. Cover with plastic film and refrigerate for at least 1 hour, or until well chilled.

3. While the soup is chilling, prepare the stuffing "croutons." Heat the oil in a medium frying pan over low heat. When hot, add the Stuffing Mix and garlic halves. Cook, stirring frequently, for about 5 minutes, or until the Stuffing Mix is crisp and lightly browned. Remove from heat. Remove and discard the garlic and set croutons aside to cool.

4. When ready to serve, divide the diced tomato, bell pepper, cucumber, and egg among 6 chilled, shallow soup bowls.

5. Ladle the chilled soup into the bowls. Top with the stuffing croutons and serve.

Chicken Noodle Soup

7 cups chicken broth

1 cup water

1 cup diced carrots

1/2 cup diced celery

1/4 cup diced onion

Salt and freshly ground white pepper to taste

KELLOGG'S ALL-BRAN Noodles (recipe follows)

2 cups diced cooked chicken

2 tablespoons minced fresh parsley

Noodles made with KELLOGG'S ALL-BRAN enrich this chicken soup with new flavor. Although the noodles make a great addition to a soup, they are also delicious served on their own with a bit of olive oil or butter and a grating of cheese. SERVES 6

1. Combine the broth and water in a large saucepan over medium-high heat. Add the carrots, celery, and onions. Season with salt and pepper to taste and bring to a boil. Lower the heat, cover, and simmer for 5 minutes.

2. Uncover, raise the heat, and add the noodles. Bring to a boil; then lower the heat and simmer, stirring occasionally, for 10 minutes, or until the noodles are tender.

3. Stir in the chicken and cook for an additional minute.

4. Remove from the heat, stir in the parsley, and serve hot.

ALL-BRAN® NOODLES

1 cup KELLOGG'S ALL-BRAN

1/2 cup whole wheat flour

1/2 cup all-purpose flour

1/2 teaspoon salt

1/4 cup fat-free milk

2 large egg whites

All-purpose flour for rolling and dusting

NOTE: If the noodles are not used in the chicken soup recipe, they can be cooked for about 10 minutes in 6 cups of boiling, salted water.

1. Combine the ALL-BRAN, whole wheat flour, all-purpose flour, and salt in a mixing bowl. Stir in the milk and egg whites. If necessary, add more all-purpose flour, a tablespoon at a time, to make a stiff dough.

2. Lightly flour a clean work surface. Scrape the dough onto the floured surface and lightly flour the top of the dough. Using a rolling pin, roll the dough out to 1/16-inch thickness. Allow to dry for 1 hour.

3. Cut dough into 3-inch-wide strips. If dough seems a bit tacky, lightly dust with flour.

4. Stack 4 to 5 dough strips on top of one another and then cut the stack crosswise into 1/4-inch-wide noodles.

5. Lightly flour a clean, flat surface. Spread the noodles out on the floured surface and allow to dry for 2 hours before cooking. (See note.)

Minestrone

2 tablespoons olive oil

$^1/_2$ cup finely diced leeks

3 tablespoons finely chopped onion

1 clove garlic, peeled and minced

$1^1/_2$ cups diced zucchini

$1^1/_2$ cups diced carrots

$1^1/_2$ cups diced potatoes

$^1/_2$ cup diced celery

One 28-ounce can diced tomatoes with their juices

One 16-ounce can Great Northern or cannellini beans with their liquid

5 cups chicken broth

2 sprigs fresh parsley

1 bay leaf

1 teaspoon minced fresh basil leaves

Salt and freshly ground pepper to taste

One 10-ounce package frozen peas

1 cup KELLOGG'S ALL-BRAN

3 tablespoons grated Parmesan cheese, optional

1 tablespoon minced fresh parsley, optional

This great-tasting soup incorporates ALL-BRAN along with fresh veggies and beans to provide extra fiber to a traditional favorite. SERVES 9

1. Heat the oil in a large saucepan over medium heat. Add the leeks, onion, and garlic and sauté for 2 minutes.

2. Add the zucchini, carrots, potatoes, and celery and cook, stirring frequently, for 5 minutes.

3. Add the tomatoes, beans, chicken broth, parsley sprigs, bay leaf, and basil. Season with salt and pepper to taste and bring to a simmer. Simmer, stirring occasionally, for 20 minutes. Add the peas and simmer for an additional 10 minutes, or until all of the vegetables are tender.

4. Remove from heat. Remove and discard the parsley and bay leaf. Stir in the ALL-BRAN and serve, garnished with Parmesan cheese and minced parsley, if desired.

Tabbouleh

1 cup uncooked bulgur wheat (see note)

4 cups peeled, seeded, and chopped very ripe tomatoes

1 cup KELLOGG'S ALL-BRAN

1 cup loosely packed parsley leaves, minced

1 cup loosely packed fresh mint leaves, minced

3/4 cup sliced scallions, with some green part

1/2 cup fresh lemon juice

2 tablespoons olive oil

Salt and freshly ground pepper to taste

Tabbouleh is a traditional Middle Eastern salad made with bulgur, wheat kernels that have been steamed, dried, and crushed. The addition of KELLOGG'S ALL-BRAN to this classic adds more texture and deeper flavor. It can be served alone with pita bread and extra virgin olive oil or as a side dish for a summer barbeque. SERVES 8

1. Place the bulgur in a medium mixing bowl and cover with cold water. Using your fingers, swish the bulgur around to rinse. Drain well.

2. Return the bulgur to the bowl and add 4 cups of cold water. Set aside to soak for 2 hours, or until al dente (firm to the bite).

3. Drain the swollen bulgur well and transfer to a clean kitchen towel. Pull up the sides of the towel and twist to ring out any remaining water.

4. Place the bulgur in a large salad bowl. Add the tomatoes, ALL-BRAN, parsley, mint, and scallions, tossing to blend.

5. Sprinkle on the lemon juice and olive oil. Season with salt and pepper to taste and toss until well combined.

6. Cover with plastic film and refrigerate for about 3 hours before serving.

NOTE: Bulgur is available at Middle Eastern markets, at specialty food stores, or in the pasta or rice section of many supermarkets.

Catfish Salad Supreme

3 cups tomato juice

1/4 cup chopped onion

1 tablespoon fresh lemon juice

1 teaspoon dried oregano

1/4 teaspoon garlic salt

1 pound skinless catfish fillets

8 cups torn mixed salad greens such as spinach, romaine, or leaf lettuce, well washed and dried

DRESSING

1/2 cup red wine vinegar

1/4 cup water

2 packets artificial sweetener, or 4 teaspoons sugar

1/4 teaspoon dried oregano

Salt and freshly ground pepper to taste

2 cups peeled, seeded, and diced tomatoes

1/4 cup sliced scallions

1 cup KELLOGG'S ALL-BRAN Extra Fiber cereal or Savory Spoon-Ons (see page 228)

Cooking the fish in a savory liquid gives the finished salad a very rich flavor. Don't be afraid to try bitter winter greens such as chicory in the base, since the heat of the warm vinegar will soften them. You could also substitute other fish, poultry, or lean pork for the catfish, cooking it in the tomato broth until done. Whatever you use, the salad will be a hit. SERVES 6

1. Combine the tomato juice, onion, lemon juice, 1 teaspoon oregano, and garlic salt in a medium nonreactive saucepan over medium heat. Bring to a boil, stirring frequently.

2. When the liquid comes to a boil, immediately add the catfish. Cover and simmer for 10 minutes, or until the catfish flakes apart when poked with a fork. Remove from the heat and set aside to cool in the liquid for 30 minutes.

3. When cool, using a slotted spoon, lift the catfish from the cooking liquid. Flake the fish and place in a container with a lid. Cover and refrigerate.

4. Place the greens in a large salad bowl. Set aside.

5. To make the dressing, combine the vinegar, water, sweetener, 1/4 teaspoon oregano, and salt and pepper to taste in a small nonreactive saucepan over medium heat. Cook, stirring constantly, for a couple of minutes, or just until the sweetener has dissolved. Remove from the heat and drizzle over the greens. Cover the bowl with plastic film and let stand for 1 minute.

6. Uncover the bowl and toss in the tomatoes, scallions, and chilled catfish.

7. When well combined, place an equal portion in each of 6 salad bowls. Sprinkle with ALL-BRAN or Savory Spoon-Ons and serve.

Turkey-Spinach Salad

3 large egg whites

2 cups KELLOGG'S CRUNCHY BLENDS Low Fat Granola

Salt and freshly ground pepper to taste

1½ pounds boneless, skinless turkey breast, in one piece

3 tablespoons olive oil

6 cups torn spinach leaves, well washed and dried

One 11-ounce can mandarin oranges, well drained

2 scallions, some green included, washed, trimmed, and cut crosswise into thin slices

½ cup sliced celery

½ cup diced cucumber

Honey Vinaigrette (recipe follows)

This is a marvelous main course salad. Turkey breast presented in this manner is also great simply seasoned with some fresh lemon juice. SERVES 4

1. Preheat oven to 350°F.

2. Line a baking pan with aluminum foil. Lightly coat with nonstick cooking spray. Set aside.

3. Place the egg whites in a shallow bowl and whisk until frothy. Place the granola in another shallow bowl. Season with salt and pepper to taste and set aside.

4. Using a sharp knife, cut the turkey, with the grain, into 4 equal pieces. Place each piece between two sheets of wax paper and, using a meat mallet, small frying pan, or other heavy, flat object, pound each piece to ½-inch thickness.

5. Remove the wax paper and, working with one piece at a time, first dip the turkey into the egg whites, taking care that each side is coated. Then immediately press it into the granola, turning to coat both sides completely.

6. Place the coated turkey pieces on the prepared baking sheet and lightly drizzle with the olive oil.

7. Bake in the preheated oven for about 25 minutes, or until cooked in the center and crisp and golden brown. Remove from oven and set aside.

8. Combine the spinach with the mandarin oranges, scallions, celery, and cucumber in a large mixing bowl. Toss to blend well. Divide the mixture among 4 plates.

9. Working with one piece at a time, carefully slice the turkey on the bias and fan the slices over the salad on one of the plates. When all of the salads are assembled, drizzle the vinaigrette over them and serve.

HONEY VINAIGRETTE

¹/₄ cup honey

¹/₄ cup cider vinegar

2 tablespoons soy sauce

1 teaspoon Dijon mustard

Combine the honey, vinegar, soy sauce, and mustard in a small container with a lid. Cover tightly and shake. Set aside until ready to use, or refrigerate for up to 5 days. Bring to room temperature before serving.

Lemony Apple-Bran Salad

¹/₂ cup lemon low-fat yogurt

1 tablespoon minced fresh parsley

Salt to taste

2 cups chopped unpeeled red-skinned apples

¹/₂ cup thinly sliced celery

¹/₂ cup sliced seedless grapes (red or green), or raisins

¹/₂ cup KELLOGG'S ALL-BRAN

6 lettuce leaves

This is our version of an old-fashioned Waldorf salad, adding ALL-BRAN for crunch. SERVES 6

1. Combine the yogurt with the parsley and salt in a small mixing bowl, whisking to blend well.

2. Combine the apples, celery, and grapes in a medium mixing bowl. Add the yogurt mixture and stir to blend. Cover and refrigerate till ready to serve.

3. Just before serving, stir in ALL-BRAN and serve immediately on a bed of lettuce.

Wilted Lettuce Salad

2 tablespoons olive oil

1 tablespoon sesame seeds

³/₄ teaspoon paprika

¹/₄ teaspoon garlic salt

1 cup KELLOGG'S ALL-BRAN or ALL-BRAN BRAN BUDS

2 tablespoons grated Parmesan cheese

2 medium heads iceberg lettuce, pulled apart, torn into small pieces, well washed and dried

1 large tomato, peeled, cored, seeded, and diced

¹/₄ cup sliced scallions

¹/₂ teaspoon dried oregano

¹/₄ teaspoon freshly ground pepper

6 slices bacon

¹/₄ cup red wine vinegar

2 teaspoons sugar

Many, many years ago, wilted salads were extremely popular—particularly in farming communities with German heritage. They gradually lost favor to crisp, tossed greens. We think that this wilted salad just might be the one to bring wilted salads back onto the menu. SERVES 6

1. Heat the olive oil in a medium frying pan over medium heat. Add the sesame seeds, paprika, and garlic salt and stir to blend well. Add the ALL-BRAN (or BRAN BUDS) and sauté for about 2 minutes, or until the cereal is well coated, crisp, and lightly browned. Remove from heat. Add the Parmesan cheese and toss to blend. Set aside.

2. Combine the lettuce with the tomato, scallions, oregano, and pepper. Set aside.

3. Place the bacon in a cold frying pan over medium-high heat. Fry, turning occasionally, for about 5 minutes, or until crisp. Remove the bacon from the pan and crumble it into small pieces. Set aside.

4. Add the vinegar and sugar to the bacon fat in the frying pan. Place over medium heat and cook, stirring constantly, for about 2 minutes, or until the sugar has dissolved.

5. Remove from heat and pour over the salad mix, tossing to coat well. Cover with plastic film and let stand for 1 minute.

6. Place an equal portion of the salad in each of 6 salad bowls. Sprinkle the reserved ALL-BRAN mix and bacon over them and serve immediately.

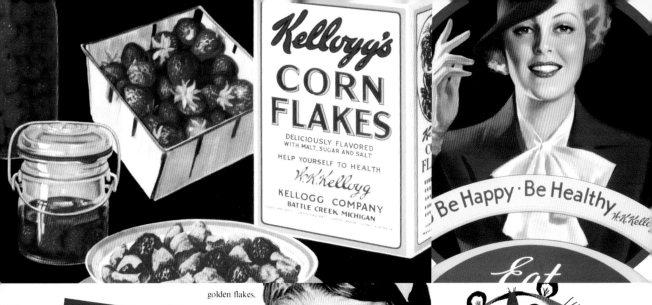

ENTRÉES

Double-Coated Chicken

7 cups KELLOGG'S CORN FLAKES, or 1³/₄ cups KELLOGG'S Corn Flake Crumbs

1 large egg

1 cup fat-free milk

1 cup all-purpose flour

¹/₂ teaspoon salt

¹/₄ teaspoon pepper

3 pounds broiler chicken pieces, with or without skin, rinsed and patted dry

3 tablespoons butter or margarine, melted

This is one of Kellogg Company's most popular recipes. Consumers have made it the number one Corn Flakes recipe. SERVES 6

1. Preheat oven to 350°F.

2. Line a baking pan with aluminum foil or lightly coat with nonstick cooking spray. Set aside.

3. Place the Corn Flakes in a resealable plastic bag. Seal the bag and, using a rolling pin, crush the flakes to a fine crumb. Open the bag and measure the crumbs; you should have 1³/4 cups. You may have to do this in batches.

4. Place the crumbs in a shallow dish or pan. Set aside.

5. Combine the egg and milk in a medium mixing bowl and beat slightly. Add the flour, salt, and pepper and mix until smooth.

6. Working with one piece at a time, dip the chicken into the batter and then coat the battered piece with cereal crumbs.

7. Place the coated chicken in a single layer in the prepared baking pan. When all of the chicken has been coated, drizzle the butter over the top.

8. Bake the chicken in the preheated oven for about 1 hour, or until the chicken is tender and no longer pink and juices run clear. Do not cover pan or turn chicken while baking.

9. Remove from oven and serve hot.

Hot and Spicy Chicken Quesadillas

Sixteen 8-inch flour tortillas

1¹/₂ pounds grilled chicken breast, cut into strips

12 ounces Mexican-style cheese, shredded

One 7-ounce can chopped green chilies, drained

¹/₂ bunch fresh cilantro, stems removed, well washed, and chopped

5 ounces (¹/₂ box) CHEEZ-IT Hot & Spicy crackers

Guacamole, optional

Salsa, optional

Quesadillas make great party fare for both children and adults. This is an extremely simple recipe to put together once you have all of the ingredients on hand. It makes a great lunch, late-night or afternoon snack, or Sunday-afternoon football munchie. The quesadillas will make an even bigger hit if served with guacamole and salsa and, of course, a bowl of CHEEZ-IT crackers! SERVES 8

1. Preheat broiler.

2. Lay 8 of the tortillas out on a clean, flat surface. Place an equal portion of chicken in the center of each tortilla, spreading it out to cover the tortilla.

3. Sprinkle equal portions of the cheese, chilies, cilantro, and crackers over the tortillas. Top with remaining tortillas.

4. Place the quesadillas on a broiler-proof pan and broil, turning once, for about 5 minutes, or until each side is slightly browned or grilled and the cheese has melted. (You may have to do this in batches.)

5. Remove from the broiler, cut into wedges, and serve hot with guacamole, salsa, and more CHEEZ-IT crackers, if desired.

Chicken Italienne

7 cups KELLOGG'S CORN FLAKES

One 8-ounce can tomato sauce

1 teaspoon chopped fresh basil

$1/4$ teaspoon dried oregano

$1/2$ teaspoon garlic salt

Freshly ground pepper to taste

3 pounds broiler chicken pieces, with or without skin, rinsed and patted dry

This is an extension of our famous Double-Coated Chicken. The chicken is dipped in an Italian seasoned tomato sauce rather than a batter, and then coated with KELLOGG'S CORN FLAKES crumbs. A side dish of spaghetti with marinara sauce and a tossed green salad would round out a perfect trattoria meal. SERVES 6

1. Preheat oven to 350°F.

2. Line a baking pan with aluminum foil or lightly coat with nonstick cooking spray. Set aside.

3. Place the KELLOGG'S CORN FLAKES in a resealable plastic bag. Seal the bag and, using a rolling pin, crush the flakes to a medium-fine crumb. Open the bag and measure the crumbs; you should have $2^1/2$ cups. You may have to do this in batches. Place the crumbs in a shallow dish.

4. Combine the tomato sauce, basil, oregano, garlic salt, and pepper in a small mixing bowl.

5. Working with one piece at a time, dip the chicken into the tomato sauce mixture and then roll in the crumbs, taking care to completely cover.

Production of KELLOGG'S CORN FLAKES began at W. K. Kellogg's newly formed Battle Creek Toasted Corn Flake Company in 1906.

6. Place the coated chicken in a single layer in the prepared baking pan. When all of the chicken has been coated, place the chicken in the preheated oven and bake for about 1 hour, or until the chicken is tender and no longer pink and juices run clear. Do not cover pan or turn chicken while baking.

7. Remove from oven and serve.

THE bugle call that brings all the little troopers eagerly around the mess-table is Kellogg's Toasted Corn Flakes.

Kellogg's—the Original Toasted Corn Flakes, remain as original as ever — light, and dainty, appetizing in flavor, with a melting crispness on the tongue.

Imitations come and go!
They change their name
They change their form
Some do both
Why?

W. K. Kellogg

Kellogg's TOASTED CORN FLAKES

Crisp Orange-Baked Chicken

3 pounds skinless broiler chicken pieces, rinsed and patted dry

²/₃ cup fresh orange juice

1 clove garlic, peeled and minced

½ teaspoon freshly grated orange zest

4 cups KELLOGG'S CORN FLAKES

2 tablespoons minced fresh parsley

2 large eggs

Salt and freshly ground pepper to taste

½ cup all-purpose flour

Crispy, citrusy, and very delicious, this is a simple-to-make but worthy-of-company dish. It is particularly good served with orange-flavored sweet potatoes and a crisp green vegetable. SERVES 6

1. Place the chicken in a single layer in a glass baking dish.

2. Combine the orange juice with the garlic and zest in a small bowl, whisking to blend. Pour over the chicken, turning to coat each piece well.

3. Cover the dish with plastic film and refrigerate, turning occasionally, for 2 hours.

4. Preheat oven to 350°F.

5. Place the KELLOGG'S CORN FLAKES in a resealable plastic bag. Seal the bag and, using a rolling pin, crush the flakes to a fine crumb. Open the bag and measure the crumbs; you should have 1 cup. You may have to do this in batches. Place the crumbs in a shallow dish. Stir in the parsley and set aside.

6. Combine the eggs with salt and pepper to taste in a shallow bowl, whisking to blend well.

7. Line a baking pan with aluminum foil or lightly coat with nonstick cooking spray. Set aside.

8. Place the flour in a shallow bowl.

9. Remove the chicken from the refrigerator. Unwrap and, working with one piece at a time, shake off excess liquid and roll in the flour to just lightly coat. Then dip the floured chicken into the eggs and, finally, roll it in the cereal mixture.

10. Place the coated chicken in a single layer in the prepared baking pan. Bake in the preheated oven for about 1 hour and 10 minutes, or until the chicken is tender and no longer pink and juices run clear. Do not cover pan or turn chicken while baking.

11. Remove from oven and serve.

Norman Rockwell created the "Kellogg Kids" for KELLOGG'S CORN FLAKES packaging in the 1950s.

Lemon-Herb Chicken

1/4 cup canola oil

1/4 cup ketchup

2 tablespoons fresh lemon juice

2 tablespoons soy sauce

1/2 teaspoon dried rosemary

1/2 teaspoon dried thyme

1/2 teaspoon dried marjoram

Salt and freshly ground pepper to taste

3 pounds broiler chicken pieces, with or without skin, rinsed and patted dry

5 cups KELLOGG'S CORN FLAKES

With this crispy chicken, you can double the marinade, reserve half of it in the refrigerator, and then cook it to be used as a dipping sauce. If you happen to have fresh herbs on hand, do use them—double the amount called for in the recipe—for garden-fresh flavor. SERVES 6

1. Combine the canola oil, ketchup, lemon juice, soy sauce, rosemary, thyme, and marjoram with salt and pepper to taste in a large bowl, whisking to blend well. Add the chicken and turn to evenly coat. Cover with plastic film and refrigerate, turning occasionally, for 4 hours.

2. Line a baking pan with aluminum foil or lightly coat with nonstick cooking spray. Set aside.

3. Place the KELLOGG'S CORN FLAKES in a resealable plastic bag. Seal the bag and, using a rolling pin, crush the flakes to a coarse crumb. Open the bag and measure the crumbs; you should have 3 cups. You may have to do this in batches. Place the crumbs in a shallow dish.

4. Preheat oven to 350°F.

5. Remove the chicken from the refrigerator. Unwrap and, working with one piece at a time, shake off excess liquid and roll in the crumbs.

6. Place the coated chicken in a single layer in the prepared baking pan. Bake in the preheated oven, without turning, for about 1 hour, or until the chicken is tender and no longer pink and juices run clear.

7. Remove from oven and serve.

Chicken Kiev

$1/2$ cup butter, softened

$1/2$ cup finely chopped fresh spinach

2 cloves garlic, peeled and finely minced

1 teaspoon salt

$1/4$ teaspoon freshly ground pepper

1 cup KELLOGG'S Corn Flake Crumbs

2 large egg whites or 1 large egg

3 whole chicken breasts, skin on, halved and boned

This is another elegant party dish that can be made early in the day and baked at the last minute to make entertaining a breeze. SERVES 6

1. Preheat oven to 350°F.

2. Line a baking pan with aluminum foil or lightly coat with nonstick cooking spray. Set aside.

3. Combine the butter and spinach in a small mixing bowl. Add the garlic, $1/2$ teaspoon of the salt, and $1/8$ teaspoon pepper and stir to blend completely. Set aside.

4. Combine the KELLOGG'S Corn Flake Crumbs with the remaining $1/2$ teaspoon salt and $1/8$ teaspoon pepper in a shallow bowl. Set aside.

5. Place the egg whites in a shallow bowl and whisk to blend.

6. Working from one side and with one piece at a time, carefully lift the chicken skin from the flesh, taking care not to pull the skin totally away from the flesh. Insert a portion of the spinach mixture between the skin and flesh in each breast piece, keeping the skin attached.

7. Dip the skin side of the stuffed breast into the egg whites and then into the crumbs.

8. Place the stuffed, coated breasts skin side up in the prepared baking pan. When all of the breasts are in the pan, place in the preheated oven and bake, without turning, for about 1 hour, or until the chicken is cooked through and the skin is crisp and golden.

9. Remove from oven and serve.

Jean-Georges Vongerichten, V Steakhouse, New York City

Crunchy Baked Chicken

$^1/_2$ cup KELLOGG'S RICE KRISPIES

$^1/_2$ cup KELLOGG'S CORN FLAKES

$^1/_2$ cup KELLOGG'S SPECIAL K

$^1/_2$ cup KELLOGG'S COMPLETE Wheat Bran Flakes

$^1/_2$ cup olive oil

6 tablespoons minced shallots

2 tablespoons minced garlic

$1^1/_2$ cups white wine

$^3/_4$ cup fresh lemon juice

$^1/_2$ cup soy sauce

$^1/_2$ cup unsalted butter, cut into pieces

2 teaspoons sesame oil

1 teaspoon salt

$^1/_2$ teaspoon white pepper

One 3-pound chicken, split in half, skin on

8 large egg yolks (see note)

1 teaspoon ground dried red chili peppers

Chef Jean-Georges Vongerichten's restaurant empire reaches all over the world. He is best known for replacing traditionally rich French sauces with light vegetable and fruit juice–based emulsions and adding Asian ingredients to classic dishes. In this recipe, classic KELLOGG'S cereals are used in combination with Asian ingredients to create a very tasty chicken dish. We have adapted this very special restaurant dish for easier cooking at home. SERVES 6

1. Combine the RICE KRISPIES, Corn Flakes, SPECIAL K, and COMPLETE in a broad mixing bowl. Crush lightly, tossing to blend well. Set aside.

2. Heat 2 tablespoons of the olive oil in a medium saucepan over medium heat. Add the shallots and garlic and cook, stirring, for about 6 minutes, or until golden brown. Add the wine, lemon juice, and 6 tablespoons of the soy sauce and bring to a simmer. Lower the heat and simmer, stirring occasionally, for about 30 minutes, or until thick and syrupy. Whisk in the butter, a bit at a time, beating until slightly thickened and well emulsified. Whisk in $1^1/2$ teaspoons of the sesame oil. Taste and, if necessary, season with salt and pepper. Transfer to the top half of a double boiler placed over barely simmering water to keep warm.

3. While the sauce is cooking, wash chicken and pat dry.

4. Preheat oven to 450°F.

5. Using about 1 tablespoon of the olive oil, lightly coat a baking pan. Set aside.

6. Using a whisk, combine the egg yolks and chilies with the remaining 2 tablespoons of soy sauce and $^1/2$ teaspoon sesame oil in a large, shallow bowl. Set aside.

7. Heat the remaining olive oil in a large sauté pan over high heat. Season the chicken with salt and pepper and place, skin side down, into the hot pan. Lower the heat and cook for about 5 minutes, or until the skin is crisp and golden brown.

8. Remove from heat and when cool enough to handle, dip the chicken halves, skin side down, into the egg yolk mixture, pressing down to coat well.

9. Immediately press the chicken, skin side down, into the cereal mixture, taking care that it is thickly and evenly coated.

10. Place the chicken halves, skin side up, into the prepared baking pan. Bake in the preheated oven for about 25 minutes, or until an instant-read thermometer inserted into the thickest part reads 155°F (the chicken will continue cooking once taken from the oven and will reach the required 165°F).

11. Remove the chicken from the oven and place on a serving platter. Serve immediately with the warm sauce on the side.

NOTE: You may use egg whites in place of the egg yolks. Add a tablespoon of cornstarch plus ¼ cup water and whisk until smooth.

Deep-Dish Chicken Pie

2 cups cubed cooked chicken

2 cups diced carrots

2 cups diced potatoes

1 cup diced onion

One 10-ounce package frozen peas, thawed

One 10 3/4-ounce can low-sodium, low-fat condensed cream of mushroom soup

1 cup fat-free milk

1 cup water

1/4 teaspoon poultry seasoning

1 1/2 teaspoons salt

1/4 teaspoon freshly ground pepper

2 cups KELLOGG'S CORN FLAKES

One 11-ounce package pie crust mix

7 tablespoons cold water

Approximately 1/4 cup all-purpose flour

This is probably the easiest chicken pie you'll ever make. If your family likes this meal in a dish, when roasting a whole bird make an extra bird or pieces so you will have chicken at the ready to make a pie. The ingredients are easy to keep on hand, which makes it very simple to surprise your family with this bit of old-fashioned cooking. SERVES 10

1. Combine the chicken with the carrots, potatoes, onions, and peas in a 9 x 13 x 2-inch glass baking dish. Set aside.

2. Combine the soup, milk, water, poultry seasoning, and salt and pepper in a small mixing bowl, whisking to combine. Pour the soup mixture over the chicken mixture.

3. Preheat oven to 375°F.

4. Place the KELLOGG'S CORN FLAKES in a resealable plastic bag. Seal the bag and, using a rolling pin, crush the flakes to a fine crumb. Open the bag and measure the crumbs; you should have 1/2 cup.

5. Combine the crumbs with the pie crust mix in a medium mixing bowl. Add the water, stirring with a fork until the dough comes together. If necessary, add no more than an additional 2 teaspoons of water to bring dough together.

6. Using all-purpose flour, lightly flour a clean work surface. Transfer the dough to the floured surface and, using a rolling pin, roll the dough out to 1/4-inch thickness in a rectangle large enough to cover the baking dish.

7. Place the dough over the chicken mixture, pressing along the edges to seal. Using a small, sharp knife, cut steam slits in the top of the dough.

8. Bake in the preheated oven for about 1 hour, or until the crust is golden and the pie filling is bubbling.

9. Remove from oven and serve.

Chicken-Vegetable Crêpes

1½ cups chopped cooked chicken

2 cups chopped fresh broccoli, steamed

½ cup sliced button mushrooms, steamed

¼ cup thinly sliced carrots, steamed

1 cup plain low-fat yogurt

3 tablespoons chopped fresh parsley

2 tablespoons minced red onion

¼ teaspoon lemon pepper

Salt to taste

12 ALL-BRAN Crêpes (recipe follows)

Crêpes always seem just a bit "fancy." So what better way to impress than to prepare these chicken-filled, fiber-rich crêpes? The vegetables can be replaced by any that particularly appeal to you, but it is always nice to keep the mushrooms, as they add a nice, earthy flavor to this "company's coming" dish. SERVES 6

1. Preheat oven to 350°F.

2. Combine the chicken with the broccoli, mushrooms, and carrots in a large mixing bowl.

3. Combine ½ cup of the yogurt with 2 tablespoons of the parsley and the red onion and lemon pepper. Pour the yogurt mixture over the chicken mixture and season with salt to taste, stirring to combine.

4. Lightly coat a glass baking dish large enough to hold 12 rolled crêpes with nonstick cooking spray.

5. Working with one piece at a time, lay a crêpe out on a clean, flat surface. Spoon about 1/4 cup of the chicken mixture into the center of the crêpe. Roll the crêpe up and over the filling and then place the rolled crêpe, seam side down, in the prepared baking dish.

6. When all of the crêpes have been rolled, place the dish in the preheated oven and bake for about 12 minutes, or until heated through.

7. Remove from oven and serve, 2 per person, garnished with a drizzle of the remaining yogurt and a sprinkle of the remaining parsley.

ALL-BRAN® CRÊPES

1/2 cup KELLOGG'S ALL-BRAN
1/4 cup all-purpose flour
1 tablespoon sugar
3 large egg whites
2/3 cup fat-free milk

1. Place the ALL-BRAN, flour, sugar, egg whites, and milk in a blender jar and process on medium for about 30 seconds, or until smooth, scraping down the sides of the jar with a spatula. Transfer to a small bowl, cover with plastic film, and refrigerate for 1 hour.

2. When ready to make the crêpes, remove the batter from the refrigerator, uncover, and whisk to blend.

3. Heat a 7-inch nonstick crêpe pan or frying pan over medium heat. Lightly coat with nonstick cooking spray.

4. Pour 2 tablespoons of the batter into the hot pan, swirling to completely cover the bottom of the pan. Cook for about 1 minute, or until brown on the bottom. Carefully turn and cook the other side for about 30 seconds, or until set.

5. Place on a double layer of paper towel to cool. When crêpes are cool, stack them, separated by waxed paper, until ready to fill. Crêpes may be stacked and then frozen, well wrapped in freezer wrap, for up to 3 months. Thaw before using.

Apricot-Glazed Chicken

One 12-ounce jar apricot preserves

2 tablespoons fat-free mayonnaise

1 tablespoon ketchup

¼ teaspoon dry mustard

8 boneless, skinless chicken breast halves

2 tablespoons canola oil

½ cup finely diced onion

½ cup finely diced celery

½ cup thinly sliced button mushrooms

1¼ cups KELLOGG'S ALL-BRAN

½ cup chicken broth

One 8-ounce can water chestnuts, drained and chopped

¼ teaspoon dried sage

Salt and freshly ground pepper to taste

This dish is perfect for a dinner party, as it can be put together well in advance of cooking and then put in the oven just as your guests arrive, leaving you free to be a gracious host. ALL-BRAN stuffing adds fiber. Served with a rice pilaf, this chicken makes a very elegant meal. SERVES 8

1. Preheat oven to 350°F.

2. Combine the preserves with the mayonnaise, ketchup, and mustard in a small mixing bowl, whisking to blend. Set aside.

3. Working with one piece at a time, place the chicken breasts between two sheets of wax paper and, using a meat mallet, small frying pan, or other heavy, flat object, pound each piece to ⅛-inch thickness, taking care not to tear the meat. Set aside.

4. Heat the oil in a large sauté pan over medium heat. Add the onions and celery and sauté for about 4 minutes, or until crisp-tender. Add the mushrooms and continue to sauté for another 3 minutes. Remove from the heat.

5. Combine ALL-BRAN with the chicken broth in a medium bowl. Set aside for about 1 minute, or until the cereal absorbs the broth.

6. Stir the reserved vegetable mixture along with water chestnuts, sage, and salt and pepper to taste into the ALL-BRAN.

7. Working with one piece at a time, place about ¼ cup of the ALL-BRAN filling into the center of the chicken. Fold the bottom up and over the filling, then fold in the sides and roll the chicken around the filling to make a neat packet.

8. Place the chicken rolls in a 12 x 8-inch baking dish, seam side down. Season with salt and pepper to taste and spoon the reserved apricot sauce over the top. Bake in the preheated over for about 45 minutes, or until the chicken is tender and no longer pink.

9. Remove from oven and serve immediately.

Chicken Enchilada Casserole

4 corn tortillas

4 cups diced cooked chicken

1 cup KELLOGG'S COMPLETE Wheat Bran Flakes or KELLOGG'S PRODUCT 19

1 cup (about 4 ounces) shredded mozzarella cheese

One 10-ounce jar enchilada sauce

One 8-ounce can tomato sauce

Salt and freshly ground pepper to taste

2/3 cup plain low-fat yogurt

2 cups shredded iceberg lettuce

1/2 cup diced tomatoes

1/3 cup sliced scallions

Great for a busy day! The casserole can be put together in the morning, covered, and refrigerated until just before dinner. The tortillas can be prepared, and the lettuce, tomato, and scallions can be cut and placed in plastic bags ready to use at the last minute. SERVES 8

1. Preheat oven to 350°F.

2. Place the tortillas on a baking sheet in the preheated oven and bake, turning occasionally, for about 10 minutes, or until crisp. Remove from oven and set aside to cool. Do not turn off the oven.

3. When the tortillas are cool, break into small pieces and set aside.

4. Combine the chicken with the cereal and mozzarella in a 1½-quart casserole. Add the enchilada and tomato sauces and stir to blend. Season with salt and pepper to taste.

5. Place the casserole in the preheated oven and bake for 30 minutes.

6. Remove the casserole from the oven. Spoon a layer of yogurt over the top, followed by a layer of lettuce. Sprinkle the tomatoes and scallions over the lettuce and top with the reserved crumbled tortillas. Serve immediately.

Baked Chicken Supreme

4 cups KELLOGG'S RICE KRISPIES

1 teaspoon paprika

1 large egg

3/4 cup fat-free milk

3/4 cup all-purpose flour

1 teaspoon poultry seasoning

Salt and freshly ground pepper to taste

3 pounds frying chicken pieces, rinsed and patted dry

3 tablespoons butter or margarine, melted

This is a better way of cooking chicken that tastes as though it has been fried. If you are a family that does not like much spice, eliminate the paprika and poultry seasoning, but make sure that the batter is nicely flavored with salt and pepper. SERVES 6

1. Line a baking pan with aluminum foil or lightly coat with nonstick cooking spray. Set aside.

2. Place RICE KRISPIES in a resealable plastic bag. Seal the bag and, using a rolling pin, crush the cereal to a coarse crumb. Open the bag and measure the crumbs; you should have 2 cups. Place the crumbs in a shallow dish and stir in paprika.

3. Combine the egg and milk in another shallow dish, whisking to blend. Add the flour, poultry seasoning, and salt and pepper to taste and stir to make a smooth batter.

4. Working with one piece at a time, dip the chicken into the batter and then into the crumbs, taking care to cover completely.

5. Place the coated chicken in a single layer in the prepared baking pan.

6. When all of the chicken has been coated, drizzle a bit of the melted butter over every piece. Bake in the preheated oven, without turning, for about 1 hour, or until the chicken is tender and no longer pink and juices run clear.

7. Remove from oven and serve.

Nachos Casserole

One 4-ounce can chopped green chilies

1 cup chunky taco sauce

1 pound lean ground turkey

$1/2$ cup finely diced onion

1 cup refried beans

$1/2$ cup plain nonfat yogurt

$1/4$ teaspoon ground cumin

1 cup shredded reduced-fat Cheddar cheese

$1/4$ cup water

4 cups KELLOGG'S SPECIAL K or KELLOGG'S CORN FLAKES

OPTIONAL GARNISHES

$3/4$ cup diced tomatoes

2 tablespoons sliced scallions

2 tablespoons sliced olives

Low-fat sour cream

This casserole is like a trip to your local Mexican restaurant. Great flavors and a little spice, but with KELLOGG'S SPECIAL K replacing the crunchy tortillas, and turkey, nonfat yogurt, and reduced-fat cheese adding their measure of good eating. The dish can be put together early in the day and baked just before dinner. SERVES 6

1. Combine the green chilies and taco sauce in a small bowl. Set aside.

2. Place the turkey and onions in a nonstick frying pan over medium heat. Fry, stirring frequently to break up the meat, for about 12 minutes, or until the meat has browned and the onions are cooked. Stir in the beans, yogurt, and cumin. When well blended, add one half each of the cheese and reserved taco sauce mixture along with the water. Cook, stirring frequently, for about 4 minutes, or until flavors have blended.

3. Preheat oven to 350°F.

4. Lightly coat a 2-quart casserole with nonstick cooking spray. Place 2 cups of the SPECIAL K in the bottom of the casserole. Spoon the meat mixture over the cereal. Top with the remaining taco sauce mixture and sprinkle with the remaining 2 cups of cereal.

5. Bake in the preheated oven for 35 minutes, or until very hot and bubbling. Sprinkle with the remaining $1/2$ cup of cheese and bake for an additional 5 minutes.

6. Remove from oven and serve, garnished with tomatoes, scallions, sliced olives, and sour cream, if desired.

Ground Turkey and Spinach Roll

1¹⁄₂ pounds lean ground turkey

One 8-ounce can tomato sauce

2 large egg whites

1 cup KELLOGG'S ALL-BRAN

¹⁄₂ cup finely diced onion

1 teaspoon minced garlic

1 teaspoon dry mustard

¹⁄₂ teaspoon dried oregano

Salt and freshly ground pepper to taste

One 10-ounce package frozen chopped spinach, thawed and well drained

¹⁄₂ cup shredded mozzarella cheese

1 teaspoon bottled horseradish, well drained

1 tablespoon chopped fresh parsley

To save time, this elegant dish can also be cooked in the microwave. Place in a microwave-safe dish and cook on high, turning once, for 12 minutes. Add the tomato sauce and then cook on high for an additional minute. The roll will still need to rest for 10 minutes before cutting. SERVES 8

1. Preheat oven to 350°F.

2. Line a shallow baking pan at least 12 inches long with aluminum foil. Set aside.

3. Combine the turkey with ¹⁄₄ cup of the tomato sauce, egg whites, ALL-BRAN, onions, garlic, mustard powder, oregano, and salt and pepper to taste in a large mixing bowl.

4. Place a 12 x 10-inch piece of aluminum foil on a flat surface. Mound the turkey mixture in the center and then push it out to form a 12 x 8-inch rectangle. Spread the spinach evenly over the meat and then sprinkle with the cheese.

5. Starting with the shortest side, roll the meat up and over the spinach and cheese, using the foil to help hold the roll together. Place the roll, seam side down, in the prepared pan.

6. Bake in the preheated oven for about 55 minutes, or until cooked through and golden brown.

7. Remove from oven, transfer to a serving platter, and let rest for 10 minutes before serving.

8. While the turkey roll is resting, place the remaining tomato sauce in a small saucepan over medium heat. Add the horseradish and bring to a boil. Lower the heat and simmer for 10 minutes.

9. Pour the hot tomato sauce over the turkey roll and sprinkle the parsley over the top. Serve immediately.

Creole Turkey on a Bun

1 pound lean ground turkey

¹/₂ cup finely diced onion

¹/₂ cup finely diced red or green bell pepper

One 14¹/₂-ounce can whole tomatoes and their juices

1¹/₂ cups KELLOGG'S PRODUCT 19

¹/₄ cup ketchup

1 tablespoon Worcestershire sauce

¹/₂ teaspoon Cajun seasoning

Salt and freshly ground pepper to taste

8 hamburger buns, split and toasted

These delicious sandwiches are a bit like Sloppy Joes (see page 81) and offer great taste for children and adults alike. When preparing the turkey mix, it is a good idea to double or even triple the recipe and freeze the extra to have sandwich makings on hand at all times. SERVES 8

1. Place the turkey, onion, and bell pepper in a large nonstick frying pan over medium heat. Fry, stirring frequently to break up the meat, for about 10 minutes, or until nicely browned. Drain off all excess fat.

2. Stir in the tomatoes, using a wooden spoon to break the tomatoes into small pieces. Add PRODUCT 19, ketchup, Worcestershire sauce, Cajun seasoning, and salt and pepper to taste, stirring to combine. Cover, lower the heat, and simmer, stirring occasionally, for about 15 minutes, or until meat is cooked and flavors have blended.

3. Remove from heat. Place an equal portion of the meat mixture on the bottom of each bun, cover with the top of the bun, and serve.

The Home Economics Department was established in 1923 by Mary I. Barber (center) to standardize and develop recipes using KELLOGG'S cereals.

Busy-Day Turkey Loaf

1 cup KELLOGG'S Stuffing Mix

1/2 cup fat-free milk

2 large egg whites

1/4 cup finely diced onion

2 teaspoons Worcestershire sauce

1 pound lean ground turkey

Salt and freshly ground pepper to taste

1/4 cup ketchup

2 teaspoons brown sugar

1 teaspoon Dijon mustard

A great meat loaf—a little different in texture and flavor from the ordinary beef-based loaf. It could also be made with lean ground chicken, pork, or the standard beef. If you don't have Dijon mustard on hand use regular prepared mustard. SERVES 6

1. Combine the KELLOGG'S Stuffing Mix and milk in a small mixing bowl and set aside for 5 minutes, or until the Stuffing Mix is soft.

2. Preheat oven to 350°F.

3. Line a baking pan with aluminum foil. Lightly spray with nonstick cooking spray. Set aside.

4. Add the egg whites, onion, and Worcestershire sauce to the softened Stuffing Mix, stirring to blend well. Add the turkey along with salt and pepper to taste and mix until combined. Shape the mixture into a loaf.

5. Place the loaf in the prepared pan. Using a small, sharp knife, make about 4 diagonal slashes across the top.

6. Combine the ketchup, brown sugar, and mustard in a small mixing bowl. When well blended, pour over the turkey loaf, making sure that the sauce goes down into the grooves made by the knife.

7. Bake in the preheated oven for about 45 minutes, or until cooked through and nicely browned.

8. Remove from oven and serve.

Stir-Fry Beef and Vegetables

One 8-ounce can unsweetened pineapple chunks

1 clove garlic, peeled and minced

3 tablespoons soy sauce

1 teaspoon grated fresh gingerroot

1½ pounds beef sirloin steak, cut into long, thin strips

1¼ cups KELLOGG'S ALL-BRAN

1 teaspoon cornstarch

One 16-ounce package frozen stir-fry vegetables

2 tablespoons canola oil

3 cups cooked brown rice

ALL-BRAN is high in fiber, low in sodium, and a good source of potassium.

Almost as easy as ordering in from the neighborhood Chinese restaurant! In this dish, KELLOGG'S ALL-BRAN takes the place of flour or cornstarch in the coating and adds an unexpected richness. Served with brown rice, it makes a great meal. SERVES 5

1. Drain the pineapple, separately reserving the juice.

2. Combine 2 tablespoons of the pineapple juice with the garlic, soy sauce, and ginger in a shallow dish. Add the beef and toss to thoroughly coat. Cover with plastic film and refrigerate for 2 hours.

3. Place ALL-BRAN in a resealable plastic bag. Seal the bag and, using a rolling pin, crush the cereal to a fine crumb. Transfer the crumbs to a shallow dish.

4. Remove the marinated beef from the refrigerator and uncover. Working with a few pieces at a time, lightly coat the beef strips with the ALL-BRAN crumbs.

5. Combine the remaining pineapple juice with the cornstarch in a small bowl. If necessary, add enough water so that the mixture equals ⅓ cup. Set aside.

6. Bring 2 tablespoons of water to a boil in a wok over high heat. Add the frozen vegetables and stir-fry for about 3 minutes, or until crisp-tender. Using a slotted spoon, transfer the vegetables to a plate.

7. Wipe the wok clean with paper towel. Add the oil and place over high heat. When the oil is almost smoking, add the beef and stir-fry for about 5 minutes, or until lightly browned and beginning to crisp. Pour in the cornstarch mixture and, stir-frying constantly, bring to a boil. Add the reserved pineapple chunks and vegetables and again bring the mixture to a boil.

8. Remove from heat and serve immediately over hot brown rice.

Meat 'n' Tater Pie

4 cups KELLOGG'S CORN FLAKES or 1 cup KELLOGG'S Corn Flake Crumbs

$1/3$ cup fat-free milk

1 tablespoon prepared mustard

1 pound lean ground beef (or turkey)

Salt and freshly ground pepper to taste

2 cups well-seasoned mashed potatoes

$1/4$ cup finely diced onion

1 tablespoon minced fresh parsley

2 large eggs, lightly beaten

1 tablespoon olive oil

$1/2$ cup shredded American or Cheddar cheese

A new version of the old-fashioned shepherd's pie that makes a great family supper or take-along dish. The recipe can easily be doubled or tripled for feeding a crowd, which makes it great for parties and family gatherings. It can also be made in a 9-inch square baking pan. SERVES 6

1. Place KELLOGG'S CORN FLAKES in a resealable plastic bag. Seal the bag and, using a rolling pin, crush the flakes to a fine crumb. Open the bag and measure the crumbs; you should have 1 cup. Measure out $1/2$ cup of the crumbs and set aside the remaining $1/2$ cup.

2. Preheat oven to 350°F.

3. Combine $1/2$ cup of the crumbs with the fat-free milk and mustard in a medium bowl. When blended, mix in the beef. When well combined, season with salt and pepper to taste.

4. Gently press the meat mixture into a 9-inch pie pan, pressing to evenly cover the bottom and sides. Set aside.

5. Combine the potatoes, onion, and parsley in a medium bowl. Using your hands, work in the eggs, mixing until very well blended. Transfer the potato mixture to the meat-lined pie pan, spreading it evenly with a spatula.

6. Place the pie on a baking sheet in the preheated oven and bake for 35 minutes.

7. While the pie is baking, combine the remaining $1/2$ cup crumbs with the olive oil to make a crumbly mixture.

8. Remove the pie from the oven. Sprinkle the cheese over the top and then top with the cereal crumble.

9. Return the pie to the oven and bake for an additional 10 minutes, or until the top is golden and the cheese has melted.

10. Remove from oven, cut into wedges, and serve.

Tangy Meatballs

SAUCE

One 15-ounce can tomato sauce

1/2 cup ketchup

1/4 cup finely chopped onion

1/4 cup firmly packed brown sugar

1/4 cup sweet pickle relish

2 tablespoons Worcestershire sauce

1 tablespoon white or cider vinegar

1/4 teaspoon freshly ground pepper

MEATBALLS

1 pound lean ground beef

1 large egg

2/3 cup nonfat dry milk powder

1/4 cup finely chopped onion

2 tablespoons ketchup

1 cup KELLOGG'S RICE KRISPIES

Salt and freshly ground pepper to taste

This dish is another Kellogg favorite. Although these zesty meatballs make terrific dinner fare, they are also great as a cocktail treat served on toothpicks. For dinner, their sauce makes a very tasty "gravy" for rice, noodles, or pasta. The ground beef can be replaced with any other ground meat.

SERVES 6

1. To make sauce, combine all ingredients in a medium nonreactive saucepan over medium-low heat. Bring to a simmer and simmer for 15 minutes.

2. While the sauce is simmering, prepare the meatballs.

3. Preheat oven to 400°F.

4. Place the beef in a medium bowl. Add the egg and mix well. Add the dry milk, onion, and ketchup and mix until well combined. Add RICE KRISPIES and salt and pepper to taste and mix to just combine.

5. Form the meat mixture into small balls of equal size. You should have about 36 meatballs.

6. Place the meatballs in a nonstick baking pan in the preheated oven and bake for about 12 minutes, or until well browned.

7. Add the meatballs to the sauce and bring to a simmer over low heat. Simmer, stirring occasionally, for 10 minutes, or until hot.

8. Remove from heat and serve over hot rice or noodles, if desired.

Hamburger Pizza Pie

2 cups KELLOGG'S CORN FLAKES

1/2 cup fat-free milk

1/4 teaspoon dry minced garlic

Salt to taste

1 pound lean ground beef

One 6-ounce can tomato paste

One 3-ounce can chopped mushrooms, well drained

1 cup shredded part-skim mozzarella cheese

1 teaspoon dry minced onion

2 teaspoons dried oregano

1/2 teaspoon dried basil

1 teaspoon sugar

1/4 cup grated Parmesan cheese

Green bell pepper strips for garnish

Pimiento-stuffed green olives, sliced crosswise, for garnish

Tired of pizza? Try this new type of pizza pie and you'll be hooked again. This is another great party dish and can be assembled early in the day, refrigerated, and baked just before serving. If you miss the usual crust, serve our pie with garlic bread. SERVES 6

1. Preheat oven to 350°F.

2. Combine KELLOGG'S CORN FLAKES with the milk, garlic, and salt to taste in a medium bowl. When well combined, add the ground beef and mix until just combined. Gently press the meat mixture into a 9-inch pie pan, pressing to evenly cover the bottom and sides. Set aside.

3. Combine the tomato paste and mushrooms with 1/2 cup of the mozzarella cheese in a medium bowl. Stir in the onion, oregano, basil, and sugar. Spoon the mixture into the meat shell, spreading it out evenly with a spatula.

4. Sprinkle the top with the Parmesan cheese along with the remaining 1/2 cup of mozzarella cheese. Garnish with green bell pepper strips and sliced olives.

5. Place in the preheated oven and bake for 30 minutes, or until the meat is well done and browned.

6. Remove from oven, cut into wedges, and serve.

Spicy Tomato Mini-Loaves

3 cups KELLOGG'S CORN FLAKES

One 10³/₄-ounce can condensed tomato soup

1 large egg

¹/₄ cup finely diced onion

1 tablespoon prepared horseradish, drained, optional

1¹/₂ pounds lean ground beef

2 tablespoons firmly packed brown sugar

1 teaspoon prepared mustard

Parsley for garnish, optional

KELLOGG'S CORN FLAKES replace the breadcrumbs generally found in a traditional meat loaf. These single-serving mini-loaves make a very nice presentation. SERVES 6

1. Line a baking pan with aluminum foil and lightly coat with nonstick cooking spray. Set aside.

2. Preheat oven to 350°F.

3. Combine KELLOGG'S CORN FLAKES with ¹/₂ cup of the tomato soup, egg, onion, and horseradish, stirring to completely blend. Add the ground beef and mix until well combined.

4. Divide the mixture into 6 equal portions. Form each portion into a loaf or oval shape and place in the prepared baking pan.

5. In a small bowl, combine the remaining soup with the brown sugar and mustard. When well blended, spoon an equal amount over each meat loaf, spreading it evenly over the top.

6. Bake in the preheated oven for about 35 minutes, or until the center is cooked and the top is nicely browned.

7. Remove from oven and serve hot, garnished with parsley, if desired.

Stuffed Peppers

6 large green or red bell peppers

1 pound lean ground beef, turkey, or chicken

1 medium onion, peeled and chopped

1 clove garlic, peeled and minced

One 16-ounce can diced tomatoes, drained

One 6-ounce can tomato paste

1/2 cup sliced pitted black olives

2 teaspoons chili powder

1 teaspoon sugar

Salt and freshly ground pepper to taste

2 cups KELLOGG'S RICE KRISPIES, KELLOGG'S CORN FLAKES, or SPECIAL K

1/2 cup shredded sharp Cheddar cheese

KELLOGG'S RICE KRISPIES add extra goodness to these Mexican-flavored stuffed peppers. These make a great busy-day meal. Serve with a salad and some Italian bread or warm tortillas. SERVES 6

1. Carefully cut off the stem end of the bell peppers. Carefully remove the seeds and membrane.

2. Bring a large saucepan of salted water to a boil over high heat. Add the peppers and boil for 5 minutes. Drain and refresh under cold running water. Pat dry.

3. Line a baking pan with aluminum foil and lightly coat with nonstick cooking spray. Place the peppers in the prepared pan, cut side up. Set aside.

4. Preheat oven to 350°F.

5. Place the ground beef, onion, and garlic in a large nonstick frying pan over medium-high heat. Fry, stirring frequently, for about 10 minutes, or until the meat has browned and the onions are cooked. Carefully drain off excess fat.

6. Return the pan to medium heat and add the tomatoes, tomato paste, olives, chili powder, sugar, and salt and pepper to taste. Cook for 5 minutes. Stir in RICE KRISPIES (or other cereal) and remove from heat.

7. Spoon an equal portion of the meat mixture into each pepper, mounding slightly in the center.

8. Bake in the preheated oven for 25 minutes, or until very hot.

9. Remove from oven and sprinkle the tops with the cheese. Return to the oven and bake for about 5 minutes, or until the cheese has melted and is beginning to brown.

10. Remove from oven and serve.

Sloppy Joes

1 pound lean ground beef

One 16-ounce can diced tomatoes with their juice

$1/2$ cup diced onion

$1/2$ diced green or red bell pepper

1 tablespoon Worcestershire sauce

Salt and freshly ground pepper to taste

2 cups KELLOGG'S CORN FLAKES

8 large hamburger buns, split and toasted

The perennial favorite sandwich for kids and sports fans! Easy eating when watching a Sunday game. SERVES 8

1. Place the ground beef in a large frying pan over medium-high heat. Fry, stirring frequently, for about 10 minutes, or until nicely browned.

2. Stir in the tomatoes, onion, green pepper, Worcestershire sauce, and salt and pepper to taste. When well combined, add KELLOGG'S CORN FLAKES. Cover, lower the heat, and cook, stirring occasionally, for 15 minutes.

3. Remove from heat and spoon an equal portion on the bottom half of each bun. Top with the remaining half and serve.

The 1911 packing shift crew at the Battle Creek Toasted Corn Flakes Company.

Corn Flake Enchiladas

2 cups KELLOGG'S CORN FLAKES

1¹/₂ cups tomato paste

2 cloves garlic, peeled and minced

4 teaspoons chili powder

¹/₂ teaspoon ground cumin

4 cups water

Tabasco to taste

Salt to taste

1 pound lean ground beef, turkey, or chicken

1 medium onion, peeled and chopped

2 cups (about ¹/₂ pound) shredded Cheddar or Monterey Jack or Pepper Jack cheese

¹/₂ cup sliced pitted black olives

Twelve 7-inch corn tortillas

If you like a lot of spice, you can add some minced fresh chili (such as jalapeño or serrano) to the basic mix. If spice is not for you, eliminate the Tabasco. Assemble these early in the day, refrigerate, and bake just before dinner for an easy-to-feed-a-crowd dish. SERVES 6

1. Place KELLOGG'S CORN FLAKES in a resealable plastic bag. Seal the bag and, using a rolling pin, crush the flakes to a fine crumb. Open the bag and measure the crumbs; you should have ¹/₂ cup. Set aside.

2. Combine the tomato paste, garlic, chili powder, and cumin in a medium saucepan. Add the water, Tabasco, and salt and place over medium-high heat. Bring to a boil. Lower the heat and simmer for 20 minutes.

3. Preheat oven to 350°F.

4. Place the ground beef and onion in a nonstick frying pan over medium-high heat. Fry, stirring frequently, for about 10 minutes, or until the meat has browned and the onion is cooked. Remove from heat, drain well, and stir 1 cup of the tomato sauce, 1 cup of the cheese, the olives, and the reserved crumbs into the meat. Set aside.

5. Pour the remaining tomato sauce into a 13 x 9 x 2-inch baking pan.

6. Working with one tortilla at a time, spoon 2 tablespoons of the meat mixture down the center of the tortilla. Roll the tortilla up and around the filling and place it, seam side down, in the baking pan.

7. When all of the tortillas are in the pan, top with the remaining meat mixture. Bake in the preheated oven for about 15 minutes. Sprinkle the remaining cheese over the top. Bake about 5 minutes longer, or until the filling is very hot and the cheese has melted and is bubbly. Remove from oven and serve immediately.

Veal Cordon Bleu

1¹/₂ cups KELLOGG'S Corn Flake Crumbs

¹/₂ cup all-purpose flour

¹/₄ teaspoon ground allspice

¹/₂ teaspoon salt

¹/₄ teaspoon freshly ground pepper

2 large egg whites, beaten

6 thin slices cooked ham

6 thin slices Swiss cheese

Six 4-ounce veal (or turkey) scallops

1¹/₂ tablespoons olive oil

1 tablespoon minced fresh parsley

In 1906 W. K. Kellogg bought a full-page ad in *Ladies' Home Journal,* the most popular women's magazine of the time, and sales of KELLOGG'S CORN FLAKES leaped from 33 cases a day to 2,900.

This is a revised version of the classic French dish, made with egg whites (rather than whole eggs) and KELLOGG'S Corn Flake Crumbs. However, it is just as elegant—perhaps even more so—and is perfect for fine dining or special family meals. SERVES 6

1. Place the KELLOGG'S Corn Flake Crumbs, flour, allspice, and salt and pepper in a shallow bowl, stirring to blend well.

2. Place the egg whites in another shallow bowl.

3. Line a small baking pan with aluminum foil and lightly coat with nonstick cooking spray. Set aside.

4. Preheat oven to 350°F.

5. Working with one piece at a time, place a slice of ham and then a slice of cheese on each veal scallop. Beginning at the thinnest end, carefully roll the veal up and over the ham and cheese to make a neat roll. Secure closed with a toothpick.

6. When all the scallops are stuffed and rolled, dip them one at a time into the egg whites and then into the crumbs.

7. Place the rolls in the prepared baking pan. Drizzle the rolls with the olive oil and place in the preheated oven. Bake for about 30 minutes, or until golden brown and cooked through.

8. Remove from oven, sprinkle with parsley, and serve.

Veal Scaloppini

4 cups KELLOGG'S SPECIAL K

¼ teaspoon salt

¼ teaspoon freshly ground pepper

2 large egg whites, beaten

2 tablespoons water

¼ cup olive oil

1 clove garlic, peeled and sliced

Six 1-inch veal chops

3 cups sliced button mushrooms

1½ cups chicken broth

Juice of ½ lemon

1 tablespoon minced fresh parsley

The veal makes this easy-to-prepare dish a bit fancier and turns it into company fare, but you may substitute pork chops if you wish. SPECIAL K and the egg whites (rather than whole eggs) offer a different twist on the classic recipe. SERVES 6

1. Place SPECIAL K in a resealable plastic bag. Seal the bag and, using a rolling pin, crush the cereal to a medium-fine crumb. Open the bag and measure the crumbs; you should have 1½ cups. Transfer to a shallow dish and season with salt and pepper to taste. Set aside.

2. Combine the egg whites and water in a second shallow dish.

3. Heat 1 tablespoon of the oil in a large frying pan over medium heat. Add the garlic and sauté for about 3 minutes, or just until the oil is nicely flavored. Using a slotted spoon, remove and discard the garlic.

4. Dip the chops into the egg mixture and then into the crumbs to evenly coat. Place the coated chops into the hot pan, adding up to 2 tablespoons of the remaining oil if necessary, and fry, turning occasionally, for about 5 minutes, or until golden brown. If your pan is not capable of holding all of the chops at once, do this in batches or in two pans. When chops are golden, transfer to a plate.

5. Add the remaining 1 tablespoon oil to the frying pan. When hot, add the mushrooms and sauté for about 4 minutes, or just until slightly soft. Stir in the broth. Add the browned chops, cover, and bring to a simmer. Lower the heat and simmer for about 35 minutes, or until the veal is cooked through.

6. Remove pan from heat and transfer the chops to a serving platter. Stir the lemon juice into the sauce, taste, and, if necessary, season with additional salt and pepper.

7. Spoon the mushroom sauce over the top of the chops, sprinkle with parsley, and serve.

In 1955 Kellogg touted SPECIAL K as "the most complete cereal food on the market today," stating that "we consider it an achievement that is perhaps the greatest in our history."

Oven-Crisped Pork Chops

1 large egg

3 tablespoons milk

2 tablespoons fresh lime juice

1 teaspoon dried oregano

$^1/_4$ teaspoon garlic powder

Salt and freshly ground pepper to taste

1 cup KELLOGG'S Corn Flake Crumbs

6 center-cut pork chops about $^3/_4$ inch thick

6 lime wedges, optional

This is a terrific way to cook pork chops, leaving them crisp on the outside and tender and juicy on the inside. The hint of lime gives a nice accent to the mild flavor of the very lean pork. SERVES 6

1. Combine the egg, milk, and lime juice with the oregano, garlic powder, and salt and pepper to taste in a shallow dish.

2. Place KELLOGG'S Corn Flake Crumbs in another shallow dish.

3. Preheat oven to 350°F.

4. Line a baking pan with aluminum foil or lightly coat with nonstick cooking spray. Set aside.

5. Working with one piece at a time, dip the pork chops into the egg mixture and then into the crumbs to evenly coat.

6. Place the coated chops in the prepared pan, and when all chops are coated, bake in the preheated oven for about 1 hour, or until an instant-read thermometer inserted into the thickest part reads 160°F.

7. Remove from oven and serve with lime wedges, if desired.

Ginger Pork with Applesauce

4 cups KELLOGG'S CORN FLAKES

2 tablespoons firmly packed brown sugar

3/4 teaspoon ground ginger

1/2 teaspoon garlic powder

1/4 teaspoon dry mustard

1/4 teaspoon ground cinnamon

1 teaspoon salt

1/4 teaspoon freshly ground pepper

2 large egg whites

Six 6-ounce pork loin filets, trimmed of all fat

3 cups applesauce

If you have the time, a cinnamony homemade applesauce would be just the thing to accent the lightly spiced pork. If you can't find pork loin filets, you can substitute pork chops or pork scaloppini. For the scaloppini, the baking time will decrease to about 20 minutes. SERVES 6

1. Place KELLOGG'S CORN FLAKES in a resealable plastic bag. Seal the bag and, using a rolling pin, crush the flakes to a fine crumb. Open the bag and measure the crumbs; you should have 1 cup. Transfer the crumbs to a shallow dish.

2. Add the brown sugar, ginger, garlic powder, dry mustard, cinnamon, and salt and pepper to taste to the crumbs, stirring to blend well. Set aside.

3. Line a baking pan with aluminum foil and lightly coat with cooking spray. Set aside.

4. Preheat oven to 350°F.

5. Place the egg whites in a shallow dish and, using a whisk, beat until slightly frothy.

6. Pat the meat dry with paper towel. Working with one piece at a time, dip the meat into the egg whites and then into the crumb mixture, pressing to insure that the coating adheres to the meat.

7. Place the coated meat in the prepared baking pan. When all of the meat has been coated, bake in the preheated oven, without turning, for about 45 minutes, or until the exterior is crisp and golden and an instant-read thermometer inserted into the center reads 160°F.

8. Remove from oven and serve with applesauce on the side.

Jeweler's Purse Pork Loin

2 pounds pork loin trimmed of all excess fat

1/2 cup chopped mixed dried fruit

1/4 cup finely chopped onion

1/4 cup fresh sage leaves, or 2 tablespoons dried sage

1 tablespoon Dijon mustard

1 tablespoon olive oil

Salt and freshly ground pepper to taste

1 cup KELLOGG'S CRUNCHY BLENDS JUST RIGHT Fruit & Nut cereal

This is a very stylish dish that will entice even the pickiest of eaters. The savory paste under the sweet cereal coating makes a perfect marriage with the delicately flavored, fruit-stuffed pork. SERVES 6

1. Preheat oven to 350°F.

2. Using a sharp knife, cut a pocket about 4 inches deep into the side of the pork loin and running the length of the meat. Place the dried fruit in the pocket and, using toothpicks, pin the pocket closed.

3. Combine the onion, sage, mustard, olive oil, and salt and pepper to taste in the small bowl of a food processor fitted with the metal blade or in a small blender jar and process until smooth.

4. Place the cereal on a large plate. Set aside.

5. Using a rubber spatula, evenly spread the onion mixture over the pork loin. Then roll the coated loin in the cereal, pressing the cereal so that it adheres to the meat and forms a crust.

6. Place a wire rack on a baking pan lined with aluminum foil. Lay the coated loin on the rack and place in the preheated oven. Bake for about 50 minutes, or until an instant-read thermometer inserted into the thickest part reads 160°F.

7. Remove from oven and let rest 10 minutes.

8. Remove the toothpicks, cut roast crosswise into 1/2-inch-thick slices, and serve.

Pork Strips with Salsa

4 cups KELLOGG'S CORN FLAKES

2 tablespoons sesame seeds, optional

1/2 teaspoon seasoned salt, or to taste

1/4 cup all-purpose flour

1/4 cup fat-free milk

6 boneless pork chops, 3/4 inches thick (about 1 1/2 pounds)

Red Tomato Salsa (see page 29)

If you like a little spice, you can add a few hits of Tabasco to the milk or a little chili powder to the crumbs. Pork strips are a terrific change from the usual chicken fingers and make a great appetizer also. SERVES 6

1. Place KELLOGG'S CORN FLAKES in a resealable plastic bag. Seal the bag and, using a rolling pin, crush the flakes to a fine crumb. Open the bag and measure the crumbs; you should have 1 cup. Transfer the crumbs to a shallow dish and add the sesame seeds and seasoned salt. Set aside.

2. Place the flour in another shallow bowl and the milk in a third.

3. Preheat oven to 350°F.

4. Line a baking pan with aluminum foil or lightly spray with nonstick cooking spray. Set aside.

5. Cut each pork chop into 4 strips about 1/2 inch thick.

6. Working with one piece at a time, dip the strips first into flour, then into the milk, and finally into the cereal mixture, pressing to insure that the coating adheres to the meat.

7. Place the coated pork strips in the prepared pan, and when all are coated, bake in the preheated oven, without turning, for about 25 minutes, or until the exterior is golden brown and crisp and the interior is no longer pink.

8. Remove from oven and serve with Red Tomato Salsa or bottled salsa of your choice.

Apple-Glazed Ham Loaf

GLAZE

One 10-ounce jar apple jelly

1/4 cup firmly packed brown sugar

3 tablespoons fresh lemon juice

1/2 teaspoon dry mustard

HAM LOAF

3 cups KELLOGG'S CORN FLAKES

2 large eggs

3/4 cup fat-free milk

1/3 cup finely diced onion

1/4 cup firmly packed brown sugar

1 1/2 teaspoons dry mustard

Freshly ground pepper to taste

1 pound cooked ham, ground

1 pound ground lean pork

Salt to taste

A somewhat different meat loaf made quite savory with the slightly tart-sweet apple glaze. Perfect for an easy dinner and even better for sandwiches the next day. SERVES 12

1. Combine the jelly with 1/4 cup brown sugar, the lemon juice, and 1/2 teaspoon dry mustard in a small saucepan over medium-low heat. Cook, stirring constantly, for about 3 minutes, or until the jelly has melted. Bring to a boil and boil, stirring constantly, for 1 minute. Remove from heat and set aside to cool.

2. Preheat oven to 350°F.

3. Line a shallow baking pan with aluminum foil and lightly coat with nonstick cooking spray. Set aside.

4. Place the Corn Flakes in a resealable plastic bag. Seal the bag and, using a rolling pin, lightly crush the cereal to make a fine crumb. Open the bag and measure the crumbs; you should have 3/4 cup.

5. In a large mixing bowl, beat eggs slightly. Add the crumbs, milk, onion, 1/4 cup brown sugar, 1 1/2 teaspoons dry mustard, and pepper to taste. Beat thoroughly. When blended, add the ham and pork and stir to combine. Season with salt to taste.

6. Shape the meat mixture into a loaf and place the loaf in the prepared pan.

7. Transfer the pan to the preheated oven and bake for 45 minutes.

8. Using a pastry brush, brush the top of the loaf with the reserved apple jelly glaze. Bake for an additional 30 minutes, brushing with the glaze 2 or 3 times.

9. Remove from oven and let rest 5 minutes.

10. Cut into 1/2-inch-thick slices and serve with the remaining glaze on the side.

Ham and Cheese Monte Cristos

5 cups KELLOGG'S RICE KRISPIES

3 large egg whites

$^3/_4$ cup fat-free milk

$^1/_4$ teaspoon salt, or to taste

12 slices day-old white or wheat bread

Approximately $^1/_4$ cup Dijon mustard, or to taste

6 medium-thick slices smoked ham

6 medium-thick slices Swiss, American, or Cheddar cheese

1 tablespoon butter, melted, or olive oil

Try this take on an old favorite. RICE KRISPIES replace the crunch of the fried bread and provide an interesting texture to bite into. You can use different cheeses and mustards to give these your own stamp. SERVES 6

1. Place RICE KRISPIES in a resealable plastic bag. Seal the bag and, using a rolling pin, lightly crush the cereal to make a medium crumb. Open the bag and measure the crumbs; you should have 2 cups. Transfer the crumbs to a shallow dish and set aside.

2. Preheat oven to 450°F.

3. Line a baking pan with aluminum foil and lightly coat with nonstick cooking spray. Set aside.

4. Place the egg whites, milk, and salt in a shallow bowl. Using a whisk, beat until foamy.

5. Place 6 slices of bread on a flat surface. Using a spatula, coat the bread with a layer of mustard—as thick or as thin as you like. Place a piece of ham and then a slice of cheese on top of each piece. Top each with a remaining slice of bread.

6. Working with one at a time, dip the sandwiches into the egg mixture, turning to coat both sides. Quickly press each side into the crumbs, pressing down to insure that the crumbs adhere to the bread.

7. Place the coated sandwiches in the prepared baking pan. When all sandwiches are in the pan, give a light drizzle of melted butter (or olive oil) to each one.

8. Bake in the preheated oven, without turning, for about 15 minutes, or until crisp and golden brown.

9. Remove from oven and serve with additional mustard on the side.

Catfish Southern Shores

2¹/₂ cups KELLOGG'S COMPLETE Wheat Bran Flakes

1 teaspoon onion powder

1 teaspoon garlic powder

1 teaspoon dried lemon peel

¹/₂ teaspoon cayenne pepper, or to taste

¹/₂ teaspoon dried thyme

¹/₂ teaspoon dried basil

¹/₂ teaspoon dried dill

Salt to taste

¹/₃ cup all-purpose flour

¹/₃ cup cold water

1 pound catfish fillets, cut lengthwise into 1-inch-wide strips

4 lemon wedges, optional

The bran flake crust adds crunch and the herbs and cayenne add real oomph to what is otherwise a fairly standard dish. Any other mild white fish fillet can replace the catfish. SERVES 4

1. Place the COMPLETE Wheat Bran Flakes in a resealable plastic bag. Seal the bag and, using a rolling pin, lightly crush the cereal to make a coarse crumb. Open the bag and measure the crumbs; you should have 1 cup.

2. Combine the crumbs with the onion and garlic powders, lemon peel, cayenne, thyme, basil, dill, and salt to taste in a shallow dish. Set aside.

3. Preheat oven to 350°F.

4. Line a small baking pan with aluminum foil. Lightly coat with nonstick cooking spray. Set aside.

5. Combine the flour and water in a small mixing bowl, whisking until smooth.

6. Working with one piece at a time, dip the fillets into the flour mixture, allowing any excess to drip off. Then press the fish into the crumb mixture, turning to evenly coat both sides.

7. Place the coated fillets in the prepared pan. When all of the fillets have been coated, bake in the preheated oven, without turning, for 20 minutes, or until the fish is cooked through and flakes easily with a fork.

8. Remove from the oven and serve with lemon wedges, if desired.

'21' CLUB, New York City

Pan-Roasted Crisp Sea Bass

SPICE MIX

1 tablespoon sugar

1/4 teaspoon ground ginger

1/4 teaspoon ground star anise

1/4 teaspoon ground coriander

1/4 teaspoon cayenne pepper

1/4 teaspoon ground cinnamon

1/4 teaspoon sea salt

1/8 teaspoon ground white pepper

SEA BASS

1 large egg

1/4 cup heavy cream

1 cup KELLOGG'S RICE KRISPIES

Six 7-ounce black sea bass steaks, skin removed (see note, next page)

1 teaspoon sea salt

1/8 teaspoon freshly ground pepper

1/4 cup plus 3 tablespoons canola oil

3 sprigs fresh thyme, plus more for garnish

6 heads Belgian endive or Boston (Bibb) or red leaf lettuce, well washed and dried, cut lengthwise into halves

1 tablespoon chopped fresh chives

2 tablespoons aged balsamic vinegar

3 tablespoons finely diced fresh tomato

Manhattan's '21' Club is one of America's dining icons, dating back to speakeasy times. It is known for its clubby atmosphere and its focus on great American food, with recipes like this delicious fish dish, which combines exotic spiciness with ever-popular KELLOGG'S RICE KRISPIES.

SERVES 6

1. For the Spice Mix, combine all ingredients in a small bowl and set aside.

2. Combine the egg with the heavy cream in a shallow bowl, whisking to blend. Set aside.

3. Place the KELLOGG'S RICE KRISPIES in another shallow bowl. Set aside.

4. Season the fish with salt and pepper to taste. Using a pastry brush, lightly coat the side of the fish from which the skin has been removed with the egg mixture. Then immediately press the egg-washed side of the fish into the cereal, gently pushing down to insure that the cereal adheres to the fish.

5. Heat 1/4 cup of the oil in a large sauté pan over medium-high heat. When oil is very hot but not smoking, carefully place the fish, cereal side down, into the pan. Cook for 2 minutes. Turn the fish and add the 3 thyme sprigs to the pan. Cook for an additional 3 minutes, or until the fish is just cooked through.

6. Using a spatula, carefully remove the fish from the pan and place on a warm platter. Lightly tent with aluminum foil to keep warm.

7. Heat the remaining 3 tablespoons oil in a large sauté pan over medium-high heat. Add the endive, tossing to coat with the oil. Stir in the Spice Mix along with the chives and cook, stirring constantly, for 1 minute.

8. Remove the endive from the heat. Remove and discard the thyme. Place a serving of endive in the center of each of 6 dinner plates. Place the fish on top of the endive. Drizzle each plate with a bit of the balsamic vinegar and sprinkle a bit of tomato around the edge of the fish. Garnish with a sprig of thyme and serve.

NOTE: If sea bass is not available, use mahi mahi, grouper, or halibut.

Fish Nuggets with Creole Sauce

7 cups KELLOGG'S CORN FLAKES

½ teaspoon paprika

½ teaspoon onion powder

1 large egg, or 2 large egg whites

1 cup fat-free milk

1 pound boneless, skinless fish nuggets (catfish, fillet of sole, snapper, grouper)

Creole Sauce (recipe follows)

This is a very tasty dish to entice non-fish eaters to the table. SERVES 6

1. Place KELLOGG'S CORN FLAKES in a resealable plastic bag. Seal the bag and, using a rolling pin, lightly crush the cereal to make a medium-fine crumb. This may have to be done in batches. Open the bag and measure the crumbs; you should have 2 cups. Combine the crumbs with the paprika and onion powder in a shallow dish. Set aside.

2. Whisk egg and milk together in another shallow dish.

3. Line a small baking pan with aluminum foil and lightly coat with nonstick cooking spray. Set aside.

4. Preheat oven to 350°F.

5. Working with one piece at a time, dip the fish nuggets into the egg mixture and then into the crumb mixture, taking care that they are evenly coated.

6. Place the coated nuggets in the prepared pan. When all of the fish has been coated, bake in the preheated oven for about 20 minutes, or until golden brown and crisp.

7. Remove the nuggets from the oven and transfer to a serving platter. Serve with hot Creole Sauce either spooned over the top or as a dipping sauce.

CREOLE SAUCE

1 tablespoon canola oil

1 clove garlic, peeled and minced

$^1/_2$ cup diced onion

$^1/_2$ cup diced green bell pepper

$^1/_2$ cup diced celery

1 tablespoon sugar

Salt to taste

Crushed red pepper flakes to taste

One 6-ounce can tomato paste

$^1/_2$ cup water

1. Heat the oil in a medium saucepan over medium heat. Add the garlic and sauté for 1 minute. Stir in the onion, bell pepper, and celery. Season with the sugar and salt and red pepper flakes to taste. Cook, stirring occasionally, for about 3 minutes.

2. Add the tomato paste and water, raise the heat, and bring to a boil. Lower the heat, cover, and simmer for about 15 minutes, or until flavors have blended nicely. Taste and, if necessary, season with additional salt and red pepper flakes.

Vegetable-Stuffed Fish Rolls

$^1/_4$ cup olive oil

$^3/_4$ cup finely diced button mushrooms

$^3/_4$ cup finely diced carrots

$^3/_4$ cup finely diced celery

$^1/_4$ cup finely diced onion

1 teaspoon minced garlic

1 teaspoon lemon zest

$^1/_2$ teaspoon salt

$^1/_8$ teaspoon freshly ground pepper

6 cups KELLOGG'S SPECIAL K

2 large egg whites

$1^1/_2$ pounds white fish fillets (such as haddock, cod, fillet of sole)

$^1/_4$ cup butter

2 tablespoons lemon juice

1 tablespoon chopped fresh parsley

The crisp coating that SPECIAL K gives these aromatic fish rolls makes this a particularly appealing dish. The fish, the olive oil–scented stuffing, and the baked-not-fried cooking method together make this recipe a wonderful addition to your repertoire. The melted butter that sauces the cooked rolls can easily be replaced with a squeeze of fresh lemon juice. SERVES 6

1. Heat 2 tablespoons of the olive oil in a large frying pan over medium heat. Add the mushrooms, carrots, celery, onion, garlic, and lemon zest and sauté for about 7 minutes, or until the vegetables are crisp-tender. Season with salt and pepper and remove from heat.

2. Preheat oven to 400°F.

3. Generously coat the bottom of a rectangular glass baking dish with cooking spray. Set aside.

4. Place the SPECIAL K in a resealable plastic bag. Seal the bag and, using a rolling pin, lightly crush the cereal to make a medium-fine crumb. This may have to be done in batches. Open the bag and measure the crumbs; you should have 2 cups. Transfer the crumbs to a shallow dish. Set aside.

5. Place the egg whites in another shallow dish, whisking until frothy.

6. Lay the fillets out on a flat surface. Working with one piece at a time, spoon a portion of the vegetable mixture over the fillet. Beginning at the narrow end, roll the fillet into a tight packet. Secure the roll closed with a toothpick or two.

7. When all the rolls are stuffed, dip them one at a time into the egg whites and then into the crumbs.

8. Place the coated rolls in the prepared baking dish and drizzle with the remaining 2 tablespoons olive oil.

9. Bake in the preheated oven for about 20 minutes, or until the rolls are cooked in the center and very hot.

10. While the fish is baking, place the butter in a small saucepan over low heat. Add the lemon juice and cook until butter is just melted. Set aside and keep warm.

11. Remove the fish from the oven and transfer to a serving platter. Stir the parsley into the melted butter and either pour the butter over the fish or serve it on the side. Serve immediately.

Tuna Croquettes with Dill-Mustard Sauce

One 7-ounce can albacore tuna packed in water, undrained and flaked

1 cup KELLOGG'S ALL-BRAN

2 egg whites

3 tablespoons finely diced celery

1/4 cup finely chopped fresh parsley

1 tablespoon fresh lemon juice

Salt and freshly ground pepper to taste

1 teaspoon canola oil

Dill-Mustard Sauce (recipe follows)

This is the KELLOGG'S version of the old-fashioned favorite croquette. ALL-BRAN adds fiber and the vegetables add a little crunch. The Dill-Mustard Sauce is the finishing touch, but the croquettes can also be served with just a drizzle of lemon juice. SERVES 4

1. Combine the tuna with 1/2 cup of ALL-BRAN along with the egg whites, celery, parsley, lemon juice, and salt and pepper to taste in a medium mixing bowl. Stir to blend well. Set aside.

2. Place the remaining 1/2 cup ALL-BRAN in a resealable plastic bag. Seal the bag and, using a rolling pin, crush the flakes to a medium crumb. Open the bag and measure the crumbs; you should have 1/4 cup. Place the crumbs in a shallow dish along with the canola oil, stirring to blend. Set aside.

3. Preheat oven to 350°F.

4. Line a 9-inch square baking pan with aluminum foil or lightly coat with nonstick cooking spray. Set aside.

5. Working with 1/2 cup at a time, shape the tuna mixture into 4 cone-shaped croquettes and then immediately roll the croquettes into the crumb mixture to evenly coat. Place the croquettes in the prepared baking pan.

6. When all of the croquettes are coated, bake in the preheated oven for 25 minutes, or until dark golden brown.

7. Remove from oven, transfer to a serving plate, spoon Dill-Mustard Sauce over the top, and serve.

DILL-MUSTARD SAUCE

1 cup skim milk

2 tablespoons all-purpose flour

2 teaspoons prepared mustard

Salt and freshly ground pepper to taste

1 tablespoon lemon juice

1/2 teaspoon dried dill weed

1. Place the milk in a small saucepan. Whisk in the flour and when blended, place over medium heat. Add the mustard and salt and pepper to taste and bring to a simmer, whisking constantly. Simmer, whisking constantly, for about 4 minutes, or until thickened.

2. Whisk in the lemon juice and dill and keep warm until ready to serve. (Alternately, make the sauce early in the day and store, covered and refrigerated, until ready to use. When ready to serve, reheat in a small saucepan over low heat.)

CHEF DAVID BURKE, davidburke & donatella, New York City

Shrimp with Black Pepper–Seasoned CORN POPS®

1/4 cup olive oil

1 1/2 cups KELLOGG'S CORN POPS

1 tablespoon cracked black pepper

1/3 cup minced shallots

1 tablespoon minced garlic

36 large shrimp, cleaned and deveined

6 plum tomatoes, peeled, cored, seeded, and finely diced

2 cups nonfat chicken broth

Juice of 2 lemons

1/2 teaspoon salt

1/4 teaspoon freshly ground pepper

1/4 cup butter, softened

2 tablespoons minced fresh chives

18 spears asparagus, trimmed, blanched, and cut into thirds

David Burke is one of America's most inventive chefs. He is known for introducing everyday ingredients into haute cuisine with playfulness and fun, but always with great flavor and taste. KELLOGG'S CORN POPS in this dish add an unexpected note, with just the right amount of crunch and a hint of sweetness. The seasoned cereal can also be used as a great topping for salads, soups, or chili. SERVES 10

1. Heat 1 tablespoon of the olive oil in a medium sauté pan or skillet. Add CORN POPS and season with cracked black pepper. Sauté for about 3 minutes, or just until the cereal is well coated with the pepper. Using a slotted spoon, transfer the cereal to a double layer of paper towel to drain. Set aside.

2. Heat the remaining 3 tablespoons olive oil in a large sauté pan or skillet over medium-high heat. Add the shallots and garlic and sauté for about 3 minutes, or until very soft and translucent. Add the shrimp and sauté for 2 minutes. Stir in the tomatoes, broth, and lemon juice, season with salt and pepper, and cook for another 3 minutes. Bring to a boil, reduce heat, and simmer until shrimp is fully cooked. (The sauce should begin to thicken.)

3. Beat in the butter. When emulsified, stir in the chives and asparagus.

4. Spoon equal portions of the shrimp mixture into shallow soup bowls. Garnish each serving with black pepper–seasoned CORN POPS and serve immediately.

NOTE: This shrimp dish is also wonderful served over rice.

Seafood Fondue

½ cup all-purpose flour

1 teaspoon salt

½ teaspoon freshly ground pepper

3 large egg whites

1¼ cups KELLOGG'S Corn Flake Crumbs

12 ounces small shrimp, peeled and deveined

12 ounces fresh sea scallops

12 ounces white fish fillets, cut into 1 x 2-inch strips

4 cups canola oil

Tartar Sauce (recipe follows)

This is a great dish to make for a relaxed party with good friends. You can add fresh vegetables such as mushrooms, pearl onions, broccoli florets, or any other that you like to the fondue pot to make a complete fondue meal. You can also serve a variety of sauces to add some interest. SERVES 9

1. Combine the flour with salt and pepper in a shallow dish.

2. Place the egg whites in a second shallow dish and whisk until frothy.

3. Place the crumbs in a final dish.

4. Working with one piece at a time, dip the shrimp, scallops, and fish strips in the flour, then in the eggs, and finally in the crumbs, taking care that each piece is evenly coated. Place the coated seafood on a platter.

5. Heat the oil in a metal fondue pot on the stove top over medium heat until it reaches 375°F on an instant-read thermometer (or a bread cube turns golden brown in 30 seconds). Carefully transfer the hot pan to the portable fondue burner.

6. Working with a few pieces at a time, drop the coated seafood into the hot oil and cook for about 3 minutes, or until golden. You can do this on metal skewers if you like.

7. Eat the seafood as it is cooked, dipped into Tartar Sauce or another savory sauce.

TARTAR SAUCE

1 cup fine-quality mayonnaise

3 tablespoons chopped dill or sweet pickles or pickle relish

1 teaspoon grated onion

A few drops lemon juice

Combine the mayonnaise, chopped pickle (or relish), onion, and lemon juice in a small mixing bowl. When blended, serve or cover with plastic film and store, refrigerated, until ready to use.

Crispy Lemon-Dill Fish Fillets

4 cups KELLOGG'S CORN FLAKES

1 teaspoon chopped fresh dill, or
1/2 teaspoon dried dill weed

Salt and freshly ground pepper to taste

1/4 cup butter, melted

1 teaspoon lemon zest

Six 6-ounce white fish fillets such as haddock, cod, or fillet of sole, patted dry

6 lemon wedges, optional

The dill and lemon add a fresh flavor to this baked, not fried, yet still crispy and crunchy fish dish. Serve with a savory rice pilaf and a tossed green salad and you have a very appetizing meal. As a variation, you can replace the lemon zest with orange zest and the dill with tarragon and serve the fish garnished with fresh orange slices. SERVES 6

1. Place KELLOGG'S CORN FLAKES in a resealable plastic bag. Seal the bag and, using a rolling pin, crush the flakes to a medium crumb. Open the bag and measure the crumbs; you should have 2 cups. Place the crumbs in a shallow dish. Season with the dill and salt and pepper to taste. Set aside.

2. Combine the butter and lemon zest in another shallow dish.

3. Line a baking pan with aluminum foil. Lightly coat with nonstick cooking spray. Set aside.

4. Preheat oven to 375°F.

5. Working with one piece at a time, dip the fillets into the butter mixture and then into the crumb mixture, taking care that the fish is evenly coated on all sides. Place the coated fillets in the prepared pan.

6. When all of the fillets have been coated, bake in the preheated oven, without turning, for about 25 minutes, or until fish easily flakes with a fork.

7. Remove from oven and serve immediately with lemon wedges, if desired.

Garden-Fresh Lasagna

One 28-ounce can whole peeled tomatoes with their juice

One 8-ounce can tomato sauce

One 6-ounce can tomato paste

1½ cups sliced button mushrooms

1 cup diced onion

1 tablespoon minced garlic

1 tablespoon minced fresh parsley

1 tablespoon minced fresh basil

1 teaspoon dried oregano

Salt and freshly ground pepper to taste

1¼ cups KELLOGG'S ALL-BRAN

1 pound part-skim ricotta cheese

⅓ cup nonfat dry milk powder

8 ounces lasagna noodles, cooked and drained

Two 10-ounce packages frozen chopped spinach, thawed and squeezed dry

8 ounces shredded mozzarella cheese

3 tablespoons grated Parmesan cheese

Garden-Fresh is its name simply because this lasagna does not contain any meat—just tomatoes, herbs, spinach, and cheeses. The addition of fiber from KELLOGG'S ALL-BRAN replaces some of the texture that would normally come from ground meats and adds to the total goodness of the dish. SERVES 12

1. Combine the tomatoes, tomato sauce, and tomato paste in a large nonreactive saucepan over medium heat. Stir in the mushrooms, onion, garlic, parsley, basil, and oregano. Season with salt and pepper to taste and bring to a simmer. Lower the heat and simmer for 15 minutes.

2. Combine ¾ cup of ALL-BRAN with the ricotta and dry milk in a small mixing bowl, stirring until very well blended. Set aside.

3. Lightly coat the interior of a 13 x 9 x 2-inch baking dish with nonstick cooking spray.

4. Preheat oven to 375°F.

5. Place a layer of noodles in the bottom of the dish. Using about one third of each ingredient, make a layer of the ricotta cheese mixture, followed by a layer of spinach, then the tomato sauce, and finally a layer of mozzarella cheese. In the same order, make two more complete layers, ending with mozzarella cheese.

6. Sprinkle the mozzarella with the remaining ½ cup ALL-BRAN and then with the Parmesan cheese.

7. Loosely cover the entire dish with aluminum foil and place in the preheated oven. Bake for 35 minutes. Then remove the foil and bake for an additional 10 minutes, or until the lasagna is bubbling and the cheese has melted.

8. Remove from oven and set aside to rest for 15 minutes before cutting into squares and serving.

"Sprouting Out" Custard Pie

CRUST

1 cup KELLOGG'S ALL-BRAN

$^1/_2$ cup whole wheat flour

$^1/_4$ cup all-purpose flour

1 tablespoon sugar

$^1/_4$ cup butter or margarine

2 tablespoons water

1 large egg white

FILLING

1 tablespoon water

1 cup sliced button mushrooms

$^1/_2$ cup diced green or red bell pepper

2 tablespoons diced onion

1 teaspoon minced garlic

Salt and freshly ground pepper to taste

1 cup low-fat cottage cheese

One 12-ounce can evaporated skim milk

$^1/_2$ teaspoon dry mustard

4 large egg whites

1 tablespoon all-purpose flour

$^3/_4$ cup shredded mozzarella cheese

GARNISH

1 medium ripe tomato, peeled, cored, and cut crosswise into thin slices

$1^1/_2$ cups alfafa sprouts

This is a "quiche" that real men will love! And so will everyone else! It is full of flavor and great taste. The tomato and sprouts make a beautiful garnish but are not necessary to complete the dish. SERVES 6

1. Preheat oven to 350°F.

2. To make the crust, combine the ALL-BRAN with the whole wheat flour, $^1/_4$ cup all-purpose flour, and sugar in a medium mixing bowl. Add the butter and cut it into the dry ingredients until coarse crumbs form. Stir in 2 tablespoons water and mix until a stiff dough forms.

3. Lightly coat the interior of a 9-inch pie pan with nonstick cooking spray. Transfer the dough to the pie pan and, using your fingertips, press the dough into the pan to evenly cover.

4. Place 1 egg white in a small bowl and whisk until frothy. Using a pastry brush, lightly coat the dough with the egg white.

5. Place the crust in the preheated oven and bake for 6 minutes, or until lightly browned. Remove from the oven and set aside.

6. Reduce the oven temperature to 325°F.

7. To make the filling, place the remaining 1 tablespoon water in a nonstick frying pan over medium heat. Add the mushrooms, bell pepper, onion, and garlic along with salt and pepper to taste and cook, stirring frequently, for about 5 minutes, or until tender. Remove from the heat and drain well through a fine sieve, discarding the liquid. Set the vegetables aside.

8. Combine the cottage cheese, 1/2 cup of the evaporated milk, the mustard, the 4 egg whites, and 1 tablespoon all-purpose flour in the bowl of a food processor fitted with the metal blade. Season with salt and pepper to taste and process until smooth. Add the remaining cup of evaporated milk and process to incorporate.

9. Using a spatula, spread the reserved vegetable mixture over the baked crust. Layer the mozzarella cheese over the vegetables. Pour the cottage cheese mixture into the crust, spreading it out evenly.

10. Bake the pie in the preheated oven for 45 minutes, or until the center is set.

11. Remove from oven and let rest for 10 minutes before cutting.

12. Garnish the top of the pie with the tomato slices and sprouts, cut into wedges, and serve.

Eggs Chimay

2 tablespoons olive oil

1/4 cup minced onion

3/4 cup finely chopped mushrooms

3 tablespoons all-purpose flour

1/2 cup hot chicken broth or whole milk or fat-free milk

1 teaspoon minced fresh parsley

1/4 teaspoon salt

1/4 teaspoon freshly ground pepper

6 hard-cooked eggs, peeled

1 large raw egg, separated

1 cup KELLOGG'S Corn Flake Crumbs

This dish is based on a classic French recipe but is a bit less rich than the usual since the eggs are baked without the classic Mornay sauce. Eggs Chimay makes a great light dinner served with a salad. SERVES 6

1. Heat the oil in a medium sauté pan over medium heat. Add the onion and sauté for 3 minutes. Stir in the mushrooms and cook, stirring frequently, for about 5 minutes, or until the mushrooms are very soft and slightly dry.

2. Add the flour and stir to blend. Stir in the hot broth (or milk) and cook, stirring frequently, until the mixture thickens.

3. Remove from the heat, stir in the parsley, and season with salt and pepper.

4. Preheat oven to 375°F.

5. Line a small baking pan with aluminum foil and lightly coat with nonstick cooking spray. Set aside.

6. Cut the hard-cooked eggs in half lengthwise, keeping the two halves matched for easier filling. Carefully scoop out the yolks. Set the whites aside and add the yolks to the mushroom mixture along with the raw egg yolk. Stir until very well blended.

7. Place the raw egg white in a shallow dish and whisk until frothy. Place the Corn Flake Crumbs in a separate shallow dish.

8. Working with one at a time, carefully stuff each egg white half with mushroom mixture. Place 2 halves together to make a whole egg.

9. Carefully roll the "whole" egg in the beaten egg white and then in the crumbs. Place the coated egg in the prepared baking pan. Repeat.

10. When all of the eggs are in the pan, lightly spray each egg with nonstick cooking spray.

11. Bake the eggs in the preheated oven for about 15 minutes, or until golden brown and heated through.

12. Remove from oven and serve as is or with a light tomato sauce.

SIDE DISHES

Summer Squash and Chilies Bake

4 tablespoons butter, softened

3 cups thinly sliced zucchini

3 cups thinly sliced yellow squash

1/2 cup chopped onion

One 4-ounce can chopped green chilies, drained

2 tablespoons all-purpose flour

1/2 teaspoon salt, or to taste

1/4 teaspoon pepper, or to taste

1 1/2 cups shredded Monterey Jack cheese

1 cup low-fat cottage cheese

1 large egg, lightly beaten

2 tablespoons chopped fresh parsley

3 cups KELLOGG'S RICE KRISPIES

1/2 cup grated Parmesan cheese

This is a terrific side dish that can also be used as a vegetarian main course or as a marvelous addition to a party buffet table. The crunchy RICE KRISPIES topping adds just the right note to elevate the dish to party fare.

SERVES 10

1. Preheat oven to 400°F.

2. Lightly spray a 12 x 7 1/2 x 2-inch (2-quart) glass baking dish with nonstick cooking spray. Set aside.

3. Heat 2 tablespoons of the butter in a 12-inch frying pan over medium heat. Add the zucchini, yellow squash, and onion and sauté for about 5 minutes, or just until crisp-tender. Remove from the heat.

4. Fold in the chilies, flour, salt, and pepper, tossing to combine. Scrape the mixture into the prepared baking pan. Sprinkle the top with the Monterey Jack cheese. Set aside.

5. Combine the cottage cheese, egg, and parsley in a medium mixing bowl. When well combined, spread the mixture over the Jack cheese in the baking dish.

6. Place the baking dish in the preheated oven and bake for about 20 minutes, or until golden brown and bubbling.

7. While the squash is baking, prepare the topping. Melt the remaining 2 tablespoons of butter in a large frying pan over medium heat. Remove from heat, add the RICE KRISPIES, and stir just until the cereal is well coated with the butter. Stir in the Parmesan cheese.

8. Remove the baking dish from the oven and sprinkle the top with the RICE KRISPIES. Return the dish to the hot oven and bake for an additional 10 minutes, or until the topping is golden brown and crusty.

9. Remove from oven and serve hot.

CHEF CHARLIE PALMER, Aureole, New York City

Vanilla-Scented Baked Winter Squash and Apples

2 cups KELLOGG'S SPECIAL K Vanilla Almond

2 large butternut squashes, peeled, seeded, and grated

3 cooking apples, cored, peeled, and grated

1 medium onion, peeled and grated

1/2 cup chopped toasted almonds

1 teaspoon minced fresh sage

1 teaspoon salt

1/2 teaspoon freshly ground pepper

1/2 cup apple cider

1/4 cup pure maple syrup

1 teaspoon pure vanilla extract

1/4 cup melted unsalted butter

Charlie Palmer is a proponent of what he calls "progressive American cuisine." He is one of America's most well-known and respected chefs, with his Aureole Restaurants in New York and Las Vegas leading a list of more than ten restaurants across the country. In this dish, he adds KELLOGG'S SPECIAL K Vanilla Almond to a lovely fall vegetable side dish that would be perfect for the holiday table. SERVES 12

1. Preheat oven to 350°F.

2. Lightly coat a 4-quart baking dish with nonstick cooking spray. Sprinkle 1 cup of the SPECIAL K Vanilla Almond over the bottom. Set aside.

3. Combine the squashes, apples, onion, almonds, sage, and salt and pepper in a large mixing bowl.

4. Combine the cider, syrup, and vanilla in a small bowl, stirring to blend. Pour the cider mixture over the squash mixture, tossing to combine.

5. Spoon the mixture over the cereal in the prepared dish, taking care that all of the liquid is poured into the dish. Sprinkle the remaining cup of cereal over the top and then drizzle the melted butter over all.

6. Bake in the preheated oven for 45 minutes, or until the top is golden brown and the edges are beginning to pull away from the sides of the dish.

7. Remove the dish from the oven and allow to rest for 5 minutes before cutting into squares and serving.

Zucchini and Tomatoes

3/4 cup KELLOGG'S COMPLETE Wheat Bran Flakes

2 teaspoons plus 2 tablespoons olive oil

1/2 teaspoon grated lemon zest

4 medium zucchini (about 1 1/4 pounds), well washed, trimmed, and cut crosswise into 1/4-inch-thick slices

3 medium tomatoes (about 3/4 pound), peeled, cored, seeded, and cut into wedges

1 tablespoon fresh lemon juice

Salt and freshly ground pepper to taste

The lemon adds a jolt of freshness to this standard vegetable combo. The mild zucchini is balanced by the acidic tomatoes, and the lemony cereal crumbs add just the right note of texture to the finished dish. SERVES 6

1. Place the COMPLETE Wheat Bran Flakes in a resealable plastic bag. Seal the bag and, using a rolling pin, crush the flakes to a fine crumb. Set aside.

2. Heat 2 teaspoons of the oil in a small frying pan over low heat. Add the crumbs and cook, stirring constantly, for about 4 minutes, or until lightly colored. Remove from the heat and stir in the lemon zest. Set aside.

3. Heat the remaining 2 tablespoons of oil in a large frying pan over medium heat. Add the zucchini and sauté for about 5 minutes, or until almost tender. Stir in tomatoes and lemon juice along with salt and pepper to taste. Cook, stirring frequently, for about 3 minutes, or until just hot.

4. Remove from heat and transfer to a serving bowl. Sprinkle the reserved crumb mixture over the top and serve.

Oven-Fried Onion Rings

1/4 cup all-purpose flour

2 large egg whites

2 tablespoons cold water

4 cups KELLOGG'S CORN FLAKES or 1 cup KELLOGG'S Corn Flake Crumbs

1 teaspoon garlic salt

1/2 teaspoon dried oregano, optional

1 large onion, peeled and cut crosswise into 1/2-inch-thick slices

Here is a new take on the usual deep-fat-fried onion rings. We coat them in cereal crumbs to add crispness, eliminate the egg yolks, and bake instead of fry. They are deliciously crunchy and make a great side dish for a burger. SERVES 6

1. Place the flour in a shallow dish.

2. Combine the egg whites and water in a second shallow dish and, using a whisk, beat until frothy.

3. Place KELLOGG'S CORN FLAKES in a resealable plastic bag. Seal the bag and, using a rolling pin, crush the flakes to a fine crumb. You should have 1 cup.

4. Transfer the crumbs to a third shallow bowl. Combine crumbs with the garlic salt and oregano.

5. Line a baking pan with aluminum foil and lightly coat with nonstick cooking spray. Set aside.

6. Preheat oven to 400°F.

7. Separate the onion slices into rings. Working with one at a time, first dip the onion rings into the flour, then into the egg white mixture, and finally into the crumb mixture. Carefully repeat the dipping into the egg white mixture and then the crumbs to double-coat completely.

8. As each ring is coated, place it on the prepared baking pan. When all of the rings have been coated and placed on the pan, lightly coat the tops with nonstick cooking spray.

9. Bake in the preheated oven for about 8 minutes, or until the onion rings are golden.

10. Remove from oven and serve.

Stuffed Zucchini Boats

3 medium zucchini, trimmed and well washed

1/2 cup finely diced celery

3 tablespoons minced onion

1/4 cup water

3/4 cup finely diced button mushrooms

1/2 cup canned chicken broth

1 teaspoon dried basil

1 teaspoon dried thyme

Salt and freshly ground pepper to taste

1 cup diced fresh tomato

1/2 cup KELLOGG'S ALL-BRAN

2 teaspoons grated Parmesan cheese

Although these delectable stuffed zucchinis make a marvelous accompaniment to roasts, they also make a terrific luncheon dish. Delicious hot, they may also be served at room temperature. SERVES 6

1. Place the whole zucchini in a steamer basket over boiling water, cover, and steam for about 15 minutes, or until crisp-tender. Remove from the steamer and set aside to cool slightly.

2. When cool enough to handle, cut in half lengthwise and, using a tablespoon or melon baller, carefully scoop out the interior pulp, leaving a 1/4-inch-thick shell. Set the shells aside.

3. Roughly chop the pulp and set aside.

4. Preheat oven to 350°F.

5. Line a baking pan with aluminum foil. Lightly spray with nonstick cooking spray. Set aside.

6. Combine the celery and onion with the water in a medium saucepan over medium heat. Cook, stirring frequently, for about 4 minutes, or until the onion is very soft. Stir in the mushrooms along with the reserved zucchini pulp and cook for 2 minutes.

7. Add the chicken broth, basil, and thyme and bring to a boil. Season with salt and pepper to taste and remove from the heat.

8. Stir in the tomato and ALL-BRAN. When well combined, generously mound the stuffing into the zucchini shells. Sprinkle with Parmesan cheese and transfer to the prepared baking pan.

9. Bake in the preheated oven for about 25 minutes, or until very hot and golden on the top. Remove from oven and serve immediately.

Winter Vegetables au Gratin

3 cups KELLOGG'S CORN FLAKES

2 tablespoons butter or margarine, melted

1/8 teaspoon garlic powder

One 1-pound package frozen carrots, cauliflower, and broccoli mix, cooked to crisp-tender according to package directions and drained

2 cups Cheese Sauce (recipe follows)

Although the recipe calls for a frozen vegetable mix, you can certainly use any combination of vegetables you like, fresh or frozen (see note). Just make sure that they are cooked only until crisp-tender when combined with the sauce so that they don't get limp and soggy when baked.

If you want to add a little zest to the mix, season the Cheese Sauce with Tabasco or other hot sauce or with chili powder. SERVES 6

1. Combine KELLOGG'S CORN FLAKES, butter, and garlic powder in small bowl. Set aside.

2. Preheat oven to 350°F.

3. Lightly spray a 1 1/2-quart casserole with nonstick cooking spray.

4. Combine the cooked vegetables with the Cheese Sauce in the mixing bowl. When blended, transfer to the prepared casserole, spreading out to an even layer. Sprinkle the reserved cereal mixture over the top.

5. Bake the casserole in the preheated oven for about 30 minutes, or until bubbling and golden brown.

6. Remove from oven and serve immediately.

The KELLOGG'S SWEETHEART OF THE CORN, who first appeared in 1907, continues to be almost as recognizable a company symbol on the box as Mr. Kellogg's signature.

CHEESE SAUCE

¹/₄ cup butter

¹/₄ cup all-purpose flour

2 cups milk

¹/₂ pound American cheese, cubed (see note)

Salt and freshly ground pepper to taste

1. Place the butter in a medium, heavy-bottomed saucepan over medium-low heat. When melted, stir in the flour and cook, stirring constantly, for 1 minute.

2. Stirring constantly, slowly add the milk, stirring until smooth. Increase heat to medium and cook, stirring constantly, until the mixture boils. Continue cooking and stirring 1 minute longer.

3. Add the cheese and cook, stirring constantly, just until the cheese has melted. Season with salt and pepper to taste.

4. Remove from heat and use as directed in a specific recipe.

NOTE: This recipe works particularly well with one of the following: carrots (4 cups); cauliflower (4 cups florets); a mix of broccoli (2 cups florets) and corn (2 cups well-drained, thawed frozen kernels); or spinach (one 10-ounce package frozen chopped, thawed, and well drained) mixed with 2 large eggs. If using spinach, add only about 1¼ cups of the Cheese Sauce.

The American cheese can be replaced with Cheddar, either full-fat or reduced-fat, or other hard cheeses such as Swiss, again either full-fat or reduced-fat.

Turnip-Apple Bake

1 cup canned chicken broth

1 teaspoon minced onion

2 cups sliced (about 1 large) yellow turnip (rutabaga)

3 tablespoons butter

1/8 teaspoon freshly ground nutmeg

2 tablespoons all-purpose flour

1 cup 2% milk

1/2 teaspoon salt

1/8 teaspoon freshly ground pepper

1 cup sliced tart apples

1/2 cup KELLOGG'S Corn Flake Crumbs

This is a great holiday side dish. The casserole can be put together the day before, covered with plastic film, and refrigerated until ready to bake. It can also be baked the day before and reheated in a 300°F oven or in a microwave. This is such a tasty dish that we guarantee you'll get even the most suspicious diner to eat turnips. SERVES 8

1. Lightly spray a 2-quart casserole with nonstick cooking spray. Set aside.

2. Place the broth in a medium saucepan over medium heat. Add the onion and bring to a boil. Immediately add the turnip and bring to a simmer. Simmer for about 20 minutes, or until crisp-tender.

3. Using a slotted spoon, transfer the turnip to the prepared casserole dish. Set aside.

4. If the broth has not reduced to 1/4 cup, return the saucepan to medium heat and simmer the broth until it has reduced to that amount. If the broth has already reduced to 1/4 cup, add the butter and nutmeg and return to medium heat. Add the flour, stirring until well blended.

5. Stirring constantly, gradually add the milk. Cook, stirring constantly, until the mixture comes to a boil. Season with salt and pepper and remove from heat.

6. Preheat oven to 350°F.

7. Add the apples to the turnip in the prepared casserole. Pour the sauce over the top and sprinkle with the crumbs. Lightly spray the top with nonstick cooking spray.

8. Bake the casserole in the preheated oven for about 20 minutes, or until bubbling hot and golden.

9. Remove from oven and serve immediately.

Corn Fritters

2 cups KELLOGG'S COMPLETE Wheat Bran Flakes

1/2 cup all-purpose flour

1/2 teaspoon baking powder

2 large egg whites

1/4 cup fat-free milk

1/2 teaspoon butter, melted

1 1/2 cups thawed frozen corn, well drained

1 teaspoon salt

1/8 teaspoon freshly ground pepper

2 tablespoons canola oil

This is a recipe you can truly make your own. You can use almost any KELLOGG'S flaked cereal, even those with a bit of sweetness; you can add some heat with fresh chilies, chili powder, or curry; you can serve the fritters with salsa, Asian sauces, or a bit of honey or maple syrup. SERVES 6

1. Place the COMPLETE Wheat Bran Flakes in a resealable plastic bag. Seal the bag and, using a rolling pin, crush the flakes to a fine crumb. Open the bag and measure the crumbs; you should have 1/2 cup.

2. Combine the crumbs with the flour and baking powder in a medium bowl. Add the egg whites, milk, and butter, stirring to combine. Stir in the corn and season with salt and pepper to taste.

3. Heat the oil in a large frying pan over medium heat. When very hot but not smoking, drop in the corn batter by the heaping tablespoonful. Using a spatula, slightly flatten the batter. Fry, turning once, for about 5 minutes, or until golden brown on both sides and cooked through. Add more oil if necessary.

4. Transfer to a double layer of paper towel to drain. Serve hot.

Bacon-Spinach Stuffed Tomatoes

6 large ripe tomatoes, well washed and cored

2 cups KELLOGG'S SPECIAL K

4 slices uncooked bacon, chopped

2 cloves garlic, peeled and minced

1/3 cup chopped onion

3 cups coarsely chopped raw spinach leaves

3 tablespoons grated Parmesan cheese

1 1/2 cups grated part-skim mozzarella cheese

1/2 teaspoon salt

1/4 teaspoon freshly ground pepper

Although these stuffed tomatoes make a marvelous side dish, they also work well as a main course for a light lunch or as part of a brunch buffet. The stuffing could also go into cherry tomatoes to be used as an hors d'oeuvre. Turkey bacon is a good alternative for the traditional pork bacon. SERVES 6

1. Using a sharp knife, carefully cut about 1/4 inch off the top of each tomato. With a tablespoon, scoop out the pulp. Chop the pulp and set aside.

2. Turn the tomato shells upside down on a double layer of paper towel to drain.

3. Place the SPECIAL K in a resealable plastic bag. Seal the bag and, using a rolling pin, crush the flakes to a fine crumb. Open the bag and measure the crumbs; you should have 1/2 cup. Set aside.

4. Preheat oven to 350°F.

5. Lightly coat a 9 x 13 x 2-inch glass baking dish with nonstick cooking spray. Set aside.

6. Combine the bacon, garlic, and onion in a medium frying pan over medium heat. Fry, stirring frequently, for about 5 minutes, or until the bacon is crisp. Drain off excess fat. Add the spinach along with the tomato pulp. Cook over medium-high heat, stirring frequently, until all of the moisture has evaporated.

7. Remove from heat and stir in the crushed cereal along with the Parmesan cheese and 1/2 cup of the mozzarella. Add the salt and pepper.

8. Invert the tomato shells and, working with one at a time, carefully place an equal portion of the bacon-spinach mixture into each one. Top with reserved mozzarella and place in prepared baking dish.

9. Bake in the preheated oven for about 30 minutes, or until tomatoes are hot and cheese is melted.

10. Remove from oven and serve.

Oven-Fried Green Tomatoes

1/4 cup all-purpose flour

2 large egg whites

2 tablespoons cold water

4 cups KELLOGG'S CORN FLAKES, crushed to 1 cup (see pages xiv–xv), or 1 cup KELLOGG'S Corn Flake Crumbs

1 teaspoon garlic salt

1/2 teaspoon dried oregano

2 large green tomatoes, cored and cut crosswise into 1/2-inch-thick slices

Everybody who has ever tasted them loves fried green tomatoes. A little tart, juicy, and crunchy—they're the perfect side dish for a steak, barbecued ribs, or chicken.
SERVES 6

1. Place the flour in a shallow dish.

2. Combine the egg whites and water in a second shallow dish and, using a whisk, beat until frothy.

3. Combine the crumbs, garlic salt, and oregano in a third shallow dish.

4. Line a baking pan with aluminum foil. Lightly coat with nonstick cooking spray. Set aside.

5. Preheat oven to 400°F.

6. Working with one at a time, first dip the tomato slices into the flour, then into the egg white mixture, and finally into the crumb mixture. Carefully repeat the dipping into the egg white mixture and then the crumbs to double-coat completely.

7. As each slice is coated, place it in the prepared baking pan. When all of the rings have been coated and placed in the pan, lightly coat the tops with nonstick cooking spray.

8. Bake in the preheated oven for about 8 minutes, or until the tomato slices are golden.

9. Remove from oven and serve.

Mallow-Whipped Sweet Potatoes

Two 23-ounce cans sweet potatoes, well drained

6 tablespoons butter, melted

3 tablespoons firmly packed brown sugar

1 teaspoon ground cinnamon

1/4 teaspoon ground nutmeg

Salt to taste

2 cups miniature marshmallows

2 cups KELLOGG'S RICE KRISPIES

The crunch of RICE KRISPIES adds texture to this standard Thanksgiving side dish. Canned sweet potatoes make this dish a breeze to prepare. SERVES 8

1. Preheat oven to 350°F.

2. Lightly coat a 10 x 6 x 2-inch (1 1/2-quart) glass baking dish with nonstick cooking spray. Set aside.

3. Combine the sweet potatoes with 1/4 cup of the melted butter along with 2 tablespoons of the brown sugar, cinnamon, nutmeg, and salt to taste in a medium mixing bowl. Using a wooden spoon, beat until very well blended. Stir in 1 cup of the marshmallows.

4. Transfer the mixture to the prepared baking dish, smoothing out the top with a spatula. Place the remaining 1 cup marshmallows over the top.

5. Combine the remaining 2 tablespoons melted butter and brown sugar with the RICE KRISPIES, tossing to coat well. Sprinkle the cereal mixture over the marshmallows.

6. Bake in the preheated oven for about 20 minutes, or until potatoes are very hot and topping is golden brown.

7. Remove from oven and serve immediately.

NOTE: RICE KRISPIES can be replaced with lightly crushed CRACKLIN' OAT BRAN for a different texture and flavor.

Cheese Potato Crisps

2 cups KELLOGG'S CORN FLAKES

3 large baking potatoes, peeled and cut lengthwise into 1/4-inch-thick slices

Salt to taste

1 cup shredded Cheddar cheese

1/2 teaspoon paprika

1/4 cup sliced scallions

These are better than French fries! We guarantee that once you try them, you'll make these cheesy potatoes a standard at your table. Using different cheeses such as Monterey Jack, American, Swiss, or grated Parmesan cheese, and a bit of chili powder easily adds variety and keeps the dish interesting. SERVES 6

1. Place the KELLOGG'S CORN FLAKES in a resealable plastic bag. Seal the bag and, using a rolling pin, crush the flakes to a medium crumb. Open the bag and measure the crumbs; you should have 1 cup. Set aside.

2. Preheat oven to 375°.

3. Lightly coat a large baking sheet with nonstick cooking spray.

4. Lay the potatoes on the prepared baking sheet in a single layer. Lightly coat with nonstick cooking spray.

5. Sprinkle the coated potatoes with salt to taste. Sprinkle each potato slice with some of the cheese. Top with the crumbs and a sprinkling of paprika.

6. Bake in the preheated oven, without turning, for about 25 minutes, or until the potatoes are cooked through and golden brown.

7. Remove from oven and transfer to a serving platter. Garnish with the scallions and serve.

Potato-Onion Casserole

1½ cups KELLOGG'S SPECIAL K

¼ cup butter, melted

1 pound potatoes, peeled and thinly sliced

1 large onion, peeled and thinly sliced

Salt to taste

¼ cup all-purpose flour

Freshly ground pepper to taste

Paprika to taste

2 cups fat-free milk

This is an updated version of the classic scalloped potato. The cereal topping adds a nice crunchy texture that heightens the mellowness of the potatoes. The onions could be replaced with leeks, and a bit of garlic can be added for flavor. You can add zest to this dish by using fresh herbs, chilies, or spices. SERVES 8

1. Place the KELLOGG'S SPECIAL K in a resealable plastic bag. Seal the bag and, using a rolling pin, crush the flakes to a medium crumb. Open the bag and measure the crumbs; you should have ³/₄ cup.

2. Place the crumbs in a small bowl. Stir in 1 tablespoon of the melted butter and set aside.

3. Lightly coat a 1½-quart glass baking dish with nonstick cooking spray. Set aside.

4. Preheat oven to 350°F.

5. Place the potatoes and onion in a medium saucepan and cover with cold salted water. Cover pan and bring to a boil over medium-high heat. Lower the heat and simmer for 5 minutes. Remove from heat and drain well. Set aside.

6. Place the remaining 3 tablespoons melted butter in a medium saucepan over medium heat. Stir in the flour and season with salt, pepper, and paprika to taste. When well blended, gradually add the milk, stirring constantly. Cook, stirring constantly, for about 5 minutes, or until the mixture comes to a boil. Remove from heat.

7. Place half the potato-onion mixture into the prepared dish, spreading it out in an even layer. Pour half the sauce over the layer of potatoes and onions. Top with another even layer of the potato-onion mixture and pour the remaining sauce over the top. Sprinkle the reserved cereal mixture over the top.

8. Bake in the preheated oven for about 30 minutes, or until the potatoes are very tender and the top is golden brown.

9. Remove from oven and serve.

Stuffed Potatoes

3 large Idaho potatoes, baked

3 slices uncooked bacon, chopped

1/4 cup finely diced onion

1 cup grated reduced-fat Cheddar cheese

1 teaspoon salt

1/2 teaspoon freshly ground pepper

2 cups KELLOGG'S CORN FLAKES, crushed to 1/2 cup (see pages xiv–xv), or 1/2 cup KELLOGG'S Corn Flake Crumbs

1 tablespoon butter, melted

Perfect sitting alongside a grilled steak or chop or served as is for lunch or a light supper. The cereal topping adds just the right touch of crunch to these richly flavored potatoes. SERVES 6

1. Preheat oven to 400°F.

2. Cut the potatoes in half lengthwise and carefully scoop out the pulp, reserving the shells.

3. Place the pulp in a medium mixing bowl and coarsely mash with a fork. Set aside.

4. Place the bacon in a large skillet over medium heat. Fry, stirring frequently, for about 5 minutes, or until partially cooked. Add the onion and continue frying for about 5 minutes, or until the bacon is crisp and the onion is soft. Drain off excess fat.

5. Scrape the bacon mixture into the mashed potatoes. Stir in the cheese along with salt and pepper.

6. When the mixture is well blended, divide it equally among the potato shells.

7. Combine the crumbs with the melted butter, tossing to blend well. Generously top each potato half with crumb mixture.

8. Place the stuffed potatoes in a baking pan in the preheated oven and bake for about 20 minutes, or until piping hot and crusty.

9. Remove from oven and serve.

Savory Bran-Rice Pilaf

Approximately 2 cups chicken broth

½ cup uncooked white or brown rice

Salt to taste

2 tablespoons butter or canola oil

¼ cup chopped onion

¼ cup chopped celery

½ cup sliced button mushrooms

¼ cup sliced canned water chestnuts

1 cup KELLOGG'S ALL-BRAN

¼ cup chopped pimientos

½ teaspoon dried basil

¼ teaspoon ground sage

Freshly ground pepper to taste

A terrific change from a dish of plain rice, this pilaf is a great accompaniment to roasts. The celery and water chestnuts add crunch and ALL-BRAN adds flavor and fiber. SERVES 6

1. Place 1 cup of the chicken broth in a medium saucepan over high heat. Bring to a boil. Add the rice and salt to taste, cover, and return to a boil. Lower the heat and simmer for about 20 minutes (about 35–45 minutes for brown rice), or until the rice is cooked. Remove from heat.

2. Heat the remaining cup of broth in a small saucepan over low heat until hot. Remove from heat and keep warm.

3. Heat the butter in a medium sauté pan over medium heat. Add the onion, celery, mushrooms, and water chestnuts and sauté for about 5 minutes, or until the celery is crisp-tender. Remove from heat.

4. Stir the cooked rice, cereal, pimientos, basil, sage, and salt and pepper to taste into the vegetable mixture. Add just enough of the reserved hot broth to make a moist mixture. Taste and, if necessary, season with additional salt and pepper. Serve immediately.

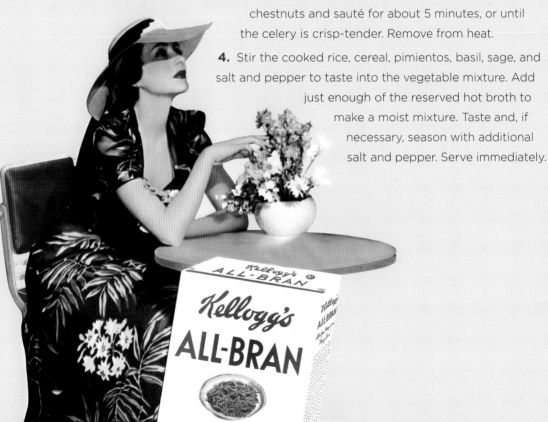

Grits Casserole

3/4 cup KELLOGG'S Corn Flake Crumbs

3 tablespoons butter, melted

2 large eggs

1/4 cup milk

4 cups water

1 cup quick-cooking grits

Salt to taste

2 cups shredded Cheddar or American cheese

1/2 pound bacon, fried and crumbled

Freshly ground pepper to taste

This very tasty casserole could be the centerpiece of a brunch table or a substantial breakfast dish for a hungry group. With a salad, it would make a great supper dish also. SERVES 6

1. Preheat oven to 300°F.

2. Lightly coat a 12 x 7 1/2 x 2-inch (2-quart) glass baking dish with nonstick cooking spray. Set aside.

3. Combine the crumbs with the melted butter, tossing to coat well. Set aside.

4. Combine the eggs and milk in a small mixing bowl, whisking to combine well. Set aside.

5. Bring the water to a boil in a medium saucepan. Stir in the grits and season with salt to taste. Return to a boil and cook, stirring constantly, for 5 minutes.

6. Remove the grits from the heat and beat in the cheese. When melted, stir in the crumbled bacon along with the egg mixture. Season with salt and pepper to taste. Pour the grits into the prepared baking dish and sprinkle the reserved crumb mixture over the top.

7. Place in the preheated oven and bake for about 45 minutes, or until very hot and bubbling.

8. Remove from oven and let rest for 10 minutes before serving.

Parmesan Noodles

2 cups KELLOGG'S CORN FLAKES

1 cup grated Parmesan cheese

One 12-ounce package broad egg noodles

1/4 cup butter

2 tablespoons chopped fresh parsley

Salt and freshly ground pepper to taste

Certainly more interesting and twice as tasty as plain buttered noodles, this is a crowd-pleasing side dish. The cheese, butter, and KELLOGG'S CORN FLAKES add great flavor and texture. SERVES 8

1. Place the KELLOGG'S CORN FLAKES in a resealable plastic bag. Seal the bag and, using a rolling pin, crush the flakes to a fine crumb. Open the bag and measure the crumbs; you should have 1/2 cup.

2. Combine the crumbs with the cheese in a small bowl. Set aside.

3. Cook the noodles according to package directions. Drain thoroughly. Do not rinse.

4. Return the noodles to the saucepan in which they were cooked. Add the butter and parsley, tossing to coat. Quickly add the reserved crumb mixture, season with salt and pepper to taste, and again toss to coat.

5. Transfer to a warm serving bowl and serve.

KELLOGG KITCHENS developed complete menus and manuals for children's camps. The 1950 "My Vacation at Camp" included favorite campfire songs.

Shrimp Stuffing

2 tablespoons canola oil

1 pound raw shrimp, cleaned, deveined, and cut into bite-size pieces

1/2 cup finely diced celery

1/2 cup finely diced onion

1/4 cup finely diced red or green bell pepper

One 10 3/4-ounce can condensed cream of mushroom soup

3/4 cup water

1 teaspoon dry mustard

1 teaspoon fresh lemon juice

1/2 teaspoon Cajun seasoning

One 6-ounce package KELLOGG'S Stuffing Mix

Salt and freshly ground pepper to taste

1/2 cup shredded part-skim mozzarella cheese

Although this recipe is called a stuffing, it is so nicely balanced with vegetables that it could almost be a meal by itself. SERVES 8

1. Heat the oil in a large frying pan over medium heat. Add the shrimp and sauté for about 4 minutes, or just until the shrimp begins to change color.

2. Stir in the celery, onion, and bell pepper. When blended, add the soup and water. When combined, stir in the mustard, lemon juice, and Cajun seasoning. Then add the Stuffing Mix and salt and pepper to taste, tossing just to moisten. Cover and lower the heat. Cook for 5 minutes. Do not overcook or the shrimp will toughen.

3. Remove from heat and stir in the cheese. Serve immediately.

NEWSPAPER
DEALER AD MATS

...and a winning team of
TV ADVERTISING

...up" with *Kellogg's* Sweet Eatin' Cereal Bowl-ers

Kellogg's
Sweet Eatin'
CEREAL Bowl-ers
PROMOTION

Kellogg's
ALL-BRAN

Kellogg's
ALL-BRAN

Kellogg's
for
crispness

The ORIGINAL
MORE PUNCH
'TIL LUNCH!
NT
NET
1 POUN
EAT BETTER · LIVE LONGER —

· SUGAR, SALT AND MALT FLAVORING · VITAMIN B₁, NIACIN
provides these percentages of minimum daily adult requirements Vitami
Riboflavin 0.55%, Calcium 0.11%, Phosphorus 1.5%, Iron 5%, and 0.6 mg. Ni
KELLOGG COMPANY, BATTLE CREEK, MI

DESSERTS

Kellogg's
RICE
KRISPIES

RICE KRISPIES TREATS® with Variations

3 tablespoons butter or margarine

One 10-ounce package regular marshmallows or 4 cups miniature marshmallows

6 cups KELLOGG'S RICE KRISPIES or KELLOGG'S COCOA KRISPIES

TO MICROWAVE: Heat the marshmallows and butter (or margarine) in a large microwave-safe bowl at high for 2 minutes. Stir and heat on high for an additional minute. Remove from the microwave and stir until smooth. Then follow steps 3 and 4.

NOTE: For best results, use fresh marshmallows. Marshmallows may be replaced with one 7-ounce jar marshmallow crème. Diet, reduced-calorie, or tub margarine is not recommended. Store no more than 2 days in an airtight container.

Without a doubt, this is the most popular recipe in our cereal recipe box! Everybody seems to love these sticky, sweet treats—a favorite rainy day project with children, a traditional birthday party grab-bag special, and a backpackers' afternoon revive-me treat. The basic recipe is so simple that the mixture lends itself to being formed into a variety of shapes, tinted in any color you choose, trimmed with a wild array of icings, candies, or sugars, and/or garnished with ice cream, yogurt, or pudding. You name it and RICE KRISPIES TREATS can do it! MAKES 2 DOZEN

1. Lightly coat a 13 x 9 x 2-inch baking pan with nonstick cooking spray. Set aside.

2. Melt the butter in a large saucepan over low heat. Add the marshmallows and stir until completely melted. Remove from heat.

3. Add KELLOGG'S RICE KRISPIES. Stir until well coated.

4. Using a buttered spatula or waxed paper, press mixture evenly into the prepared pan. Cut into 2-inch squares when cool. Best if served same day.

VARIATIONS

Birthday Fun Cups: Divide one batch of warm RICE KRISPIES TREATS mixture into 2½-inch-diameter muffin pan cups coated with nonstick cooking spray. Fit the mixture down into and up the sides of the cups, leaving a hollow center to form individual cups. Set aside to cool. When ready to serve, invert the muffin pan and tap the cups free. Fill with your favorite pudding, flavored yogurt and fruit, ice cream, or frozen yogurt. Serve immediately after being filled. Yield: 16 cups

Candy Canes: Divide one batch of warm RICE KRISPIES TREATS mixture in half and quickly shape each half into a 12-inch candy cane. Wrap red licorice strings around the canes to form stripes. Secure the licorice with toothpicks or frosting. (Caution: remove toothpicks before serving and/or eating.) Yield: 2 canes

Egg Nests: Prepare one batch of RICE KRISPIES TREATS, adding 1/2 cup green-tinted coconut flakes to the cereal mixture. While still warm, shape the mixture into sixteen 3-inch nests. Set aside to cool. Fill the cooled nests with jelly beans, chocolate or other candy eggs, or miniature marshmallows. Yield: 16 nests

Fun Balls: Prepare one batch of RICE KRISPIES TREATS. If desired, food coloring may be added to the marshmallow mixture before adding cereal. While cereal mixture is still warm, and working with 1/2 cup at a time, shape the

mixture into 12 balls. Immediately roll the balls in coconut or drizzle with melted chocolate, if desired. Create face features with miniature marshmallows, candies, or frosting. Yield: 12 balls

Pumpkin Faces: Prepare one batch of RICE KRISPIES TREATS. If desired, orange food coloring (orange may be created by mixing red and yellow food coloring) may be added to the marshmallow mixture before adding cereal. While cereal mixture is still warm, and working with 1/2 cup at a time, shape the mixture into 12 pumpkins. Create eyes, nose, mouth, and ears with candy corn, jellied orange slices, and frosting. Use jellied candies or pieces of licorice for the stem. Yield: 12 pumpkins

Chocolate Wafer Stack-Ups

2 cups KELLOGG'S RICE KRISPIES

1½ cups all-purpose flour

¾ teaspoon salt

½ cup butter or margarine, softened

1 cup sugar

1 large egg

1 teaspoon pure vanilla extract

Two 1-ounce squares unsweetened chocolate, melted

¾ cup coarsely chopped walnuts, plus more for garnish, if desired

Vanilla Icing (recipe follows)

The SNAP! CRACKLE! POP! RICE KRISPIES characters made their television debut in the early 1960s with the first of their many songs.

This is it—a homemade version of the bestselling chocolate sandwich cookie. MAKES 3 DOZEN

1. Preheat oven to 325°F.

2. Place the RICE KRISPIES in a resealable plastic bag. Seal the bag and, using a rolling pin, lightly crush the cereal. Open the bag and and measure the crumbs; you should have 1 cup. Set aside.

3. Lightly coat 2 cookie sheets with nonstick cooking spray. Set aside.

4. Combine the flour and salt in a small bowl. Set aside.

5. Place the butter in the bowl of a standing electric mixer and beat on medium until light. Add the sugar and beat until very light and fluffy. Beat in the egg and vanilla. When well blended, add the melted chocolate and beat to blend.

6. When blended, add the reserved flour mixture and crumbs along with the nuts, beating until well combined.

7. Drop the dough by the rounded teaspoon onto the prepared cookie sheets. Using the bottom of a cup or glass, lightly press on the dough to make even, flat rounds.

8. Bake the cookies in the preheated oven for about 10 minutes, or until set. Remove from oven and let cool slightly before transferring to wire racks to cool completely.

9. When cookies are cool, working with one at a time and using a spatula, spread an even layer of the Vanilla Icing on half of the cookies. Top each iced cookie with another cookie to make a sandwich. Lightly coat the top of each cookie sandwich with icing. If desired, while the icing is still soft, sprinkle the tops with chopped walnuts or candy sprinkles.

VANILLA ICING

1½ cups confectioners' sugar

2 tablespoons butter or margarine, softened

5 teaspoons milk

1 teaspoon pure vanilla extract

Place the sugar in a mixing bowl. Add the butter, milk, and vanilla, beating with a wooden spoon until completely smooth. (This may also be done with an electric mixer.) Use immediately, before the icing begins to dry.

Chocolate Scotcheroos

1 cup light corn syrup

1 cup sugar

1 cup peanut butter

6 cups KELLOGG'S RICE KRISPIES or KELLOGG'S COCOA KRISPIES

1 cup semisweet chocolate morsels

1 cup butterscotch morsels

This is one of the all-time favorite back-of-the-box recipes. All of the popular dessert flavors are wrapped up in one bar—peanut butter, chocolate, and butterscotch. Who could ask for anything more? MAKES 48 BARS

1. Lightly coat a 13 x 9 x 2-inch pan with nonstick cooking spray. Set aside.

2. Combine the corn syrup and sugar in a large, heavy-bottomed saucepan over medium heat. Cook, stirring frequently with a wooden spoon, until the sugar begins to dissolve and the mixture starts to boil. Remove from heat.

3. Stir the peanut butter into the hot syrup, beating to blend well. Add the cereal, stirring to coat completely.

4. While mixture is still warm, press it into the prepared pan to make an even layer. Set aside.

5. Combine the chocolate and butterscotch morsels in a small saucepan over low heat. Cook, stirring constantly, until completely melted.

6. With a rubber spatula, spread the chocolate mixture over the cereal mixture to evenly coat. Let stand until firmed.

7. When firm, cut the cookies into 48 even bar shapes.

RICE KRISPIES® Cookies

1 cup all-purpose flour

1/2 teaspoon baking soda

1/4 teaspoon baking powder

1/4 teaspoon salt

1/2 cup butter or margarine, softened

1/2 cup granulated sugar

1/2 cup firmly packed brown sugar

1 large egg

1/2 teaspoon pure vanilla extract

1 cup KELLOGG'S RICE KRISPIES

1 cup quick-cooking oats

1/2 cup shredded coconut

Not your traditional oatmeal cookie—an even better one! RICE KRISPIES add that extra crunch and the coconut supplies extra sweetness. If you want to really take them over the top, add chopped nuts and/or raisins. MAKES ABOUT 2 1/2 DOZEN

1. Preheat oven to 350°F.

2. Lightly coat 2 large cookie sheets with nonstick cooking spray. Set aside.

3. Combine the flour, baking soda, baking powder, and salt in a mixing bowl. Set aside.

4. Place the butter in the bowl of a standing electric mixer and beat on medium until light and fluffy. Add the white and brown sugars and beat until blended. Add the egg and vanilla, beating to incorporate.

5. Stir in the reserved flour mixture. When well combined, stir in the cereal, oats, and coconut.

6. Drop the mixture by level measuring tablespoon onto the prepared cookie sheets, leaving room between cookies.

7. Transfer the sheets to the preheated oven and bake for about 12 minutes, or until the cookies are lightly browned.

8. Remove from oven and transfer cookies to wire racks to cool.

9. When cool, store in an airtight container.

Ginger Disks

3 cups KELLOGG'S RICE KRISPIES

2¹/₂ cups all-purpose flour

1 teaspoon baking soda

1 teaspoon ground ginger

1 teaspoon ground cinnamon

¹/₂ teaspoon ground cloves

¹/₄ teaspoon salt

1¹/₄ cups firmly packed brown sugar

¹/₄ cup butter or margarine, softened

2 large egg whites, at room temperature

¹/₄ cup unsweetened applesauce

¹/₄ cup molasses

¹/₄ cup granulated sugar

SNAP!

These are deliciously sweet-spicy cookies that are perfect "dunkers" with coffee, tea, or milk. MAKES 4 DOZEN

1. Preheat oven to 350°F.

2. Place the RICE KRISPIES in a resealable plastic bag. Seal the bag and, using a rolling pin, lightly crush the cereal to a fine crumb. Open the bag and measure the crumbs; you should have ³/₄ cup. Set aside.

3. Lightly coat 2 cookie sheets with nonstick cooking spray. Set aside.

4. Combine the reserved crumbs with the flour, baking soda, ginger, cinnamon, cloves, and salt in a medium bowl. Set aside.

5. Combine the brown sugar and butter in the bowl of a standing electric mixer and beat on medium until thoroughly combined. Turn the mixer speed to low and add the egg whites, applesauce, and molasses, beating until combined.

6. Add the reserved flour mixture and beat until well blended.

7. Place the granulated sugar in a shallow dish.

8. Working with one piece at a time, drop the dough by the level tablespoon into the granulated sugar, rolling to completely coat.

9. Transfer the sugar-coated dough to the prepared cookie sheets. Working with one at a time, dip the bottom of a measuring cup into the sugar and then lightly press on the dough to make even, flat rounds.

10. Bake the cookies in the preheated oven for about 8 minutes, or until lightly browned. Remove from oven and transfer to wire racks to cool.

Cream Cheese Cookies

2 cups KELLOGG'S RICE KRISPIES

2 cups all-purpose flour

2 teaspoons baking powder

1/4 teaspoon salt

One 8-ounce package cream cheese, softened

1/2 cup butter or margarine, softened

1 cup sugar

2 teaspoons freshly grated orange zest

Orange Glaze (recipe follows)

The RICE KRISPIES make these marvelous teatime cookies special. The cream cheese base keeps them moist, and the orange offers a fragrant touch. MAKES 4 DOZEN

1. Preheat oven to 350°F.

2. Lightly coat 2 cookie sheets with nonstick cooking spray. Set aside.

3. Place the RICE KRISPIES in a resealable plastic bag. Seal the bag and, using a rolling pin, lightly crush the cereal to a medium crumb. Open the bag and measure the crumbs; you should have 1 cup.

4. Place 3/4 cup of the crumbs in a shallow dish. Set aside.

5. Combine the remaining 1/4 cup of crumbs with the flour, baking powder, and salt. Set aside.

6. Combine the cream cheese, butter (or margarine), sugar, and orange zest in the bowl of a standing electric mixer and beat on medium until very well blended. Add the reserved flour mixture, beating to blend. The mixture will be quite stiff.

7. Working with one piece at a time, scoop out a level teaspoon of dough and, using the palms of your hands, roll the dough into a ball. Then roll the ball in the reserved cereal crumbs, taking care to evenly coat the dough.

8. Place the balls about 2 inches apart on the prepared cookie sheets. Using the bottom of a glass or measuring cup, lightly press on the dough to slightly flatten.

CRACKLE!

POP!

9. Bake the cookies in the preheated oven for about 8 minutes, or until the top springs back when lightly touched.

10. Remove from oven and transfer to wire racks to cool.

11. When cool, drizzle the glaze over the top of each cookie.

12. When the glaze has set, store tightly covered, in layers separated by waxed paper.

ORANGE GLAZE

1¹/₂ cups confectioners' sugar
3 tablespoons fresh orange juice
1 teaspoon grated orange zest

1. Combine the sugar with the juice and zest in a small bowl, stirring with a wooden spoon until very smooth.

2. Drizzle over cookies. Use immediately, before glaze begins to firm.

Jumbo KELLOGG'S CORN FLAKES® Cookies

6 cups KELLOGG'S CORN FLAKES
1³/₄ cups all-purpose flour
1 teaspoon baking powder
¹/₂ teaspoon baking soda
¹/₄ teaspoon salt
1 cup butter or margarine, softened
1 cup sugar
2 large eggs
¹/₂ teaspoon pure vanilla extract
¹/₂ cup milk chocolate morsels
¹/₂ cup peanut butter morsels

These are great big delicious lunchbox favorites! You can, if you like, add some chopped nuts and use whatever flavor morsels appeal to you—all of one kind or a mix including coated candies. The KELLOGG'S CORN FLAKES crumbs should not be too fine, as you want them to add a slightly crunchy bite to the cookies. MAKES 16

1. Place KELLOGG'S CORN FLAKES in a resealable plastic bag. Seal the bag and, using a rolling pin, lightly crush the flakes to a coarse crumb. Open the bag and measure the crumbs; you should have 4 cups. Set aside.

2. Preheat oven to 350°F.

3. Lightly coat 2 cookie sheets with nonstick vegetable spray. Set aside.

4. Combine the flour, baking powder, baking soda, and salt. Set aside.

5. Place the butter in the bowl of a standing electric mixer and beat on medium for a couple of minutes to lighten. Add the sugar and continue beating until light and fluffy.

6. Add the eggs, one at a time, along with the vanilla, beating to incorporate.

7. Begin beating in the reserved flour mixture, mixing until just combined. Beat in 2 cups of the reserved crumbs along with the chocolate and peanut butter morsels.

8. Place the remaining crumbs in a shallow dish.

9. Working with one piece at a time, portion the dough into a 1/4-cup measure. Form the dough into a ball and then roll it in the crumbs to completely coat.

10. Place the coated dough on the prepared cookie sheets, using a fork to flatten to a circle about 3 inches in diameter.

11. When all of the cookies have been placed on the cookie sheets, transfer them to the preheated oven and bake for about 15 minutes, or until golden brown.

12. Remove from oven and transfer to wire racks to cool. When cool, store in an airtight container.

"Oh boy! Kellogg's CORN FLAKES for me"

Almond Macaroons

2 large egg whites

½ teaspoon pure vanilla extract

¼ teaspoon almond flavoring

¾ cup sugar

2 cups KELLOGG'S CORN FLAKES

1 cup chopped almonds

A little bit different from a traditional macaroon but, we think, even better. A couple of these macaroons and a cup of tea offer a perfect afternoon break on a busy day.

MAKES 3 DOZEN

1. Preheat oven to 350°F.

2. Line 2 cookie sheets with parchment paper or coat with cooking spray. Set aside.

3. Place the egg whites, vanilla, and almond flavoring in the bowl of a standing electric mixer fitted with the whip. Beat on medium until foamy. Increase the speed and gradually add the sugar, beating on high until stiff and glossy.

4. Fold in KELLOGG'S CORN FLAKES and almonds.

5. Drop the batter by the rounded tablespoon onto the prepared cookie sheets, leaving about 1 inch between cookies.

6. Bake in the preheated oven for about 10 minutes, or until lightly browned.

7. Remove from oven and immediately transfer to wire racks to cool.

8. When cool, place in an airtight container. Make sure that the cookies are very cool when storing or they will get soggy.

Cherry Dot Cookies

2²/₃ cups KELLOGG'S CORN FLAKES, or
1¹/₃ cups KELLOGG'S Corn Flake Crumbs

2¹/₄ cups all-purpose flour

2 teaspoons baking powder

¹/₂ teaspoon salt

³/₄ cup butter or margarine, softened

1 cup sugar

2 large eggs

2 tablespoons fat-free milk

1 teaspoon pure vanilla extract

1 cup chopped nuts

1 cup finely chopped dates

¹/₃ cup finely chopped maraschino cherries

15 maraschino cherries, cut into quarters

These are one of Kellogg Company's all-time favorite cookies. They were first introduced in the 1940s and remain one of our most requested recipes. MAKES 5 DOZEN

1. Preheat oven to 350°F.

2. Lightly coat 2 cookie sheets with nonstick cooking spray. Set aside.

3. Place KELLOGG'S CORN FLAKES in a resealable plastic bag. Seal the bag and, using a rolling pin, crush the flakes to a fine crumb. Open the bag and measure the crumbs; you should have 1/3 cups. Place the crumbs in a shallow dish. Set aside.

4. Combine the flour, baking powder, and salt in a mixing bowl. Set aside.

5. Combine the butter and sugar in the bowl of a standing electric mixer. Beat on medium until light and fluffy.

6. Add the eggs, one at a time, beating to incorporate.

7. Add the milk, along with the vanilla, followed by the reserved flour mixture, beating to blend.

8. Stir in the nuts, dates, and 1/3 cup chopped cherries.

9. Form the dough into balls about 1 inch in diameter. Working with one piece at a time, roll the dough in the reserved crumbs.

10. Place the coated balls about 2 inches apart on the prepared cookie sheets. Top each cookie with a cherry quarter.

11. Bake in the preheated oven for about 10 minutes, or until lightly browned. Remove from oven and immediately transfer to a wire rack to cool.

12. When cool, store in an airtight container.

Frosted Lemon Bars

2 cups KELLOGG'S CORN FLAKES

1 cup plus 2 tablespoons all-purpose flour

1¹/₃ cups firmly packed brown sugar

¹/₃ cup butter or margarine, softened

¹/₄ teaspoon salt

2 large eggs, lightly beaten

¹/₂ teaspoon pure vanilla extract

1¹/₂ cups flaked coconut

1 cup chopped walnuts or pecans

Lemon Icing (recipe follows)

These are very elegant cookies, lightly scented with lemon. KELLOGG'S CORN FLAKES add a delicate flavor to the crust that is a perfect balance to the citrus. Frosted Lemon Bars are great for lunch bags or as an accompaniment to lemon sorbet to make a pleasant ending to an evening meal. MAKES 3 DOZEN

1. Preheat oven to 275°F.

2. Lightly coat a 13 x 9 x 2-ich baking pan with nonstick cooking spray. Set aside.

3. Place KELLOGG'S CORN FLAKES in a resealable plastic bag. Seal the bag and, using a rolling pin, crush the flakes to a fine crumb. Open the bag and measure the crumbs; you should have ¹/₂ cup.

4. Combine the crumbs with 1 cup of the flour in a mixing bowl. Add ¹/₃ cup of the brown sugar and stir to blend. Blend the butter into the dry ingredients until well combined.

5. Transfer the mixture to the prepared pan and press the dough into the pan to make an even layer.

6. Bake in the preheated oven for about 10 minutes, or until golden and set.

7. Remove from oven and set aside.

8. Increase oven temperature to 350°F.

9. Combine the remaining 2 tablespoons flour with the salt. Set aside.

10. Combine the eggs, the remaining cup of brown sugar, and the vanilla in the bowl of a standing electric mixer. Beat until well blended. Beat in the coconut.

11. Add the reserved flour mixture and the nuts and mix well.

12. Spoon the mixture into the crust-filled pan, spreading out with a rubber spatula to cover evenly.

13. Bake in the preheated oven for about 20 minutes, or until lightly browned and set.

14. Remove from oven and set aside to cool slightly.

15. While bars are still warm, pour on the Lemon Icing, spreading it out with a rubber spatula to make an even layer of icing.

16. Set aside to cool completely.

17. When cool, cut into 36 bars of equal size.

LEMON ICING

1 cup confectioners' sugar

1 tablespoon butter or margarine, melted

1 tablespoon fresh lemon juice

1. Combine the sugar with the butter and lemon juice in a small mixing bowl, beating until smooth.

2. Use as directed.

The first World's Longest Breakfast Table event was held in Battle Creek in 1956 in celebration of the fiftieth anniversary of Kellogg.

Whole Wheat Apple Bars

4 cups KELLOGG'S CORN FLAKES

$^{1}/_{2}$ cup whole wheat flour

$^{1}/_{2}$ cup all-purpose flour

$^{1}/_{2}$ cup firmly packed brown sugar

2 teaspoons ground cinnamon

$^{1}/_{2}$ teaspoon ground nutmeg

$^{1}/_{2}$ teaspoon baking soda

$^{1}/_{4}$ teaspoon salt

1 large egg

1$^{1}/_{2}$ cups grated unpeeled tart apple

$^{1}/_{2}$ cup light corn syrup

2 tablespoons canola oil

$^{1}/_{2}$ cup raisins

1 tablespoon confectioners' sugar

These moist bar cookies are a delicious and very satisfying after-school snack. MAKES 2 DOZEN

1. Preheat oven to 350°F.

2. Lightly coat a 9-inch square baking pan with nonstick cooking spray. Set aside.

3. Place KELLOGG'S CORN FLAKES in a resealable plastic bag. Seal the bag and, using a rolling pin, crush the flakes to a fine crumb. Open the bag and measure the crumbs; you should have 1 cup.

4. Combine the crumbs with the whole wheat and all-purpose flours, brown sugar, cinnamon, nutmeg, baking soda, and salt. When blended, stir in the egg, apple, corn syrup, and oil. When combined, fold in the raisins.

5. Spread the mixture into the prepared baking dish, spreading out with a rubber spatula to make an even layer.

6. Bake in the preheated oven for about 35 minutes, or until a cake tester inserted into the center comes out clean.

7. Remove from oven and cool in pan on a wire rack.

8. Sift the confectioners' sugar over the top and cut into 24 bars of equal size. Store in airtight container in refrigerator.

Holiday Wreaths

1/3 cup butter or margarine

One 10-ounce package regular marshmallows, or 4 cups miniature marshmallows

1 teaspoon green food coloring (see note)

6 cups KELLOGG'S CORN FLAKES or KELLOGG'S FROSTED FLAKES

Cinnamon red hot candies

Prepared vanilla frosting

NOTE: Use fresh marshmallows for best results. Children should be supervised. Green paste food coloring makes the best color for wreaths.

Come Christmas and you will find these cookies in every state of the union. The recipe, first devised in the 1950s, has been passed down from generation to generation and seems to be enjoyed just as much as ever today. Some cooks make the wreaths to eat and others to use as table decoration only. Whichever you choose, this recipe is a very simple way to bring some holiday cheer to your kitchen. MAKES 16 SMALL WREATHS OR 1 LARGE WREATH

1. Melt butter in a large saucepan over low heat. Add marshmallows. Cook, stirring constantly, until the marshmallows are completely melted. Remove from the heat. Stir in the food coloring.

2. Add KELLOGG'S CORN FLAKES, stirring until well coated. Do not stir vigorously, as you want the flakes to remain as intact as possible.

3. If making individual wreaths, lightly coat a 1/4-cup measuring cup with nonstick cooking spray. (If making one large wreath, go to step 7.)

4. Working quickly, as the mixture will set up quite fast, portion out sixteen 1/4 cups of the warm cereal mixture onto a clean, flat work surface.

5. Continuing to work quickly, use your sprayed fingertips to shape each portion into an individual wreath shape.

6. Dot the back of a cinnamon candy with a touch of the prepared frosting and set it into the wreath to simulate a berry. Place as many "berries" as you wish on each wreath.

7. If making one large wreath, lightly coat a 51/2-cup ring mold with nonstick cooking spray and lightly press the warm cereal mixture into the mold. Let set before unmolding, then decorate as above. You can also form the large wreath in the same free-form manner as for individual wreaths.

8. Store in an airtight container in a single layer.

Raspberry Streusel Bars

1 cup KELLOGG'S ALL-BRAN
³/₄ cup all-purpose flour
³/₄ cup whole wheat flour
³/₄ cup firmly packed brown sugar
¹/₂ teaspoon baking soda
¹/₄ teaspoon ground cinnamon
¹/₄ teaspoon salt
¹/₄ cup butter or margarine
¹/₄ cup water
¹/₂ cup red raspberry preserves
1 teaspoon confectioners' sugar

These bars are very easy to make and are great to have on hand for unexpected company. They taste and look a bit like an old-fashioned Viennese cookie, but they are even better with the addition of ALL-BRAN. MAKES 2 DOZEN

1. Preheat oven to 350°F.

2. Lightly coat a 9-inch square baking pan with nonstick cooking spray. Set aside.

3. Combine ALL-BRAN with the all-purpose and whole wheat flours, brown sugar, baking soda, cinnamon, and salt in a medium mixing bowl.

4. Using a pastry blender or two forks, blend in the butter until the mixture resembles coarse crumbs. Stir in the water. The mixture should be crumbly.

5. Measure out 1 cup of the crumbly mixture to use as topping. Set aside.

6. Transfer the remaining mixture to the prepared pan. Using the back of a spoon, press the mixture into the pan to make a smooth, even layer.

7. Using a rubber spatula, spread the raspberry preserves evenly over the top of the mixture. Sprinkle the reserved crumbly mixture over the preserves.

8. Bake in the preheated oven for about 25 minutes, or until lightly browned.

9. Remove from oven and cool in pan on a wire rack.

10. When cool, sift the confectioners' sugar over the top and cut into 24 bars of equal size.

Brownies

²/₃ cup all-purpose flour

¹/₂ cup cocoa powder

¹/₄ teaspoon salt

2 large eggs

1 cup sugar

¹/₂ cup KELLOGG'S ALL-BRAN

¹/₂ cup butter or margarine, melted, cooled

1 teaspoon pure vanilla extract

¹/₂ cup chopped walnuts or pecans

¹/₂ cup semisweet chocolate morsels, optional

Could brownies be better than these? We don't think so. ALL-BRAN adds a rich, deep flavor to make these possibly the best brownies ever. You can, of course, add ¹/₂ cup chocolate (or other flavored) morsels to give even more interest to this all-time favorite bar cookie. MAKES 2 DOZEN

1. Preheat oven to 350°F.

2. Lightly coat an 8-inch square baking pan with nonstick cooking spray. Set aside.

3. Combine the flour, cocoa, and salt. Set aside.

4. Place the eggs in the bowl of a standing electric mixer and beat until very light. Gradually add the sugar, beating until fluffy.

5. Remove the bowl from the mixer and fold in the cereal, butter, and vanilla. Fold in the reserved flour mixture. Lastly, fold in the walnuts (and, if using, chocolate morsels).

6. Using a rubber spatula, evenly spread the mixture in the prepared baking pan. Bake in the preheated oven for about 30 minutes, or until a cake tester inserted into the center comes out clean.

7. Remove from oven and cool in pan on a wire rack.

8. When cool, cut into 24 bars of equal size.

ALL-BRAN® Icebox Cookies

1½ cups all-purpose flour

1 teaspoon baking powder

½ cup butter or margarine, softened

1 cup firmly packed brown sugar

1 large egg

¼ teaspoon pure vanilla extract

½ cup KELLOGG'S ALL-BRAN

1 cup finely chopped dates

½ cup finely chopped walnuts, pecans, or almonds

NOTE: When freezing this dough, you can freeze an entire roll, wrapped in freezer wrap and labeled. To use the frozen roll, bring it to cuttable temperature, cut into slices, and bake according to recipe directions.

Icebox cookies are the baker's most convenient have-on-hand goody. The rolls can be made anytime, chilled, and then frozen. The cookies can then be popped into the oven whenever needed (see note). You can use a bit of orange or lemon zest to add a fresh flavor. MAKES 4 DOZEN

1. Combine the flour and baking powder and mix together in a small bowl. Set aside.

2. Place the butter in the bowl of a standing electric mixer, beating until light. Add the sugar and continue beating until light and fluffy.

3. Beat in the egg and vanilla. When blended, add the cereal.

4. Beat in the reserved flour mixture. When combined, stir in the dates and nuts.

5. Remove the dough from the bowl and knead it for a couple of minutes; then shape the dough into 2 rolls about 1½ inches in diameter. Wrap in waxed paper, taking care that the ends are covered so the dough does not dry out.

6. Place in the refrigerator and let rest for 8 hours or overnight.

7. When ready to bake, preheat oven to 425°F.

8. Remove the cookie rolls from the refrigerator. Unwrap and, using a sharp knife, cut crosswise into ¼-inch-thick slices.

9. Place the cookies on ungreased cookie sheets. Transfer to the preheated oven and bake for about 10 minutes, or until golden brown.

10. Remove from oven and transfer to wire racks to cool.

11. Store in an airtight container.

KELLOGG'S® CRACKLIN' OAT BRAN®
Raisin Spice Cookies

2 cups KELLOGG'S CRACKLIN' OAT BRAN

1³/₄ cups all-purpose flour

1 teaspoon baking soda

1 teaspoon ground cinnamon

¹/₂ teaspoon ground nutmeg

¹/₄ teaspoon salt

¹/₂ cup butter or margarine, softened

¹/₂ cup sugar

¹/₂ cup firmly packed brown sugar

2 large eggs

1 teaspoon pure vanilla extract

¹/₂ cup seedless raisins

This is our version of an old-fashioned oatmeal-raisin cookie. KELLOGG'S CRACKLIN' OAT BRAN adds crunch that is lacking in the traditional cookie, but otherwise the cookies are quite similar. MAKES 3 DOZEN

1. Preheat oven to 375°F.

2. Lightly coat 2 cookie sheets with nonstick vegetable spray. Set aside.

3. Place the CRACKLIN' OAT BRAN in a resealable plastic bag. Seal the bag and, using a rolling pin, lightly crush the cereal into small nuggets. Set aside.

4. Combine the flour, baking soda, cinnamon, nutmeg, and salt. Set aside.

5. Place the butter in the bowl of a standing electric mixer and beat until light. Add the sugars and continue beating until light and fluffy.

6. Beat in the eggs and vanilla. When blended, add the cereal nuggets along with the reserved flour mixture. Stir in the raisins.

7. Drop the mixture by the level tablespoon onto the prepared cookie sheets.

8. Bake in the preheated oven for about 10 minutes, or until golden brown.

9. Remove from oven and transfer to wire racks to cool.

Lemon Crunch Cookies

2 cups all-purpose flour

1/2 teaspoon baking soda

1/2 teaspoon salt

1/2 cup butter or margarine, softened

1/2 cup granulated sugar

1/2 cup firmly packed brown sugar

1 tablespoon freshly grated lemon zest

1 large egg

3 tablespoons fresh lemon juice

1 1/2 cups KELLOGG'S COMPLETE Wheat Bran Flakes

These sweet-tart cookies are crunchy and deliciously flavorful. They are perfect to serve with a hot cup of tea.

MAKES 3 DOZEN

1. Preheat oven to 350°F.

2. Lightly coat 2 cookie sheets with nonstick cooking spray. Set aside.

3. Combine the flour, baking soda, and salt. Set aside.

4. Place the butter in the bowl of a standing electric mixer and beat until light. Add the white and brown sugars and lemon zest, beating until light and fluffy. Be sure to scrape the paddle, as the zest will tend to stick to it.

5. Add the egg and lemon juice, beating to blend. Add the reserved flour mixture and the cereal, beating until well combined.

6. Drop the mixture by the level tablespoon onto the prepared cookie sheets, leaving about 2 inches between the cookies.

7. Lightly flour the bottom of a drinking glass and, working with one cookie at a time, lightly press down with the glass to flatten slightly.

8. Bake in the preheated oven for about 12 minutes, or until lightly browned.

9. Remove from oven and transfer to wire racks to cool.

Peanut Butter Cookies

3 cups KELLOGG'S COMPLETE Wheat Bran Flakes

2 cups all-purpose flour

1 teaspoon baking soda

$1/2$ teaspoon salt

$1/2$ cup butter or margarine, softened

$1/2$ cup reduced-fat peanut butter

$1^1/2$ cups firmly packed brown sugar

4 large egg whites

1 teaspoon pure vanilla extract

Here we have a traditional peanut butter cookie made even better with the addition of KELLOGG'S COMPLETE cereal flakes. If you want to make these extra special, try crunchy peanut butter or add some chopped unsalted peanuts and semisweet chocolate morsels to the mix.

MAKES 6 DOZEN

1. Preheat oven to 350°F.

2. Lightly coat 2 cookie sheets with nonstick cooking spray. Set aside.

3. Place the COMPLETE Wheat Bran Flakes in a resealable plastic bag. Seal the bag and, using a rolling pin, crush the cereal to a medium crumb. Open the bag and measure the crumbs; you should have $1^1/2$ cups. Set aside.

4. Combine the flour, baking soda, and salt. Set aside.

5. Place the butter and peanut butter in the bowl of a standing electric mixer and beat to blend. Add the sugar, beating until light and fluffy.

6. Add the egg whites and vanilla, beating to blend. Add the reserved flour mixture and the cereal crumbs, mixing to just combine.

7. Drop the mixture by the tablespoon onto the prepared cookie sheets.

8. Bake in the preheated oven for about 10 minutes, or until light golden brown.

9. Remove from oven and transfer immediately to wire racks to cool.

10. When cool, store in an airtight container.

Meringues

2 large egg whites

¾ cup sugar

½ teaspoon pure vanilla extract

3 cups KELLOGG'S CORN POPS

Easy to make and fun to serve, these are special cookies made with crisp CORN POPS. MAKES 3½ DOZEN

1. Preheat oven to 225°F.

2. Generously coat 2 cookie sheets with nonstick cooking spray. Set aside.

3. Place the egg whites in the bowl of a standing electric mixer fitted with the whip and beat until just barely stiff. Gradually add the sugar, beating until stiff and slightly glossy.

4. Fold in the vanilla and then the CORN POPS.

5. Drop the mixture by the rounded teaspoon onto the prepared cookie sheets.

6. Bake in the preheated oven for about 55 minutes, or until just very slightly browned.

7. Remove from oven and transfer to wire racks to cool.

Fiesta Cookies

2 cups KELLOGG'S FROOT LOOPS

2 cups all-purpose flour

½ teaspoon baking powder

¼ teaspoon salt

1 cup butter or margarine, softened

½ cup sugar

1 teaspoon pure vanilla extract

These are terrific butter cookies with the FROOT LOOPS coating adding fun crispiness and rainbow color. With their buttery flavor and colorful coating, they are a favorite of children. MAKES 4½ DOZEN

1. Preheat oven to 350°F.

2. Place the FROOT LOOPS on a flat surface and cover with waxed paper or plastic film. Using a rolling pin, crush to fine crumbs. Do not mix the crumbs, as you want them to transfer variegated color to the cookies.

3. Combine the flour, baking powder, and salt in a medium mixing bowl. Set aside.

4. Place the butter in the bowl of a standing electric mixer and beat until light. Add the sugar and vanilla and beat until light and fluffy. Beat in the reserved flour mixture.

5. Working with a piece at a time, shape the dough into balls about 1 inch in diameter. Carefully roll each ball into the crushed FROOT LOOPS.

6. Place the coated cookies on ungreased cookie sheets.

7. Bake in the preheated oven for about 14 minutes, or until golden.

8. Remove from oven and transfer immediately to wire racks to cool.

Circus Cookies

2 cups all-purpose flour

$^1/_2$ teaspoon baking powder

$^1/_4$ teaspoon salt

1 cup unsalted butter or margarine, softened

$^1/_2$ cup sugar

2 large eggs

$^1/_2$ cup fresh orange juice

2 cups KELLOGG'S FROOT LOOPS

Orange Icing (recipe follows)

Additional KELLOGG'S FROOT LOOPS (crushed or whole), optional

Another butter cookie with great appeal to children and with the colorful, fruity flavor of FROOT LOOPS in every bite. The icing adds a tasty touch. MAKES 4 DOZEN

1. Preheat oven to 350°F.

2. Combine the flour, baking powder, and salt. Set aside.

3. Place the butter in the bowl of a standing electric mixer and beat until light. Add the sugar and beat until light and fluffy.

4. Add the eggs and orange juice, beating until blended. Add the reserved flour mixture, beating to combine.

5. Remove the bowl from the mixer and, using a wooden spoon, stir in the FROOT LOOPS, taking care not to crush them.

6. Drop the mixture by the level tablespoon onto ungreased cookie sheets.

7. Bake in the preheated oven for about 12 minutes, or until light brown.

8. Remove from oven and transfer immediately to wire racks to cool.

9. When cool, frost with Orange Icing. If desired, while the icing is soft, decorate with additional FROOT LOOPS.

ORANGE ICING

2 cups confectioners' sugar

3 tablespoons butter, softened

2 tablespoons orange juice

1. Place the sugar in a small mixing bowl. Add the butter and juice and, using a wooden spoon, beat until smooth.

2. Use as directed.

Walnut Drop Cookies

2 cups KELLOGG'S PRODUCT 19

1¹/₂ cups all-purpose flour

¹/₂ teaspoon baking soda

1 teaspoon salt

1 cup butter or margarine, softened

1 cup granulated sugar

¹/₂ cup firmly packed brown sugar

1 large egg

1 teaspoon pure vanilla extract

1 cup chopped walnuts

Drop cookies are easy to make, and KELLOGG'S PRODUCT 19 nicely enriches these nutty gems. These cookies are great dunkers. MAKES 5 DOZEN

1. Preheat the oven to 350°F.

2. Place the PRODUCT 19 in a resealable plastic bag. Seal the bag and, using a rolling pin, crush the cereal to a medium crumb. Open the bag and measure the crumbs; you should have 1 cup. Set aside.

3. Combine the flour, baking soda, and salt. Set aside.

4. Place the butter in the bowl of a standing electric mixer and beat until light. Add the white and brown sugars and continue beating until light and fluffy.

5. Add the egg and vanilla, beating to blend. Stir in the reserved flour mixture. When well combined, stir in the reserved cereal crumbs along with the nuts.

6. Drop the mixture by the level tablespoon onto ungreased cookie sheets.

7. Bake in the preheated oven for about 14 minutes, or until golden brown.

8. Remove from oven, cool slightly, and transfer to wire racks.

As advertised, PRODUCT 19 contains only 13 vitamins and minerals, so where did the number 19 come from? The story goes that a Kellogg copywriter, John E. Matthews, was having difficulty coming up with a name for this new product. After quite a struggle, he gave up and called it PRODUCT 19 simply because it was the nineteenth product that Kellogg Company was working on at that time.

TONY THE TIGER™ Cookies

3 cups KELLOGG'S FROSTED FLAKES

1³/₄ cups all-purpose flour

¹/₂ teaspoon baking soda

¹/₂ teaspoon salt

1 cup butter or margarine, softened

1 cup sugar

2 large eggs

1 teaspoon pure vanilla extract

1 cup semisweet chocolate morsels, melted

Great cookies for your little tigers! Chocolate swirls throughout add extra enjoyment. MAKES 4 DOZEN

1. Preheat oven to 350°F.

2. Place KELLOGG'S FROSTED FLAKES in a resealable plastic bag. Seal the bag and, using a rolling pin, lightly crush the flakes to make a medium crumb. Open the bag and measure the crumbs; you should have 1¹/₂ cups. Set aside.

3. Combine the flour, baking soda, and salt. Set aside.

4. Place the butter in the bowl of a standing electric mixer and beat until light. Add the sugar and beat until light and fluffy.

5. Add the eggs and vanilla and beat until blended. Beat in the reserved flour mixture along with the reserved crumbs.

6. Remove bowl from mixer and drizzle the melted chocolate over the dough. Using a table knife, swirl the chocolate into the dough to achieve a marbled appearance.

7. Drop the dough by the tablespoon onto ungreased cookie sheets.

8. Bake in the preheated oven for about 12 minutes, or until lightly browned.

9. Remove from oven and immediately transfer to wire racks to cool.

Sour Cream Crunchies

4 cups KELLOGG'S FROSTED FLAKES

2 cups sifted all-purpose flour

1/2 teaspoon baking soda

1/2 cup butter or margarine, softened

1 cup sugar

1/2 cup sour cream

1 large egg

1 teaspoon pure vanilla extract

The sour cream adds just a hint of tartness to these moist cookies. KELLOGG'S FROSTED FLAKES coating provides a nice crispness that highlights the tender interior. MAKES 4 1/2 DOZEN

1. Preheat oven to 350°F.

2. Lightly coat 2 cookie sheets with nonstick cooking spray. Set aside.

3. Place KELLOGG'S FROSTED FLAKES in a resealable plastic bag. Seal the bag and, using a rolling pin, lightly crush the flakes to make a coarse crumb. Place the crumbs in a shallow dish. Set aside.

4. Combine the flour and baking soda. Set aside.

5. Place the butter in a large mixing bowl and beat until light. Add the sugar and continue beating until light and fluffy.

6. Add the sour cream, egg, and vanilla, beating to blend. Add the reserved flour mixture, beating to incorporate.

7. Shape about 1 heaping teaspoon of the dough into a ball. Roll the ball in the reserved cereal crumbs, taking care to evenly coat.

8. Place the coated balls on the prepared cookie sheets.

9. Bake in the preheated oven for about 12 minutes, or until lightly browned.

10. Remove from oven and transfer to wire racks to cool.

Lemon Cake

2 cups cake flour

1 cup sugar

1/2 cup KELLOGG'S Corn Flake Crumbs

2 teaspoons baking powder

1 1/2 teaspoons baking soda

1/4 teaspoon salt

1 1/4 cups reduced-fat buttermilk

1/2 cup canola oil

2 large eggs

3 tablespoons fresh lemon juice

1 tablespoon freshly grated lemon zest

Lemon Glaze (recipe follows)

This is a wonderful cake to serve after a big meal, as it is light and lemony and totally refreshing. If you don't have Corn Flake Crumbs on hand, finely crush 2 cups of KELLOGG'S CORN FLAKES with a rolling pin, which should result in 1/2 cup crumbs. MAKES 1 TUBE CAKE

1. Preheat oven to 350°F.

2. Lightly coat a 2-quart tube or Bundt pan with nonstick cooking spray. Set aside.

3. Combine the flour, sugar, crumbs, baking powder, baking soda, and salt in a large mixing bowl. Using a wooden spoon, stir in the buttermilk and oil. When blended, stir in the eggs, lemon juice, and zest, beating to incorporate.

4. Pour the mixture into the prepared pan. Bake in the preheated oven for about 50 minutes, or until a cake tester inserted near the center comes out clean.

5. Remove from oven and place on a wire rack to cool.

6. When cool, turn the cake out of the pan onto a cake plate.

7. Drizzle the Lemon Glaze over the top and serve.

LEMON GLAZE

1 cup confectioners' sugar

1 1/2 tablespoons fresh lemon juice

2 teaspoons freshly grated lemon zest

1. Combine the sugar, 1 tablespoon of the juice, and the zest in a small mixing bowl, beating until smooth. Add the remaining lemon juice as necessary to make a thin glaze.

2. Use as directed.

Favorite Chocolate Cake

2¼ cups all-purpose flour

¾ cup KELLOGG'S Corn Flake Crumbs

⅓ cup cocoa powder

1 tablespoon baking soda

½ teaspoon salt

1½ cups sugar

1½ cups fine-quality mayonnaise

1½ cups water

1½ teaspoons pure vanilla extract

Fluffy White Frosting (recipe follows)

"Favorite" is the defining word. This is one of Kellogg Company's most popular cake recipes. It is based on a mayonnaise cake that became popular during World War II when fresh eggs were scarce. The frosting is an easy version of the classic 7-minute frosting and takes far less time to make. MAKES ONE 13 X 9 X 2-INCH CAKE

1. Preheat oven to 350°F.

2. Lightly coat a 13 x 9 x 2-inch baking pan with nonstick cooking spray. Set aside.

3. Combine the flour, crumbs, cocoa, baking soda, and salt. Set aside.

4. Place the sugar and mayonnaise in a large mixing bowl and beat until well blended.

5. Add the reserved flour mixture, beating to incorporate. Add the water and vanilla, beating until smooth.

6. Pour the mixture into the prepared baking pan. Bake in the preheated oven for about 35 minutes, or until a cake tester inserted in the center comes out clean.

7. Remove from oven and place on a wire rack to cool.

8. When cool, frost with Fluffy White Frosting.

9. Place in the refrigerator for about 1 hour, or until well chilled. Cut into squares and serve cold. Cover any remaining cake with plastic film and store in the refrigerator.

FLUFFY WHITE FROSTING

2 tablespoons all-purpose flour

³/₄ cup milk

³/₄ cup butter or margarine

³/₄ cup sugar

1 teaspoon pure vanilla extract

1. Combine the flour with about ¹/₄ cup of the milk in a small saucepan over medium heat, whisking until smooth. Stirring constantly, add the remaining milk. Cook, stirring constantly, until the mixture is thick and bubbling. Remove from heat and set aside to cool completely.

2. Place the butter and sugar in the small bowl of a standing electric mixer and beat until light and fluffy. Add the cooled milk mixture along with the vanilla and beat until very smooth and no sugar granules remain.

3. Immediately frost the cake.

Applesauce Cake

2 cups KELLOGG'S CORN FLAKES

1/2 cup butter or margarine, softened

3/4 cup granulated sugar

1 large egg

1/2 cup milk

2 cups all-purpose flour

2 teaspoons baking powder

1 teaspoon ground ginger

Pinch salt

One 10-ounce jar applesauce

1/2 cup firmly packed brown sugar

1 teaspoon ground cinnamon

There is almost always a jar of applesauce and a box of KELLOGG'S CORN FLAKES in the pantry, which makes this an easy spur-of-the-moment dessert. Add some nuts and raisins to the batter if you like. A dollop of frozen yogurt or ice cream could be the perfect final touch, melting over the warm cake. MAKES ONE 8-INCH SQUARE CAKE

1. Preheat oven to 350°F.

2. Lightly coat an 8-inch square baking pan with nonstick cooking spray. Set aside.

3. Place KELLOGG'S CORN FLAKES in a resealable plastic bag. Seal the bag and, using a rolling pin, crush the flakes to fine crumbs. Open the bag and measure the crumbs; you should have 1/2 cup. Set aside.

4. Place 1/4 cup of the butter in the bowl of a standing electric mixer and beat until light. Add the granulated sugar and continue beating until light and fluffy. Add the egg and milk, beating to incorporate.

5. Combine the flour, baking powder, ginger, and salt and stir the dry ingredients into the creamed mixture.

6. Using a rubber spatula, spread half of the mixture into the prepared baking pan. Spread the applesauce in an even layer over the cake mixture. Drop the remaining batter by spoonfuls over the applesauce.

7. Combine the reserved crumbs with the brown sugar and cinnamon, then cut in the remaining 1/4 cup butter to make coarse crumbs. Sprinkle the mixture over the top of the cake.

8. Bake in the preheated oven for about 45 minutes, or until a cake tester inserted in the center comes out clean.

9. Remove from oven and serve warm.

Coffee Coconut Cake

½ cup KELLOGG'S ALL-BRAN
1 cup cold, strong coffee
1½ cups all-purpose flour
¾ cup sugar
1 teaspoon baking soda
1 teaspoon ground cinnamon
½ teaspoon salt
¼ cup canola oil
1 tablespoon vinegar
½ teaspoon almond extract
½ cup flaked coconut

This is a very interesting cake, combining ALL-BRAN, a morning cup of coffee, and tropical coconut. Although delicious as is, it is even better when served with whipped cream. MAKES ONE 8-INCH SQUARE CAKE

1. Preheat oven to 350°F.

2. Lightly coat an 8-inch square baking pan with nonstick cooking spray. Set aside.

3. Combine ALL-BRAN and coffee in a large mixing bowl. Set aside for 2 minutes, or until the cereal has softened.

4. Combine the flour, sugar, baking soda, cinnamon, and salt in another bowl. Set aside.

5. Using a wooden spoon, stir the oil, vinegar, and almond flavoring into the cereal mixture. When blended, stir in ⅓ cup of the coconut.

6. Add the reserved flour mixture, stirring until well combined.

7. Using a rubber spatula, spread the mixture in the prepared pan. Sprinkle the remaining coconut over the top.

8. Bake in the preheated oven for about 25 minutes, or until a cake tester inserted in the center comes out clean.

9. Remove from oven and serve either warm or cold.

Raisin Pumpkin Cake

2 cups all-purpose flour

2 cups granulated sugar

2 teaspoons pumpkin pie spice

2 teaspoons baking powder

1 teaspoon baking soda

$1/2$ teaspoon salt

4 large eggs

One 16-ounce can pumpkin

$3/4$ cup canola oil

2 cups KELLOGG'S ALL-BRAN

1 cup golden raisins

2 tablespoons confectioners' sugar, optional

Rather than small pumpkin loaves, this makes one delicious spicy cake. This is another cake that a dollop of whipped cream or scoop of frozen yogurt will turn into a very special dessert. MAKES ONE 10-INCH TUBE CAKE

1. Preheat oven to 350°F.

2. Lightly coat a 10-inch tube pan with nonstick vegetable spray. Set aside.

3. Combine the flour, granulated sugar, pumpkin pie spice, baking powder, baking soda, and salt. Set aside.

4. Place the eggs in a large mixing bowl and, using a whisk, beat until foamy. Add the pumpkin and oil, beating to blend well. Stir in the ALL-BRAN, beating to incorporate. Stir in the raisins. Add the reserved flour mixture, stirring only until combined.

5. Pour the mixture into the prepared pan. Bake in the preheated oven for about 1 hour and 5 minutes, or until a cake tester inserted near the center comes out clean.

6. Remove from oven and place pan on a wire rack to cool.

7. Cool completely before removing from the pan. Dust with confectioners' sugar and serve.

Mango-Pango Cheesecake

12 ounces reduced-fat cream cheese, softened

1/2 cup sugar

2 tablespoons all-purpose flour

2 tablespoons fresh lemon juice

1 tablespoon freshly grated lemon zest

1 large egg

1 cup cubed fresh mango

1 KEEBLER READY CRUST Shortbread Pie Crust

TOPPING

1/4 cup KEEBLER READY CRUST graham cracker crumbs

1 tablespoon sugar

This recipe combines the convenience of a KEEBLER READY CRUST pie shell with a luscious made-from-scratch cheesecake filling. It is a great company's-coming dessert, as it needs at least 4 hours to chill before serving.

SERVES 8

1. Preheat oven to 350°F.

2. Combine the cream cheese with 1/2 cup sugar and the flour in the bowl of a standing electric mixer and beat until fluffy. Add the lemon juice and zest and beat to blend. Add the egg, beating to just combine.

3. Remove the bowl from the mixer and, using a rubber spatula, fold the mango into the cream cheese mixture.

4. Pour the mixture into the pie crust, using a rubber spatula to spread evenly.

5. To make the topping, combine the crumbs with the sugar in a small bowl. Sprinkle the top of the cheesecake with the crumb mixture.

6. Bake in the preheated oven for 30–35 minutes, or until the center is almost set.

7. Remove from oven and place on a wire rack to cool for 1 hour.

8. When cool, transfer to the refrigerator for at least 4 hours to allow the cake to firm completely.

9. When chilled and firm, cut into wedges and serve.

NOTE: Soften cream cheese in microwave at high for 15 to 20 seconds.

Sweet Chocolate Cake

¹/₂ cup water

4 ounces sweet baking chocolate

2 cups all-purpose flour

1 teaspoon baking soda

¹/₄ teaspoon salt

1 cup KELLOGG'S ALL-BRAN

1 cup butter or margarine, softened

2 cups sugar

4 large eggs, separated

1 teaspoon pure vanilla extract

1 cup buttermilk

Coconut-Pecan Frosting (recipe follows)

Sweet Chocolate Cake is one of Kellogg Company's longtime favorite desserts. Its towering layers filled with yummy Coconut-Pecan Frosting never reveal the secret of the addition of bran cereal. MAKES ONE 3-LAYER 8-INCH CAKE

1. Place the water in a small saucepan over medium heat. Add the chocolate, stirring until melted. Set aside until cool.

2. Preheat oven to 350°F.

3. Lightly coat three 8-inch round cake pans with nonstick cooking spray and dust with flour. Set aside.

4. Combine the all-purpose flour with the baking soda and salt and sift together into a mixing bowl. Stir in ALL-BRAN and set aside.

5. Place the butter in the mixing bowl of a standing electric mixer and beat until light. Add the sugar and continue beating until light and fluffy.

6. Add the egg yolks, one at a time, beating well to incorporate. Add the reserved chocolate mixture along with the vanilla, beating to mix well.

7. Alternately add the reserved flour mixture and the buttermilk, beating well after each addition.

8. Using an electric mixer, beat the egg whites until stiff and glossy. Fold the beaten egg whites into the batter. Do not overmix or the cake will be tough.

9. Spoon equal portions of the batter into the prepared pans. Bake in the preheated oven for about 35 minutes, or until a cake tester inserted in the center comes out clean.

10. Remove from oven and cool for 10 minutes.

11. Remove the cakes from the pans and cool completely on wire racks.

12. Place one layer, top down, on a serving plate. Coat the layer with Coconut-Pecan Frosting. Top with another cake layer and spread frosting evenly over it. Place the final layer on top and frost the top and sides of the cake. Cut into wedges and serve.

COCONUT-PECAN FROSTING

1 cup evaporated milk

1 cup sugar

3 egg yolks

$^1/_2$ cup butter or margarine

1 teaspoon pure vanilla extract

1$^1/_3$ cups flaked coconut

1 cup chopped pecans

1. Combine evaporated milk, sugar, egg yolks, butter, and vanilla in a small saucepan. Cook over medium heat, stirring constantly, until mixture thickens. Remove from heat.

2. Stir in coconut and pecans. Cool, stirring occasionally, until thick enough to spread. Spread between layers and on top and sides of cake.

Golden Carrot Cake

1 cup all-purpose flour

1/2 teaspoon baking powder

1/2 teaspoon baking soda

1/2 teaspoon salt

1 teaspoon ground cinnamon

1/4 teaspoon ground ginger

1/4 teaspoon ground nutmeg

One 8-ounce can crushed pineapple

2 large eggs

1/3 cup canola oil

1 cup firmly packed brown sugar

1 1/2 cups shredded raw carrots

1/2 cup chopped walnuts

2 cups KELLOGG'S RAISIN BRAN

Pineapple Frosting (recipe follows)

What could be better than a moist, spicy carrot cake with the added benefit of KELLOGG'S RAISIN BRAN cereal? Interestingly, the cereal adds a deep, slightly nutty flavor to the cake, which only enhances its goodness. MAKES ONE 9-INCH SQUARE CAKE

1. Preheat oven to 350°F.

2. Lightly coat a 9-inch square baking pan with nonstick cooking spray. Set aside.

3. Combine the flour, baking powder, baking soda, and salt in a large mixing bowl. Stir in the cinnamon, ginger, and nutmeg. Set aside.

4. Drain the pineapple, reserving 2 tablespoons juice for the frosting.

Sunny, a happy, smiling sun face, was introduced to cereal boxes in 1966 to promote KELLOGG'S RAISIN BRAN, which had come on the market in the early 1940s.

5. Place the eggs in a large mixing bowl, beating to blend. Add the oil, beating to incorporate. Stir in the sugar. When blended, add the carrots, walnuts, and drained pineapple. Stir in KELLOGG'S RAISIN BRAN, followed by the reserved flour mixture.

6. When very well mixed, pour the batter into the prepared baking pan. Bake in the preheated oven for 40 minutes, or until a cake tester inserted in the center comes out clean.

7. Remove from oven and set aside on a wire rack to cool.

8. When cool, spread the Pineapple Frosting evenly over the cake and let stand until set.

9. Cut into pieces and serve, or store, covered and refrigerated.

PINEAPPLE FROSTING

1 cup confectioners' sugar
2 tablespoons pineapple juice

1. Combine the sugar and pineapple juice in a small mixing bowl, beating until smooth.

2. Use as directed.

Red Berry Angel Food Cake

1 cup sifted cake flour

1 1/2 cups sifted superfine sugar (see note)

1 1/2 cups egg whites (about 13 large eggs)

1/4 teaspoon salt

1 1/2 teaspoons cream of tartar

1 teaspoon pure vanilla extract

4 cups KELLOGG'S SPECIAL K Red Berries, lightly crushed to 2 cups (see pages xiv–xv)

2 cups chilled heavy cream, whipped

2 cups sliced strawberries

1 cup KELLOGG'S SPECIAL K Red Berries whole cereal flakes

Whole strawberries, well washed and dried, for garnish

A few sprigs fresh mint or mint leaves, for garnish, optional

NOTES: If you can't find superfine sugar, process regular granulated sugar in a food processor fitted with the metal blade until very fine.

To decrease calories, use whipped topping instead of whipped cream.

Angel food cake is a classic dessert that we have enhanced by incorporating KELLOGG'S SPECIAL K Red Berries into the batter. The strawberries in the cereal add a hint of strawberry flavor to the cake, and the fresh fruit adds color to the whipped cream frosting. MAKES ONE 10-INCH CAKE

1. Preheat oven to 350°F.

2. Combine the cake flour with 3/4 cup of the sugar and sift together 3 times. Set aside.

3. Combine the egg whites and salt in the bowl of a standing electric mixer fitted with the whisk, beating until foamy. Sprinkle with the cream of tartar, add the vanilla, and beat on high speed until soft peaks form. Gradually sprinkle with the remaining 3/4 cup sugar and continue beating on medium until stiff peaks form, approximately 4–5 minutes.

4. Reduce the speed to low and gradually add the flour mixture, scraping down the sides and bottom of the bowl to insure even distribution. Fold in the lightly crushed SPECIAL K Red Berries to just incorporate.

5. Pour the batter into an ungreased angel food cake pan. Cut through the batter with a kitchen knife to burst any bubbles that might have formed.

6. Place in the preheated oven and bake for 35 minutes, or until the cake has risen and is golden brown and a cake tester inserted near the center comes out clean. Cake should feel dry to the touch.

7. Remove from oven. If the pan has feet, turn it upside down. If not, invert it over the neck of a bottle. Set aside to cool for 2 hours.

8. Turn the cake right side up and carefully run a sharp knife around the sides of the pan to release the cake. Holding on to the tube, carefully lift the cake from the pan. Slowly run the knife around the tube and between the cake and the bottom to entirely release the cake from the pan.

9. Invert the cake onto a serving plate and tap it free.

10. Using a serrated knife, carefully cut the cake crosswise into 3 equal layers. Spoon one quarter of the whipped cream over the bottom layer and sprinkle with 1 cup of the sliced strawberries. Place the middle layer on top and coat it with an equal portion of the cream and berries. Place the final cake layer on top and spoon the remaining whipped cream over the top and spread it around the cake to completely cover. Sprinkle with the cereal flakes and decorate the top with whole strawberries and mint sprigs.

11. Serve immediately or refrigerate for up to 2 hours before serving.

From its inception, the Kellogg Company was a frontrunner with the use of prizes, coupons, and premiums to increase sales. During the past thirty years, baseball cards have been the most popular premium in KELLOGG'S cereal boxes.

KELLOGG'S CORN FLAKES® Pie Crust

4 cups KELLOGG'S CORN FLAKES

2 tablespoons sugar

2 tablespoons light corn syrup

2 tablespoons butter or margarine, softened

Easy to prepare as a last-minute dessert, this Corn Flakes Pie Crust has long been a consumer favorite. Fill with ice cream or pudding, chilling until firm. Garnish with ice cream topping, fruit, or whipped cream, if desired. MAKES ONE 9-INCH PIE CRUST

1. Preheat oven to 350°F.

2. Place KELLOGG'S CORN FLAKES in a resealable plastic bag. Seal the bag and, using a rolling pin, crush the cereal to very fine crumbs. Open the bag and measure the crumbs; you should have 1 cup.

3. Combine the crumbs with the sugar, corn syrup, and butter, mixing until well blended.

4. Press the mixture into a 9-inch pie pan to make an even layer over the bottom and up the sides of the pan. Bake in the preheated oven for 5 minutes, or until lightly browned.

5. Remove from oven and cool completely before filling.

Easy Bran Pie Crust

1 cup all-purpose flour
³/₄ cup KELLOGG'S ALL-BRAN
¹/₂ cup butter or margarine
2 tablespoons milk

This is a terrific, nutty-tasting pie crust that is perfect for any refrigerated or frozen pie filling. MAKES ONE 9-INCH PIE CRUST

1. Preheat oven to 400°F.

2. Combine the flour and cereal in a medium mixing bowl. Add the butter and, using a pastry blender, cut the butter into the dry ingredients to make a coarse meal. Add the milk and stir until the mixture is moist. The dough will seem crumbly.

3. Place the mixture into a 9-inch pie pan and, using the back of a spoon, press it evenly and firmly around the sides and over the bottom of the pan to form a neat crust.

4. Fill and bake pie as directed in individual recipe. Or, for prebaked crust, prick bottom and sides with fork and bake in the preheated oven for about 12 minutes, or until lightly browned.

5. Remove crust from oven and cool completely before filling.

Fruit Pizza

6 cups KELLOGG'S FROSTED FLAKES

1/2 cup butter or margarine, softened

Two 8-ounce packages light cream cheese, softened

One 7-ounce jar marshmallow crème

2–3 cups sliced fruit or berries

Whipped cream or whipped topping, optional

This is a great rainy day project with the kids! Everybody loves pizza, and our special dessert pizza will become a family favorite. You do the baking and let the children do the decorating—it's a terrific way to get them to eat fruit.

MAKES ONE 12-INCH PIE

1. Preheat oven to 325°F.

2. Place the KELLOGG'S FROSTED FLAKES in a resealable plastic bag. Seal the bag and, using a rolling pin, crush the cereal to a medium crumb. Open the bag and measure the crumbs; you should have 2 1/4 cups.

3. Combine the crumbs with the butter. When blended, transfer to a 12-inch pizza pan and press the mixture into the pan in an even layer.

4. Bake in the preheated oven for 5 minutes, or until light golden brown.

5. Remove from oven and set aside to cool completely.

6. Combine the cream cheese and marshmallow crème in a medium mixing bowl and beat until very smooth.

7. Spread the cream cheese mixture over the cooled crust. Immediately arrange fruit over the top in a decorative pattern and, if desired, garnish with dollops of whipped cream or topping. Chill until firm, about 1 hour. Cut into wedges and serve cold.

Rustic Rhubarb Tart
with Vanilla Almond Crust

2 cups KELLOGG'S SPECIAL K Vanilla Almond

One 8-ounce package light cream cheese, softened

1 cup unsalted butter, softened

1/2 teaspoon salt

1 1/2 cups all-purpose flour

6 cups diced fresh rhubarb

1 1/4 cups sugar (see note)

1/2 cup toasted slivered almonds

1/3 cup all-purpose flour

1 tablespoon freshly grated orange zest

1 teaspoon pure vanilla extract

1 large egg

1 tablespoon water

NOTE: It is often difficult to gauge the amount of sugar necessary to adequately sweeten fresh rhubarb. One cup is usually enough for very young, tender stalks, while older, tougher stalks may take up to 2 cups.

Since both vanilla and almond are flavors that work well with rhubarb, KELLOGG'S SPECIAL K Vanilla Almond seems ready-made to bring out the best of this sweet-tart dessert. A scoop of vanilla ice cream or frozen yogurt would be the perfect garnish. MAKES ONE 9-INCH TART

1. Place the SPECIAL K Vanilla Almond in a resealable plastic bag. Seal the bag and, using a rolling pin, crush the cereal to fine crumbs. Set aside.

2. Combine the cream cheese, butter, and salt in the bowl of a standing electric mixer fitted with the paddle. Beat on low until well combined. With the motor running on low, add the flour and reserved crumbs and mix until just incorporated.

3. Lightly flour a clean, flat surface. Turn the dough out onto the floured surface and, using your hands, slightly flatten it out. Using a rolling pin, roll the dough out to a rectangle about 12 x 8 inches. Wrap in plastic film and refrigerate for 8 hours or overnight.

4. Lightly flour a clean, flat surface. Unwrap the chilled dough and place it on the floured surface. Lightly flour the dough and, using a rolling pin, roll it out to a rectangle about 15 x 8 inches. Fold the dough into thirds by bringing the ends in and over the center. Turn the dough so that the open edge is facing to the right and again roll into a 15 x 8 rectangle. Repeat this folding, turning, and rolling process 3 times, turning the dough counterclockwise each time. Fold the dough in half, wrap in plastic film, and refrigerate for 1 hour.

5. Preheat oven to 450°F.

6. Combine the rhubarb, 1 cup of the sugar, almonds, flour, orange zest, and vanilla in a large mixing bowl. Set aside.

7. Remove the dough from the refrigerator and unwrap.

8. Lightly flour a clean, flat surface. Open the dough and place it on the floured surface. Using your hands, push on the corners of the dough to slightly round them. Using a rolling pin, roll the dough into a circle about 12 inches in diameter.

9. Transfer the dough to a large baking sheet or to a pizza pan.

10. Spoon the rhubarb mixture into the center of the dough and spread it out evenly, leaving about 1$\frac{1}{2}$ inches uncovered all around the edge of the dough. Using your fingers, bring the uncovered dough up and over the filling to make a rim around the edge of the tart, folding any excess dough into pleats.

11. Combine the egg and water in a small bowl, whisking to blend. Using a pastry brush, lightly coat the edge of the dough with the egg wash. Sprinkle the fruit and the dough with the remaining $\frac{1}{4}$ cup of sugar.

12. Bake in the preheated oven for 10 minutes. Lower the oven temperature to 350°F and continue to bake for an additional 30 minutes, or until the pastry is golden brown and the fruit is glazed and bubbling.

13. Remove from oven and allow to rest for about 15 minutes before cutting into wedges and serving.

Creamy Pineapple Pie
with Blueberry Sauce

2 1/2 cups KELLOGG'S CRACKLIN' OAT BRAN

3 tablespoons butter or margarine, softened

One 8-ounce package light cream cheese, softened

1 cup confectioners' sugar

One 8-ounce can crushed pineapple, undrained

2 cups frozen nondairy whipped topping, thawed

TOPPING

1 cup canned blueberry pie filling

1/4 teaspoon ground cinnamon

Beautiful to look at and even better to eat, this creamy pie is great for entertaining. MAKES ONE 9-INCH PIE

1. Preheat oven to 350°F.

2. Combine the cereal and butter in the bowl of a food processor fitted with the metal blade, using quick on and off turns to process to fine crumbs.

3. Transfer the mixture to a 9-inch pie pan and press it in an even layer over the bottom and up the sides of the pan.

4. Bake in the preheated oven for 5 minutes, or just until the crust begins to brown. Remove from oven and set aside to cool.

5. Combine the cream cheese and sugar in the bowl of a standing electric mixer and beat until smooth. Add the pineapple, mixing to blend.

6. Remove the bowl from the mixer and fold in the whipped topping.

7. Pour the mixture into the cooled crust. Using a rubber spatula, smooth the top slightly.

8. Transfer the pie to the freezer and freeze for at least 4 hours, or until firm.

9. While the pie is freezing, prepare the sauce.

10. Combine the blueberry pie filling and cinnamon, stirring to blend well. Cover with plastic film and refrigerate until ready to serve.

11. Remove the pie from the freezer 10 minutes before serving, cut it into wedges, and serve with the blueberry sauce spooned over the top.

COCOA KRISPIES®
Frozen Peanut Butter Pie

One 6-ounce package semisweet chocolate morsels

3 tablespoons butter or margarine

2/3 cup smooth peanut butter

2 cups KELLOGG'S COCOA KRISPIES

One 8-ounce package cream cheese, softened

1/2 cup confectioners' sugar

One 12-ounce container frozen nondairy whipped topping, thawed

Chocolate and peanut butter with the added crunch of COCOA KRISPIES—An "Are there seconds?" dessert for sure! MAKES ONE 9-INCH PIE

1. Combine the chocolate morsels and butter in a medium saucepan over low heat, stirring constantly until melted. Remove from heat.

2. Combine 3 tablespoons of the melted chocolate mixture with 1 tablespoon of the peanut butter in a small saucepan. Set aside.

3. Stir the COCOA KRISPIES into the remaining chocolate mixture in the pan.

4. Transfer the COCOA KRISPIES mixture to a 9-inch pie pan and press it in an even layer over the bottom and up the sides of the pan.

5. Transfer the crust to the refrigerator and chill until firm, about 1 hour.

6. Combine the remaining peanut butter with the cream cheese and sugar in the bowl of a standing electric mixer and beat until smooth. Add about one third of the whipped topping, beating to incorporate.

7. Remove the bowl from the mixer and, using a whisk, fold in the remaining whipped topping.

8. Pour the mixture into the chilled crust, smoothing out the top with a rubber spatula.

9. Heat the reserved chocolate–peanut butter mixture, stirring until smooth.

10. Immediately remove from heat and drizzle over the top of the pie.

11. Transfer to the freezer and freeze for 2 hours, or until firm.

12. Remove from the freezer, cut into wedges, and serve.

Oatmeal Raisin Cookie Pie

One 6-ounce KEEBLER READY CRUST Graham Pie Crust

1 large egg yolk, slightly beaten

3 large eggs

1/2 cup firmly packed brown sugar

1 cup light corn syrup

3 tablespoons butter or margarine, melted

3/4 cup quick-cooking oats

1 tablespoon all-purpose flour

1/4 teaspoon salt

1 teaspoon ground cinnamon

3/4 cup raisins

1 cup whipped cream or whipped topping, optional

There is nothing like KEEBLER READY CRUST to make dessert preparation a breeze. This is a marvelous pie that combines the old familiar cookie flavors of oatmeal, raisins, and spice in a newfangled pie. MAKES ONE 9-INCH PIE

1. Preheat oven to 325°F.

2. Brush bottom and sides of the crust with the beaten egg yolk. Place the crust on a baking sheet in the preheated oven. Bake 5 minutes.

3. Lightly beat the 3 eggs in the bowl of a standing electric mixer. Add the brown sugar, corn syrup, and butter and continue beating to incorporate. Add the oats, flour, salt, and cinnamon and beat to blend.

4. Remove the bowl from the mixer and fold in the raisins.

5. Pour the mixture into the pie crust.

6. Place the pie on a baking sheet in the 325° oven. Bake for about 45 minutes, or until the top is golden brown and the center is set.

7. Remove from oven and set on a wire rack to cool for about 1 hour.

8. Refrigerate at least 1 hour before serving. Cut into wedges and serve with whipped cream, if desired.

9. Store any leftover pie tightly covered and refrigerated.

Buttery Apple Tart

2 cups KELLOGG'S RICE KRISPIES

1 1/3 cups all-purpose flour

1/2 teaspoon salt

2/3 cup butter or margarine, softened

1/4 cup milk

5 cups sliced, peeled tart apples

3/4 cup granulated sugar

1 tablespoon lemon juice

1/4 teaspoon ground cinnamon

1/4 teaspoon ground nutmeg

GLAZE

1/2 cup confectioners' sugar

1 tablespoon hot water

This is a very elegant apple tart with a sweet buttery flavor that is equally at home ending a dinner party or packed into a brown bag lunch. Be sure that you use firm, juicy, tart apples to create the perfect tart-sweet balance. MAKES ONE 9-INCH TART

1. Preheat oven to 375°F.

2. Place the RICE KRISPIES in a resealable plastic bag. Seal the bag and, using a rolling pin, crush the cereal to a fine crumb.

3. Combine the crumbs with the flour and salt in a medium mixing bowl. Add the butter and, using a pastry blender, cut the butter into the mixture to make coarse crumbs. Add the milk and stir to incorporate.

4. Lightly flour a clean, flat surface. Place half of the dough on the floured surface and, using a rolling pin, roll it out to a circle about 10 1/2 inches in diameter.

5. Transfer the rolled dough to a 9-inch quiche pan, fitting it in to completely cover the bottom and sides.

6. Roll the remaining half of the dough in the same fashion. Set aside.

7. Combine the apples with the sugar, lemon juice, cinnamon, and nutmeg in a medium mixing bowl, tossing to coat well. Place the apple mixture into the crust. Cover with the remaining dough circle, crimping the edges together to make a neat top. Randomly prick the top 4 times with a fork.

8. Bake the tart in the preheated oven for about 45 minutes, or until the top is golden brown and the apples are tender.

9. Remove from oven. Glaze with mixture of confectioners' sugar and water and serve either hot or at room temperature.

Bran-Apple Crisp

1 cup KELLOGG'S ALL-BRAN

$^1/_2$ cup whole wheat flour

$^1/_4$ cup firmly packed brown sugar

$^1/_4$ cup butter or margarine, softened

6 cups sliced, unpeeled baking apples

$^1/_4$ cup granulated sugar

$^1/_2$ teaspoon ground cinnamon

Nonfat vanilla yogurt as garnish, optional

A simple dessert that includes ALL-BRAN and whole wheat flour. It's a perfect busy-day recipe just sweet enough to satisfy everyone. SERVES 8

1. Preheat oven to 325°F.

2. Combine the ALL-BRAN with the flour and brown sugar in a small mixing bowl. Add the butter and, using a pastry blender, cut the butter into the dry ingredients to make coarse crumbs. Set aside.

3. Combine the apples, granulated sugar, and cinnamon in a medium mixing bowl. Place the apples in a shallow 2-quart baking dish. Sprinkle with the reserved cereal crumbs.

4. Bake in the preheated oven for about 45 minutes, or until the apples are tender and the cereal mixture is crisp and light brown.

5. Remove from oven and serve warm with a dollop of nonfat vanilla yogurt, if desired.

In the 1980s, boxes of KELLOGG'S ALL-BRAN included a "fiber insurance" policy with guidelines for a high-fiber, low-fat diet.

Peach Crisp

2 cups KELLOGG'S CORN FLAKES

1/2 cup butter or margarine, softened

1/2 cup sugar

2 large eggs

1/2 teaspoon pure vanilla extract

1 1/2 cups toasted bread cubes

1/2 teaspoon ground nutmeg

One 16-ounce can sliced peaches, well drained

2 teaspoons fresh lemon juice

Whipped cream, frozen yogurt, or ice cream as garnish, optional

This crisp is a great winter dessert when fresh fruit is not in season. Canned peaches can be replaced by other canned soft fruits such as apricots or plums. In the summer, fresh fruit can also be used. SERVES 4

1. Preheat oven to 375°F.

2. Lightly coat a 10 x 6 x 2-inch baking dish with nonstick cooking spray. Set aside.

3. Place KELLOGG'S CORN FLAKES in a resealable plastic bag. Seal the bag and, using a rolling pin, crush the cereal to a medium crumb. Open the bag and measure the crumbs; you should have 1 cup. Set aside.

4. Place the butter in the bowl of a standing electric mixer and beat until light. Add the sugar and continue beating until light and fluffy.

5. Add the eggs, one at a time, beating to incorporate. Beat in the vanilla.

6. Remove the bowl from the mixer and stir in the reserved crumbs along with the bread cubes and nutmeg.

7. Place half of the mixture into the prepared dish. Cover with the peaches. Sprinkle with lemon juice and then cover with the remaining batter.

8. Bake in the preheated oven for about 25 minutes, or until lightly browned.

9. Remove from oven and serve warm, garnished with whipped cream, frozen yogurt, or ice cream, if desired.

Pear Dumplings

½ cup plus 2 tablespoons sugar

2 tablespoons small red hot cinnamon candies

½ teaspoon ground nutmeg

2½ cups water

1 teaspoon ground cinnamon

1 cup KELLOGG'S ALL-BRAN

¾ cup fat-free milk

1½ cups all-purpose flour

2 teaspoons baking powder

½ teaspoon salt

½ cup butter or margarine, softened

3 large ripe pears, peeled, cored, and cut in half lengthwise

The cinnamon candies add a touch of sweet heat to this old-fashioned dessert. If you can find particularly small pears, you can use 6 whole pears for a very attractive presentation. The pears can also be replaced by apples or other firm fruit. SERVES 6

1. Preheat oven to 375°F.

2. Combine ½ cup of the sugar with the cinnamon candies and ¼ teaspoon of the nutmeg in a medium saucepan. Add the water, stirring to combine. Place over medium heat and cook, stirring frequently, for about 5 minutes, or until the mixture comes to a boil. Immediately remove from the heat and set aside and keep warm.

3. Combine the remaining 2 tablespoons sugar and ¼ teaspoon nutmeg with the ground cinnamon in a small mixing bowl. Set aside.

4. Combine the ALL-BRAN and milk in a small mixing bowl. Set aside for 2 minutes, or until the cereal has absorbed the milk.

5. Combine the flour, baking powder, and salt in a medium mixing bowl. Add the butter and, using a pastry blender, cut the butter into the dry ingredients to make a coarse crumb. Add the moistened cereal, stirring with a fork just until the mixture comes together. Divide the dough into 6 equal pieces.

6. Lightly flour a clean, flat surface. Working with one piece at a time and using a rolling pin, form the dough into 6 circles approximately 7 inches in diameter.

7. Place a pear half on each circle. Sprinkle the reserved cinnamon sugar on the pears and then carefully pull the dough up and around to completely enclose each pear, taking care to seal the edges.

8. Place the dough-covered pears in a 13 x 9 x 2-inch baking pan. Pour the reserved hot cinnamon syrup over the dumplings.

9. Transfer to the preheated oven and bake, basting twice with the syrup, for about 35 minutes, or until the pears are tender and the pastry is golden brown.

10. Remove from oven and serve warm or cold.

CHEF JOHN DOHERTY with Pastry Sous-Chef Charlie Romano, Waldorf-Astoria Hotel, New York City

KELLOGG'S® Summer Strawberry Delight

1¹/₂ cups KELLOGG'S SPECIAL K

³/₄ cup quick-cooking oatmeal

¹/₃ cup lightly toasted coconut

¹/₃ cup lightly toasted sliced almonds

8¹/₂ tablespoons strawberry jam or fresh strawberry marmalade

2 quarts fresh strawberries, washed, hulled, and drained

¹/₂ teaspoon fresh lemon juice

³/₄ cup fresh raspberries

³/₄ cup sugar

6 tablespoons sour cream

1 envelope unflavored gelatin

¹/₄ cup cold water

1¹/₂ cups heavy cream

1 teaspoon pure vanilla extract

Fresh mint leaves for garnish, optional

John Doherty has overseen the kitchen of the prestigious Waldorf-Astoria Hotel since 1985. This very elegant dessert adapted from the New York landmark is ideal for summertime entertaining. SERVES 16

1. Preheat oven to 325°F.

2. Line a 9-inch square baking pan with parchment paper. Set aside.

3. Combine the SPECIAL K, oatmeal, coconut, and almonds with 2¹/₂ tablespoons of the strawberry jam in a medium mixing bowl. Using a rubber spatula, gently fold together to fully incorporate the jam.

4. Transfer the cereal mixture to the prepared pan and press it into the pan to make an even layer about ¹/₃ inch thick.

5. Place in the preheated oven and bake for about 8 minutes, or until the jam has dried somewhat and the mixture is firm but slightly soft when pressed.

6. Remove from oven and set aside to cool.

7. For the sauce, cut 8 of the larger strawberries into quarters and place in a small saucepan. Add the lemon juice along with the remaining 6 tablespoons of jam and place over medium heat. Cook, stirring frequently, for about 2 minutes, or until the jam is melted. Remove from heat and set the sauce aside to cool.

8. For the mousse, quarter enough of the remaining strawberries to make 2 cups (approximately 20 strawberries, depending on their size), and combine with the raspberries and $1/2$ cup of the sugar. Thoroughly crush this mixture until sugar is dissolved and juices are released. Combine crushed berries with sour cream and set aside.

9. In a small bowl, sprinkle gelatin over $1/4$ cup cold water; let stand one minute to soften.

10. In a large bowl, begin to whip the heavy cream. As it begins to thicken, add the gelatin mixture and continue to whip until stiff peaks form. Using a rubber spatula, fold the whipped cream into the sour cream mixture until even in texture and color. Spread the mousse over the cereal crust, cover with plastic film, and place in the freezer for at least 2 hours, or until ready to serve.

11. Cut the remaining strawberries lengthwise into thin slices and place in a medium mixing bowl. Add the remaining $1/4$ cup sugar and the vanilla extract, tossing to blend.

12. Cover with plastic film and refrigerate for at least 1 hour, or until ready to serve.

13. When ready to serve, remove the dessert from the freezer and invert it onto a cutting board. Peel off the parchment paper and then turn the dessert mousse side up. Using a serrated knife, cut the dessert into $2^{1}/4$-inch squares. Place each square on a dessert plate and top with the sauce and sliced strawberries. Garnish with mint leaves, if desired, and serve immediately.

Baked Pancake with Apples

1½ cups KELLOGG'S RICE KRISPIES

½ cup all-purpose flour

2 tablespoons granulated sugar

2 large eggs

1 cup fat-free milk

1 tablespoon canola oil

1 teaspoon confectioners' sugar

Apple Topping (recipe follows)

Based on a German dessert, this light, fluffy pancake makes a great brunch dish as well as a dessert. The topping can be made from almost any fruit, but if using soft fruits reduce the cooking time so that they don't become mushy. SERVES 6

1. Preheat oven to 425°F.

2. Place the RICE KRISPIES, flour, and granulated sugar in a blender. Add the eggs, milk, and oil and process until smooth.

3. Place a 10-inch pie plate in the preheated oven for 5 minutes, or until very hot. Remove from the oven, quickly spray with nonstick cooking spray, and pour the batter into the hot plate.

4. Place in the preheated oven and bake for about 20 minutes, or until golden brown and puffed. Remove from oven and immediately sprinkle with confectioners' sugar.

5. Cut into wedges and serve immediately with hot Apple Topping spooned over each wedge.

APPLE TOPPING

2 tablespoons butter or margarine

⅓ cup sugar

1 teaspoon ground cinnamon

3 cups thinly sliced, peeled tart apples

¼ cup water

½ cup fresh raspberries, well washed and dried, optional

½ cup fresh blueberries, well washed and dried, optional

1. Heat the butter in a large sauté pan over medium heat. Add the sugar and cinnamon, stirring to blend. Add the apples and water and bring to a simmer. Simmer, stirring frequently, for about 10 minutes, or until the apples are just tender. (The apples may be cooked up to this point and stored, covered and refrigerated, for up to 3 days. Reheat before using.)

2. Remove from the heat and, if using, stir in the raspberries and blueberries. Keep hot until ready to serve.

All-American Party Pudding

1/3 cup seedless raisins

20 pieces KELLOGG'S MINI-WHEATS Frosted Original cereal

3 large eggs

1/2 cup sugar

1/2 teaspoon salt

2 tablespoons butter or margarine

2 cups milk, scalded

1 teaspoon pure vanilla extract

Low-fat ice cream as garnish, if desired

No one can remember how this pudding got its name, but since it tastes so good, we haven't rocked the boat by changing it. However the name came about, we can guarantee that it is a favorite in the KELLOGG KITCHENS.

SERVES 6

1. Preheat oven to 300°F.

2. Sprinkle the raisins in an even layer over the bottom of a 10 x 6 x 2-inch glass baking dish. Place the MINI-WHEATS, frosted side up, in a single layer on top of the raisins. Set aside.

3. Place the eggs in a medium, heatproof mixing bowl, whisking until light and foamy. Add the sugar and salt, whisking to just blend. Add the butter and, whisking constantly, add the hot milk, beating just until the butter has melted. Stir in the vanilla.

4. Pour the hot milk mixture over the cereal in the baking dish.

5. Bake in the preheated oven for about 1 hour, or until a knife inserted into the center comes out clean.

6. Remove from oven, cut into squares, and serve with a scoop of low-fat ice cream, if desired.

Pennsylvania Fall Harvest

CRUST

3 cups KELLOGG'S CORN FLAKES

1/2 cup granulated sugar

1/2 cup butter or margarine, melted

FILLING

3 medium Granny Smith apples, peeled, cored, and sliced

3 medium peaches, peeled, pitted, and sliced

1 pint fresh raspberries, well washed and dried

1/4 cup dried currants

1 1/2 teaspoons fresh lemon juice

1/2 cup granulated sugar

1/4 cup all-purpose flour

1/2 teaspoon ground cinnamon

TOPPING

1/4 cup granulated sugar

1/3 cup firmly packed brown sugar

1/3 cup all-purpose flour

1 teaspoon ground cinnamon

1 1/2 cups KELLOGG'S CRUNCHY BLENDS Low Fat Granola, plus more for garnish, if desired

1/2 teaspoon ground nutmeg

1/2 cup butter or margarine, softened

GARNISH

Nonfat vanilla yogurt, optional

Pennsylvania Fall Harvest it is—filled with sweet fruits and accented with crunchy, good-for-you granola. This is a perfect buffet dessert that tastes just as good at room temperature as it does hot from the oven. Garnish the warm dessert with yogurt or with whipped cream, whipped topping, or low-fat ice cream or frozen yogurt. SERVES 12

1. Preheat oven to 375°F.

2. Lightly coat a 13 x 9 x 2-inch baking dish with nonstick cooking spray. Set aside.

3. Place KELLOGG'S CORN FLAKES, 1/2 cup sugar, and the melted butter in the bowl of a food processor fitted with the metal blade and process to fine crumbs.

4. Transfer the mixture to the prepared baking dish, patting it in with your fingertips to make an even layer.

5. Place in the preheated oven and bake for 8 minutes, or until lightly browned. Remove from oven and set aside. Do not turn the oven off.

6. Combine all the filling ingredients in a large bowl, stirring gently to evenly coat the fruit. Pour this mixture over the prepared crust. Set aside.

7. Combine the topping ingredients in a medium bowl and mix to blend well.

8. Sprinkle the topping over the fruit in the prepared crust. Bake in the preheated oven for 45 minutes, or until the fruit is bubbling and the top is lightly browned.

9. Remove from oven and spoon equal portions into dessert cups. If desired, top with a dollop of nonfat vanilla yogurt and a sprinkle of CRUNCHY BLENDS granola.

Fruit Shortcakes

1½ cups all-purpose flour

1 teaspoon baking powder

½ teaspoon baking soda

½ teaspoon salt

½ cup vegetable shortening

1 cup KELLOGG'S COMPLETE Wheat Bran Flakes

¾ cup low-fat buttermilk

6 cups berries and/or sliced fresh fruit, lightly sweetened with ½ cup sugar, if necessary

Whipped cream as garnish, if desired

Rather than the traditional shortcake biscuits, we've made a slightly crunchy, wedge-shaped portion that can be smothered with fresh berries or fruit. If you want a very juicy topping, crush the fruit slightly, then add a bit of lemon or orange juice, and just enough sugar to get the juices flowing. SERVES 6

1. Preheat oven to 450°F.

2. Lightly coat an 8-inch round cake pan with nonstick cooking spray. Set aside.

3. Combine the flour, baking powder, baking soda, and salt in the bowl of a food processor fitted with the metal blade. Add the shortening and process, using quick on and off turns, to make coarse crumbs. Add the cereal along with the buttermilk, processing just until the dough pulls away from the bowl.

4. Remove the dough from the processor bowl and lightly pat it into the prepared cake pan.

5. Bake in the preheated oven for about 20 minutes, or until golden.

6. Remove from oven and cut into 6 equal wedges.

7. Place a wedge on each of 6 dessert plates. Top with fruit and a dollop of whipped cream, if desired, and serve.

Andrew Dornenburg, Author/Chef

Karen's Sundae Cups

16 large marshmallows

1/4 cup butter, softened

3/4 cup smooth peanut butter

2 1/2 cups KELLOGG'S RICE KRISPIES

1/2 cup chopped semisweet chocolate

2 tablespoons heavy cream

2 ripe bananas

1 quart vanilla ice cream

1/2 cup chopped roasted, unsalted peanuts

NOTE: If necessary, coat the spatula with melted butter or cooking spray to facilitate forming the cup shape.

Andrew Dornenburg and his wife, Karen Page, are award-winning cookbook authors. When Karen was about eight years old, she kept a diary, listing in it her five favorite foods: bacon, bananas, chocolate, peanut butter, and RICE KRISPIES. In her honor, Andrew has incorporated four of her childhood favorites in this delicious dessert.

MAKES 12

1. Line the cups of a 12-cup muffin tin with aluminum foil, pressing the foil firmly into the cups to make a neat, smooth fit. Lightly coat with nonstick vegetable spray and set aside.

2. Combine the marshmallows and butter in a medium, heavy-bottomed saucepan, over medium heat. Cook, stirring constantly, for about 4 minutes, or until smooth.

3. Beat in the peanut butter and continue stirring to incorporate. Lower the heat and fold in half of the RICE KRISPIES. When incorporated, fold in the remaining cereal.

4. Working quickly, pour about 1/4 cup of the marshmallow mixture into each foil-lined cup in the muffin pan. Using a rubber spatula, press the mixture firmly into the cup to completely cover the bottom and sides to make a neat cup shape, adding a bit more of the mixture, if necessary, to build up the sides. (See note.) When all of the cups have been formed, transfer to the refrigerator for 30 minutes to set.

5. When set, remove the pan from the refrigerator. Lift the cups from the pan and peel away the foil. The cups are quite fragile, so do this very carefully. If not using them immediately, return to the refrigerator. Remove from refrigerator 15 minutes before serving.

6. Combine the chocolate and cream in a small, heavy saucepan over low heat, stirring constantly to melt. Remove from heat and keep warm.

7. Peel the bananas and cut crosswise into $1/4$-inch-thick slices.

8. Fill each RICE KRISPIES cup with a scoop of ice cream. Place some sliced bananas on top of each one. Drizzle warm chocolate sauce over the top and sprinkle with peanuts. Serve immediately.

Caramel Nut Bites

8 ounces (about 28) soft caramel candy pieces

$1/4$ cup butter or margarine, softened

2 tablespoons fat-free milk

$3^1/2$ cups KELLOGG'S CORN FLAKES

$1/2$ cup chopped toasted walnuts

$1/2$ cup shredded coconut

Absolutely delicious and so simple to prepare, Caramel Nut Bites are about as good a candy as you can make. KELLOGG'S CORN FLAKES add just the right amount of crunch to the bite! MAKES ABOUT 2 DOZEN

1. Lightly coat a cookie sheet with nonstick cooking spray. Set aside.

2. Combine the caramels, butter, and milk in a medium, heavy-bottomed saucepan over low heat. Cook, stirring constantly, for about 10 minutes, or until caramels have melted and the mixture is smooth.

3. Remove from heat and stir in the cereal, walnuts, and coconut.

4. When combined, drop by the tablespoon onto the prepared cookie sheet. Set aside to cool.

5. When cool, store tightly covered, at room temperature.

Chocolate Pecan Clusters

One 11.5-ounce package milk chocolate morsels

1 tablespoon vegetable shortening

2 cups KELLOGG'S COCOA KRISPIES or RICE KRISPIES

1 cup coarsely chopped toasted pecans

Oh so easy and oh so yummy! There are so many variations to this simple recipe that you can make a couple of batches, each tasting quite different. Use semisweet chocolate in place of the milk chocolate, add 2 teaspoons freshly grated orange zest, and/or try 1 teaspoon pure vanilla extract or rum extract or 1/2 teaspoon peppermint extract. MAKES ABOUT 3 DOZEN

1. Line a baking pan with waxed paper. Set aside.

2. Combine the chocolate morsels and shortening in a heavy-bottomed saucepan over low heat. Cook, stirring constantly, for about 5 minutes, or just until the chocolate has melted and the mixture is smooth.

3. Remove from the heat and stir in the cereal and nuts.

4. Drop the mixture by the rounded teaspoon onto the prepared baking pan. Transfer to the refrigerator and allow to chill for 30 minutes.

5. Serve, or store tightly covered and refrigerated.

HONEY SMACKS® Brittle

³/₄ cup firmly packed brown sugar

¹/₄ cup light corn syrup

1 tablespoon butter or margarine

4 cups KELLOGG'S HONEY SMACKS

¹/₂ cup peanuts

An old-fashioned peanut brittle made new with the addition of sweet KELLOGG'S HONEY SMACKS cereal.

MAKES 1 DOZEN PIECES

1. Lightly coat a 15 x 10 x 1-inch nonstick baking pan with nonstick cooking spray. Set aside.

2. Combine sugar, corn syrup, and butter in a medium, heavy-bottomed saucepan over moderate heat. Bring to a boil, stirring constantly.

3. Immediately remove from heat and quickly stir in the HONEY SMACKS and nuts and then immediately pour the mixture onto the prepared baking pan. You must work quickly, as the mixture will harden.

4. After about 30 seconds, using rubber gloves, take hold of the edge of the candy and, lifting it slightly from the pan, pull it as thin as possible.

5. Break the candy into irregular pieces. Store tightly covered.

Tiger Paws

1 pound vanilla caramels

8 teaspoons water

1 teaspoon pure vanilla extract

One 12-ounce package semisweet chocolate morsels

2 cups KELLOGG'S TIGER POWER

This is a version of the classic chocolate, caramel, and pecan candy called Turtles. We've used KELLOGG'S TIGER POWER cereal in place of the pecans so that the candy resembles TONY THE TIGER paws. You can, if you wish, add pecans to the recipe—about $1/4$ pound will give a nice nutty flavor. Combine the nuts with the cereal for the best result. MAKES ABOUT 4 DOZEN

1. Lightly coat 2 cookie sheets with nonstick cooking spray. Set aside.

2. Combine the caramels with the water and vanilla in the top half of a double boiler over boiling water, stirring until melted.

3. Remove from heat and cool slightly.

4. Place the chocolate morsels in a small, heavy saucepan over low heat and cook, stirring constantly, until melted (or microwave following manufacturer's directions). Remove from heat and set aside, but keep warm and melted.

5. Place about 10 pieces of TIGER POWER in a mound on one of the prepared cookie sheets. Spoon about 1 teaspoon of the caramel over the center of the TIGER POWER, almost covering the cereal. Continue making mounds of cereal and caramel, one mound at a time, until all of the cereal has been used. Let rest for about 10 minutes, or until the caramel has begun to firm.

6. Pour a bit of melted chocolate over each mound, covering the caramel but leaving the cereal edge exposed so that the candy looks a bit like a cat's paw.

7. Set aside until very firm.

8. Store in an airtight container, in layers separated by waxed paper.

Fruity Snowballs

1 cup KELLOGG'S ALL-BRAN

1 cup pitted dried plums (prunes)

1 cup dried apricots

1 cup seedless raisins

1 cup candied pineapple chunks

1/2 cup confectioners' sugar

These sweets are a marvelous combination of KELLOGG'S ALL-BRAN and dried fruits. They keep well and are great to have on hand for afternoon snacks or tea. MAKES ABOUT 18

1. Combine the ALL-BRAN and dried plums in the bowl of a food processor fitted with the metal blade. Process, using quick on and off turns, until the mixture is crumbly.

2. Add the apricots, raisins, and pineapple and process until the fruit is in pieces about 1/4 inch thick.

3. Place the confectioners' sugar in a resealable plastic bag.

4. Portion the fruit mixture, using a level tablespoon. Form into balls about 3/4 inch in diameter.

5. Working with a few balls at a time, drop the balls into the sugar, seal the bag, and toss to coat.

6. Serve immediately or store in layers separated by waxed paper, tightly covered and refrigerated.

7. If stored, again coat in sugar before serving, as the fruit will absorb the sugar during storage.

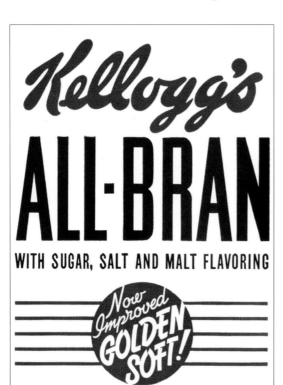

CRISPIX MIX® SWEET MINGLERS®

1 cup confectioners' sugar

1 cup semisweet chocolate morsels

¼ cup peanut butter

½ cup peanuts, optional

6 cups KELLOGG'S CRISPIX

A cinch to make and a favorite with kids and adults! If you don't have a microwave, melt the chocolate in a heavy-bottomed saucepan over low heat. MAKES ABOUT 8 CUPS

1. Place the confectioners' sugar in a 2-gallon resealable plastic bag. Set aside.

2. Place the chocolate morsels in a microwave-safe bowl and microwave on high for 1 minute. Stir and heat 30 seconds longer at high, or until melted when stirred.

3. Remove from the microwave and stir in the peanut butter and, if using, the peanuts.

4. Add the CRISPIX, stirring gently to coat well without breaking up the cereal.

5. Transfer the mixture to the sugar in the plastic bag and gently toss until all of the pieces are well coated with sugar.

6. Transfer to an airtight container and store in refrigerator.

Polly-Pops

1 tablespoon butter

4 cups KELLOGG'S CORN POPS

1 cup salted peanuts

1 cup sugar

1/2 cup light corn syrup

1 cup half-and-half

Lollipops made out of cereal? Yes indeed, and they are delicious! You will need 30 wooden skewers and a candy thermometer to make them. MAKES ABOUT 2 1/2 DOZEN

1. Lightly coat a large mixing bowl with 1 teaspoon of the butter. Add the cereal and peanuts, tossing to mix. Set aside.

2. Using the remaining butter, lightly coat a mini-muffin pan. Set aside.

3. Combine the sugar and corn syrup in a heavy-bottomed saucepan. Add the half-and-half and place over low heat. Cook, stirring constantly, for about 15 minutes, or until the mixture reaches 240°F (soft ball stage) on a candy thermometer.

4. Pour the hot syrup over the cereal mixture, tossing to coat well.

5. Press the cereal mixture into the prepared muffin pan and set aside to cool.

6. When cool, remove the hardened cereal pieces from the muffin tin and stick a wooden skewer into each one to resemble a lollipop.

7. Store tightly covered, at room temperature.

PASTRY CHEF KATE ZUCKERMAN, Chanterelle Restaurant, New York City

Milk Chocolate RICE KRISPIES® Crunchies

7 ounces fine-quality milk chocolate, broken into small pieces

2 cups KELLOGG'S RICE KRISPIES

Kate Zuckerman is the pastry chef at the elegant Chanterelle in New York City. Her flavor-focused desserts have made her one of the most acclaimed pastry chefs of her generation. Kids of all ages will enjoy these crunchies. If you can get your hands on very high quality milk chocolate, they taste all the better. MAKES APPROXIMATELY 4 DOZEN

1. Make sure that all of your equipment is very clean and dry.

2. Line a cookie sheet with parchment paper or aluminum foil. Set aside.

3. Place the chocolate in a stainless steel bowl over a pot of barely simmering water. Do not allow the bottom of the bowl to touch the water. Heat, stirring frequently, for about 5 minutes, or until the chocolate reaches 110°F on a candy thermometer. Do not allow it to go above that heat or the chocolate will be unsuitable for candy making.

4. Remove the chocolate from the heat and set aside to cool to 80°F on a candy thermometer, scraping and stirring with a rubber spatula every 5 minutes. If the chocolate seems too firm at this temperature, it can be reheated to no more than 84°F.

5. Fold the RICE KRISPIES into the chocolate, using a rubber spatula to insure that all of the cereal is coated.

6. Using 2 teaspoons, scoop up and form the chocolate candies into small mounds. Place the mounds on the prepared cookie sheet to set. Try to make the mounds high rather than wide.

7. When all of the candies are formed, set aside in a cool, dry place to set. Do not refrigerate.

8. Store in layers, tightly covered, in a cool, dry place for up to 1 week.

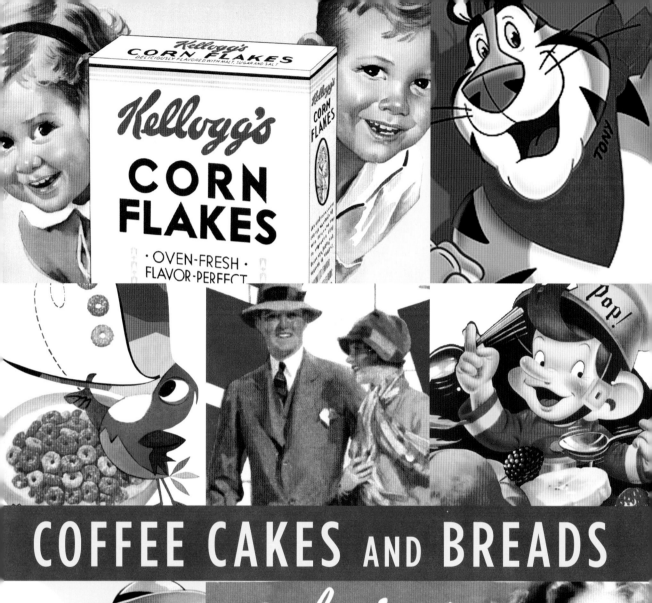

Kellogg's CORN FLAKES

Kellogg's
CORN
FLAKES
DELICIOUSLY FLAVORED WITH MALT, SUGAR AND SALT

Kellogg's CORN FLAKES
· OVEN-FRESH ·
FLAVOR-PERFECT

COFFEE CAKES AND BREADS

Delicious
with Fruits

Cinnamon Coffee Cake

TOPPING

1 cup KELLOGG'S CORN FLAKES

¹/₄ cup sugar

¹/₂ teaspoon ground cinnamon

.1 tablespoon butter or margarine, melted

CAKE

¹/₂ cup butter or margarine, softened

³/₄ cup sugar

2 large eggs, separated

²/₃ cup fat-free milk

1¹/₂ cups all-purpose flour

2 teaspoons baking powder

¹/₂ teaspoon salt

1 teaspoon ground cinnamon

There is no better way to wake the house than with the sweet-spicy smell of cinnamon coming from a freshly baked coffee cake. This is a simple recipe that couldn't be easier to make, and it will quickly become a breakfast staple in your house. MAKES ONE 9-INCH CAKE

1. Preheat oven to 350°F.

2. Lightly coat a 9-inch round cake pan with nonstick cooking spray. Set aside.

3. Place KELLOGG'S CORN FLAKES in a resealable plastic bag. Seal the bag and, using a rolling pin, crush the cereal to a coarse crumb. Open the bag and measure the crumbs; you should have ¹/2 cup.

4. Combine the crumbs with ¹/4 cup of the sugar and ¹/2 teaspoon of the cinnamon. Add the melted butter and stir to blend. Set aside.

5. Place the ¹/2 cup butter in the bowl of a standing electric mixer and beat until light. Add ³/4 cup sugar and continue beating until light and fluffy. Add the egg yolks, beating to blend. Add the milk and continue beating until well incorporated.

6. Sift together the flour, baking powder, salt, and 1 teaspoon cinnamon and add to the batter, stirring to just combine.

7. Beat the egg whites until stiff but not dry. Fold the beaten egg whites into the batter.

8. Spread the batter in the prepared pan. Sprinkle with reserved topping and place in the preheated oven. Bake for about 45 minutes, or until a cake tester inserted into the center comes out clean.

9. Remove from oven and serve.

Blueberry Kuchen

5 cups KELLOGG'S CORN FLAKES

1 cup firmly packed brown sugar

4 teaspoons ground cinnamon

¹/₄ cup butter or margarine, cold

¹/₄ cup chopped walnuts or pecans

One 20-ounce package white cake mix

1¹/₄ cups fresh blueberries, well washed, or frozen blueberries, thawed and drained

KELLOGG KITCHEN'S Blueberry Kuchen gets less than 30 percent of its calories from fat. The cereal and blueberries combine to make a very tasty breakfast. We use a packaged cake mix to save time. MAKES ONE 13-INCH CAKE

1. Preheat oven to 350°F.

2. Lightly coat a 13 x 9 x 2-inch baking pan with nonstick cooking spray. Set aside.

3. Place KELLOGG'S CORN FLAKES in a resealable plastic bag. Seal the bag and, using a rolling pin, crush the cereal to a fine crumb. Open the bag and measure the crumbs; you should have 1¹/₄ cups. Set aside.

4. Combine the sugar and cinnamon in a small mixing bowl. Add the butter and, using a fork, cut the butter into the sugar. Add the crumbs and nuts and stir to combine. Set aside.

5. Prepare the cake mix according to the package directions.

6. Sprinkle half of the cereal mixture over the bottom of the prepared pan. Spread the cake batter evenly over the cereal mixture, using a rubber spatula to smooth it out to an even layer.

7. Sprinkle the blueberries over the cake batter and then cover with the remaining cereal mixture, lightly pressing it into the batter.

8. Bake in the preheated oven for about 45 minutes, or until a cake tester inserted into the center comes out clean.

9. Remove from oven and cool in pan, on a wire rack. Serve warm or cold.

Plum-Marmalade Coffee Cake

½ cup orange marmalade

3 large purple plums, well washed, pitted, and thinly sliced

¼ cup firmly packed brown sugar

½ cup plus 2 tablespoons all-purpose flour

1 cup KELLOGG'S ALL-BRAN

1 cup fat-free milk

1 large egg

¼ cup butter or margarine, softened

½ cup whole wheat flour

¼ cup granulated sugar

2 teaspoons baking powder

½ teaspoon ground nutmeg

½ teaspoon salt

This is a beautiful and yummy upside-down coffee cake. If plums are not in season, you can use any other fresh, firm stone fruit, or even apples or pears. When all else fails, use canned plums, peaches, or apricots; just be sure to drain them well. Here again the combination of bran, whole wheat flour, and fruit add goodness to this special breakfast cake. MAKES ONE 9-INCH CAKE

1. Preheat oven to 400°F.

2. Lightly coat a 9-inch round cake pan with nonstick cooking spray. Spread the marmalade in an even layer over the bottom of the pan.

3. Combine the plums and brown sugar with 2 tablespoons of the all-purpose flour, tossing to coat well. Arrange the plum slices in a decorative pattern over the marmalade. Set aside.

4. Combine the ALL-BRAN and milk in a large mixing bowl, stirring to combine. Set aside for 2 minutes, or until the cereal has softened. Stir in the egg and butter, beating to blend.

5. Sift the remaining ½ cup all-purpose flour with the whole wheat flour, granulated sugar, baking powder, nutmeg, and salt and add to the cereal mixture, beating just until incorporated.

6. Spread the batter evenly over the plums, using a rubber spatula to smooth it out to an even layer. Bake in the preheated oven for about 25 minutes, or until the cake is golden brown and a cake tester inserted into the center comes out clean.

7. Remove from oven and immediately invert onto a serving plate. Serve warm or at room temperature.

Orange Juice Coffee Cake

TOPPING

1/2 cup KELLOGG'S CRUNCHY BLENDS JUST RIGHT Fruit & Nut

2 tablespoons firmly packed brown sugar

1 tablespoon all-purpose flour

1 tablespoon butter or margarine, softened

COFFEE CAKE

3/4 cup KELLOGG'S CRUNCHY BLENDS JUST RIGHT Fruit & Nut

1 1/2 cups all-purpose flour

2 1/2 teaspoons baking powder

1/4 teaspoon baking soda

1/3 cup butter or margarine, softened

2/3 cup granulated sugar

1 large egg, lightly beaten

1/2 cup fresh orange juice

The sweet citrusy tang of orange makes this a very inviting breakfast cake. For an extra orange kick, add 1 teaspoon freshly grated orange zest to the crumb topping. MAKES ONE 9-INCH SQUARE CAKE

1. Preheat oven to 375°F.

2. Lightly coat a 9-inch square baking pan with nonstick cooking spray. Set aside.

3. Place 1/2 cup KELLOGG'S CRUNCHY BLENDS JUST RIGHT Fruit & Nut into a resealable plastic bag. Seal the bag and, using a rolling pin, crush the cereal to coarse crumbs. Open the bag and measure the crumbs; you should have 1/4 cup.

4. Combine the cereal crumbs with the remaining topping ingredients. Mix together until crumbly. Set aside.

5. Repeat step 3 with 3/4 cup of the cereal. You should have 1/2 cup of crumbs.

6. Combine 1 1/2 cups flour with the baking powder, baking soda, and 1/2 cup of crumbs, stirring to just incorporate.

7. Place the 1/3 cup butter in the bowl of an electric mixer, beating until light. Add the sugar, egg, and orange juice, beating to blend. Add flour-cereal mixture, beating to just combine.

8. Spread the batter in the prepared pan, using a rubber spatula to smooth it out to an even layer. Sprinkle the reserved crumb mixture over the top. Bake in the preheated oven for about 30 minutes, or until a cake tester inserted in the center comes out clean.

9. Remove from oven and serve.

Almond Tea Ring

2 packages active dry yeast

1/2 cup warm (110°F) water

1 cup KELLOGG'S ALL-BRAN or BRAN BUDS

3/4 cup milk, scalded

1 cup granulated sugar

1/3 cup vegetable shortening

1 teaspoon salt

5 cups all-purpose flour

2 large eggs, beaten

1 teaspoon almond extract

1 tablespoon butter, melted

1/4 cup butter or margarine, softened

1/2 cup sliced almonds

GLAZE

1 cup confectioners' sugar

1 1/2 tablespoons fresh orange juice

1/4 teaspoon almond extract

Additional sliced almonds as garnish, optional

This coffee cake is based on a traditional European almond cake. MAKES 2 RINGS

1. Combine the yeast with the warm water in a small bowl, stirring to dissolve the yeast. Set aside.

2. Place the ALL-BRAN in a large mixing bowl. Add the hot milk, 1/2 cup of the granulated sugar, shortening, and salt, stirring until the shortening has melted. Set aside until lukewarm, about 15 minutes.

3. Add about 2 cups of the flour to the cereal mixture, stirring with a wooden spoon to make a thick batter. Add the eggs and 1 teaspoon almond extract along with the dissolved yeast, beating to blend well. Add the remaining 3 cups of flour and beat until thoroughly incorporated. (You can do this in a standing electric mixer fitted with the dough hook or by hand.)

4. Lightly coat a large mixing bowl with nonstick cooking spray. Set aside.

5. Lightly flour a clean, flat surface. Scrape the dough onto the floured surface and knead for about 10 minutes, or until smooth and elastic. Place the dough in the oiled bowl. Using a pastry brush, lightly coat the dough with 1 tablespoon melted butter. Cover with a kitchen towel and set aside in a warm, draft-free place for about 1 hour, or until doubled in volume.

6. Lightly coat 2 baking sheets with nonstick cooking spray. Set aside.

7. Punch the dough down and divide it into 2 equal pieces.

8. Lightly flour a clean, flat surface.

9. Roll one portion of the dough out into a rectangle about 22 inches long and $1/4$ inch thick. Using a spatula, lightly coat the dough with half the softened butter. Sprinkle with $1/4$ cup of the remaining granulated sugar and then sprinkle half the sliced almonds over it.

10. Roll the dough up and then bring the ends of the roll together and press to form a ring. Place the ring on one of the prepared baking sheets.

11. Repeat steps 9 and 10 with the second portion of dough.

12. Using kitchen scissors, make diagonal cuts about 1 inch apart into the upper outer edges of the rings, to within an inch of the inner circle. Do not cut all the way through. Turn each section slightly so that the cut edge is up.

13. Cover with a clean kitchen towel and set aside in a warm, draft-free place for 1 hour, or until doubled in volume.

14. Preheat oven to 350°F.

15. Uncover rings and place in the preheated oven. Bake for about 20 minutes, or until golden brown.

16. While the coffee cakes are baking, make the glaze.

17. Combine the confectioners' sugar with the orange juice and $1/4$ teaspoon almond extract, beating to blend.

18. Remove the cakes from the oven and transfer to wire racks. Drizzle the cakes with the glaze and sprinkle with additional sliced almonds, if desired.

19. Cool slightly before serving.

Corn Flake–Banana Bread

2 cups all-purpose flour

1 teaspoon baking powder

½ teaspoon baking soda

½ teaspoon salt

2½ cups KELLOGG'S CORN FLAKES

1½ cups mashed very ripe bananas

½ cup butter or margarine, softened

¾ cup sugar

2 large eggs

½ cup coarsely chopped walnuts

KELLOGG'S CORN FLAKES add great flavor and texture to this wonderful bread. MAKES ONE 9-INCH LOAF

1. Preheat oven to 350°F.

2. Lightly coat a 9 x 5 x 3-inch loaf pan with nonstick cooking spray. Set aside.

3. Sift the flour, baking powder, baking soda, and salt together. Set aside.

4. Combine the cereal and bananas in a medium mixing bowl. Set aside for 5 minutes, or until the cereal has softened.

5. Combine the butter and sugar in the bowl of a standing electric mixer and beat until well blended. Add the eggs, one at a time, beating to blend. Stir in the cereal-banana mixture. Stir in flour mixture. Blend well.

6. Remove the bowl from the mixer and stir in the nuts.

7. Scrape the batter into the prepared pan, spreading out in an even layer. Bake in the preheated oven for 1 hour, or until a cake tester inserted into the center comes out clean.

8. Remove from oven and set aside to cool for 10 minutes.

9. Turn out the bread onto a wire rack, and cool completely before slicing. Store tightly wrapped in plastic film.

Anadama Bread

4 cups KELLOGG'S CORN FLAKES or 1 cup KELLOGG'S Corn Flake Crumbs

1½ cups boiling water

½ cup molasses

⅓ cup butter, softened

1 tablespoon salt

4–4½ cups all-purpose flour

2 packages active dry yeast

1 large egg

2 tablespoons butter, melted

Anadama bread is an early American bread that is traditionally made with cornmeal and molasses. At Kellogg we use KELLOGG'S Corn Flake Crumbs in place of the usual meal to make a somewhat less dense but nonetheless delicious bread. MAKES 2 ROUND LOAVES

1. Place KELLOGG'S CORN FLAKES in a resealable plastic bag. Seal the bag and, using a rolling pin, crush the cereal to a fine crumb. Open the bag and measure the crumbs; you should have 1 cup.

2. Place the crumbs in a large, heatproof mixing bowl. Stir in the water, molasses, butter, and salt. Set aside until it cools to 120°–130°F.

3. Combine 1 cup of the flour with the yeast and stir it into the cereal mixture. When combined, beat in the egg.

4. Stir in enough of the remaining 3½ cups of flour to make a stiff dough.

5. Lightly coat a large mixing bowl with nonstick cooking spray. Set aside.

6. Lightly flour a clean, flat surface.

7. Scrape the dough onto the floured surface and knead the dough for about 8 minutes, or until smooth and elastic.

8. Transfer the dough to the oiled bowl, turning to lightly oil all sides. Cover with a kitchen towel and set aside in a warm, draft-free place to rise for 1 hour, or until doubled in bulk.

9. Remove the dough from the bowl and punch down to flatten slightly. Divide the dough into 2 equal pieces. Cover with a kitchen towel and let rest for 10 minutes.

10. Lightly coat a cookie sheet with nonstick cooking spray. Set aside.

11. Uncover the dough and, working with one piece at a time, shape the dough into two round, slightly flattened loaves. Place loaves in opposite corners of the prepared cookie sheet. Cover with a kitchen towel and set aside in a warm, draft-free place to rise for about 45 minutes, or until almost doubled in bulk.

12. Preheat oven to 375°F.

13. Uncover the breads and place the baking sheet in the preheated oven. Bake for 20 minutes. Cover loaves with aluminum foil to prevent excess browning and bake for an additional 20 minutes, or until golden brown.

14. Remove from oven and place on wire racks. Using a pastry brush, lightly coat the warm loaves with melted butter. Serve warm or at room temperature.

Lemon Poppy Seed Bread

4 cups KELLOGG'S CORN FLAKES

1³/₄ cups all-purpose flour

³/₄ cup sugar

2 tablespoons poppy seeds

1 teaspoon baking powder

¹/₂ teaspoon baking soda

¹/₂ teaspoon ground nutmeg

¹/₄ teaspoon salt

2 large egg whites

1 cup fat-free milk

3 tablespoons canola oil

2 tablespoons fresh lemon juice

1 tablespoon freshly grated lemon zest

GLAZE

¹/₄ cup light corn syrup

1 tablespoon fresh lemon juice

1 teaspoon freshly grated lemon zest

Slightly tart and deeply flavorful with the wholesomeness of KELLOGG'S CORN FLAKES and the subtle poppy seeds, this is an excellent breakfast or tea bread. MAKES ONE 8¹/₂-INCH LOAF

1. Preheat oven to 350°F.

2. Lightly coat an 8¹/₂ x 4¹/₂ x 2¹/₂-inch loaf pan with nonstick cooking spray. Set aside.

3. Place the Corn Flakes in a resealable plastic bag. Seal the bag and, using a rolling pin, crush the cereal to a fine crumb. Open the bag and measure the crumbs; you should have 1 cup.

4. Combine the crumbs with the flour, sugar, poppy seeds, baking powder, baking soda, nutmeg, and salt in a medium mixing bowl. Set aside.

5. Combine the egg whites, milk, and oil with 2 tablespoons lemon juice and 1 tablespoon lemon zest in a mixing bowl, beating with a hand-held electric mixer until light and frothy.

6. Add the egg mixture to the cereal mixture, stirring with a wooden spoon to just combine.

7. Spoon the batter into the prepared pan and bake in the preheated oven for 50 minutes, or until a cake tester inserted into the center comes out clean.

8. Prepare a glaze by combining the corn syrup with 1 tablespoon lemon juice and 1 teaspoon lemon zest.

9. Using a long-tined fork, prick the top of the hot bread 12 times. Pour the glaze over the bread.

10. Set aside on a wire rack to cool for 30 minutes.

11. Remove the bread from the pan and cool completely before serving. Store tightly wrapped in plastic film and refrigerated.

Grandma's Molasses Brown Bread

$^1/_2$ cup all-purpose flour

$^1/_2$ cup whole wheat flour

1 teaspoon baking soda

$^1/_2$ teaspoon ground cinnamon

$^1/_2$ teaspoon salt

2 large egg whites

1 cup KELLOGG'S ALL-BRAN

$^3/_4$ cup very hot water

$^1/_3$ cup molasses

2 tablespoons canola oil

$^1/_2$ cup seedless raisins

This bread is rather like an old-fashioned Boston brown bread, made even better with the addition of ALL-BRAN. It is a satisfying bread that can be served along with food or as a great snack or tea bread. Traditionally, this style of bread is baked in clean cans about 4 inches deep and 3 inches in diameter. MAKES ONE $8^1/_2$-INCH LOAF

1. Preheat oven to 350°F.

2. Lightly coat an $8^1/_2$ x $4^1/_2$ x $2^1/_2$-inch loaf pan with nonstick cooking spray. Set aside.

3. Combine the white and whole wheat flours, baking soda, cinnamon, and salt. Set aside.

4. Place the egg whites in a medium mixing bowl and, using a whisk, beat until frothy. Add the cereal, hot water, molasses, and oil. Let stand 5 minutes, or until cereal softens. Beat to blend. Stir in the raisins.

5. Add the flour mixture to the cereal mixture, beating until just combined.

6. Spoon the batter into the prepared pan and bake in the preheated oven for about 35 minutes, or until a cake tester inserted into the center comes out clean.

7. Remove pan from oven and turn out loaf onto a wire rack to cool slightly. Serve warm or cold.

8. Store tightly wrapped and refrigerated.

ALL-BRAN® Corn Bread with Bacon

½ pound uncooked bacon, diced

1 cup all-purpose flour

1 cup yellow cornmeal

2 tablespoons sugar

4 teaspoons baking powder

¼ teaspoon salt

½ cup KELLOGG'S ALL-BRAN

1 cup fat-free milk

1 large egg

This is the Kellogg version of an all-time southern favorite, corn bread, flavored with smoky bacon. ALL-BRAN adds a slightly sweet crunch to the savory bread. This corn bread is particularly delicious with breakfast or brunch. MAKES ONE 9-INCH SQUARE BREAD

1. Preheat oven to 425°F.

2. Lightly coat a 9 x 9 x 2-inch baking pan with nonstick cooking spray. Set aside.

3. Fry bacon in fry pan over medium heat until slightly crisp, stirring constantly. Drain bacon on paper towels. Reserve 2 tablespoons drippings.

4. Stir the flour, cornmeal, sugar, baking powder, and salt together.

5. Combine KELLOGG'S ALL-BRAN, milk, egg, and the 2 tablespoons bacon drippings in a large bowl. Let stand about 2 minutes, or until cereal softens.

6. Add the flour mixture, stirring to combine. Reserve 2 tablespoons of diced bacon. Stir in remaining bacon.

7. Spoon the batter into the prepared pan. Sprinkle the reserved bacon over the top. Bake in the preheated oven for about 18 minutes, or until a cake tester inserted into the center comes out clean.

8. Remove from oven, cut into squares, and serve.

Hearty Bran Rolls

1 cup KELLOGG'S ALL-BRAN

1 cup bread flour

2 tablespoons sugar

1 1/2 teaspoons salt

1 package active dry yeast

1 cup fat-free milk

1/2 cup water

2 tablespoons butter or margarine

2 large egg whites

1 1/4 cups whole wheat flour

The perfect dinner roll. If time is of the essence, the rolls can be baked when placed in the muffin pans, eliminating the second rise. They will be somewhat smaller and more compact but still delicious. MAKES 16 ROLLS

1. Combine ALL-BRAN, bread flour, sugar, salt, and yeast in the bowl of a standing electric mixer.

2. Combine the milk, water, and butter in a small saucepan over low heat. Heat to 120°–130°F.

3. Add the warm milk mixture along with the egg whites to the cereal-flour mixture, beating on low speed for about 30 seconds, or until well blended. Increase the speed to high and beat, frequently scraping down the sides of the bowl with a rubber spatula, for about 3 minutes, or until quite smooth.

3. Remove the bowl from the mixer and, using a wooden spoon, beat in the whole wheat flour to make a sticky batter.

4. Cover with a kitchen towel and set aside in a warm, draft-free place for about 1 hour, or until doubled in volume.

5. Lightly coat the 2 1/2-inch-diameter cups of two 8-cup muffin pans with nonstick cooking spray.

6. Uncover and stir down the batter. Spoon the batter into the oiled muffin cups. Cover with a kitchen towel and set aside in a warm, draft-free place for about 40 minutes, or until doubled in volume.

7. Preheat oven to 400°F.

8. Uncover the rolls and bake in the preheated oven for about 17 minutes, or until golden brown.

9. Remove from oven and serve hot.

Bran Pita Bread

1¼ cups warm (110°–115°F) water

1 package active dry yeast

1½ cups KELLOGG'S ALL-BRAN

1½ cups all-purpose flour

½ teaspoon salt

¼ cup canola oil

1 cup whole wheat flour

NOTE: You can use more than one cookie sheet, but do not place more than 2 circles on each sheet, as you don't want the pitas to stick to one another.

Who would have thought that ALL-BRAN could help you make fresh-from-the-oven pita breads? These are the perfect pocket for a lunch or breakfast. MAKES 1 DOZEN

1. Preheat oven to 450°F.

2. Place the water in the bowl of a standing electric mixer fitted with the paddle. Add the yeast, stirring to dissolve. Set aside for 5 minutes.

3. Stir in the cereal, mixing to combine.

4. With the motor running on low, gradually add 1 cup of the all-purpose flour and the salt, alternating with the oil. Raise the speed to high and beat for 3 minutes.

5. Change the paddle to the dough hook and add the whole wheat flour. Set the speed on low and begin kneading the dough. Knead for 5 minutes, or until dough is smooth and elastic. If necessary, add the remaining ½ cup all-purpose flour to make a soft dough.

6. Divide the dough into 12 equal portions.

7. Lightly flour your hands and roll each piece into a very smooth ball. Cover the balls with a damp kitchen towel and set aside to rest for 10 minutes.

8. Lightly flour a clean, flat surface and, working with one ball of dough at a time, use a rolling pin to lightly roll it into a circle about 6 inches in diameter. Do not stretch, puncture, or crease the dough. Keep the unrolled dough covered so that it does not dry out.

9. Place 2 circles on an ungreased cookie sheet and bake in the preheated oven for about 4 minutes, or until puffed and slightly firm. Using a metal spatula, turn the circles and continue baking for 2 minutes, or until lightly browned. Repeat with remaining dough. (See note.)

10. Transfer to a wire rack to cool.

11. When cool, cut in half and stuff with a vegetable or meat filling, or place in a resealable plastic bag and refrigerate until ready to use. Reheat before serving.

Bran English Muffins

1 cup milk

2 tablespoons butter

1 teaspoon salt

3/4 cup KELLOGG'S ALL-BRAN

1/4 cup warm (110°–115°F) water

1 package active dry yeast

2 3/4 cups all-purpose flour

These may not resemble the assembly-line, presplit English muffins available from the grocery store, but they will amaze you with their wonderful rich flavor. MAKES 1 DOZEN

1. Combine the milk, butter, and salt in a medium saucepan over low heat. Cook, stirring frequently, for about 3 minutes, or just until the butter has melted.

2. Remove from heat and stir in the cereal. Set aside to cool to lukewarm.

3. Lightly coat a large mixing bowl with nonstick cooking spray. Set aside.

4. Place the water in a warm, large mixing bowl. Stir in the yeast. When dissolved, stir in the cereal mixture. Gradually add 2 1/2 cups of the flour, mixing with a wooden spoon, until the dough pulls away from the sides of the bowl.

5. Coat a clean, flat work surface with the remaining 1/4 cup flour.

6. Scrape the dough onto the floured surface and knead the dough for about 5 minutes, or until smooth and elastic, adding more flour if necessary to keep the dough from sticking.

7. Transfer the dough to the oiled bowl, turning to lightly oil all sides. Cover with a kitchen towel and set aside in a warm, draft-free place for about 45 minutes, or until doubled in volume.

8. Lightly flour a clean, flat surface. Scrape the dough onto the floured surface and punch it down.

9. Lightly flour the top of the dough and, using a rolling pin, roll it out to a 1/2-inch-thick circle.

10. Using a 3-inch round biscuit cutter, cut out 12 muffins. Place on a platter and cover with a kitchen towel. Place in a warm, draft-free place and let rest for another 45 minutes, or until doubled in volume.

11. Heat a cast iron (or other heavy) frying pan over low heat until quite hot. Transfer the muffins to the frying pan, without crowding the pan, and cook for about 12 minutes, or until lightly browned. Turn once and continue cooking for another 13 minutes, or until lightly browned on both sides.

12. Transfer finished muffins to a wire rack to cool.

13. When ready to serve, split and toast. Serve with butter and orange marmalade, if desired.

Bran-Cherry Bread

2 cups all-purpose flour

3/4 cup sugar

1 tablespoon baking powder

1/2 teaspoon salt

1/2 teaspoon ground nutmeg

1 1/2 cups KELLOGG'S CRACKLIN' OAT BRAN

1 1/4 cups fat-free milk

1 large egg

2 tablespoons canola oil

One 10-ounce jar maraschino cherries, well drained and finely chopped

1 cup chopped walnuts or pecans

1 tablespoon butter or margarine, melted

This is one of Kellogg Company's often requested holiday recipes. It is such a wonderful, moist, eat-anytime bread that it makes a great from-the-kitchen gift as well as an instant snack to be served with warm drinks when friends come to call. MAKES ONE 9-INCH LOAF

1. Preheat oven to 350°F.

2. Lightly coat a 9 x 5 x 3-inch loaf pan with nonstick cooking spray. Set aside.

3. Sift the flour, 1/2 cup of the sugar, baking powder, salt, and nutmeg together. Set aside.

3. Combine the cereal and milk in a large mixing bowl. Let stand for 10 minutes, or until the cereal has softened.

4. Stir in the egg and oil, beating to blend.

5. Add the flour mixture to the cereal mixture, beating to blend.

6. Measure 2 tablespoons of the chopped cherries. Set aside.

7. Fold the remaining chopped cherries along with 3/4 cup of the nuts into the batter.

8. Spoon the batter into the prepared pan.

9. Combine the remaining 1/4 cup sugar, the remaining 1/4 cup nuts, and the reserved 2 tablespoons of cherries with the melted butter. Sprinkle the mixture over the batter.

10. Bake in the preheated oven for about 1 hour, or until a cake tester inserted in the center comes out clean.

11. Remove from oven and cool for 10 minutes; then remove from the pan and place on a wire rack to cool.

12. Serve warm or at room temperature.

Peanut Butter Bread

1½ cups all-purpose flour

1 tablespoon baking powder

½ teaspoon salt

2 cups KELLOGG'S RAISIN BRAN

1⅓ cups milk

⅓ cup smooth peanut butter

½ cup sugar

1 large egg

¼ cup chopped peanuts

This peanut-flavored bread is made even more delicious by the fiber-rich, slightly sweet KELLOGG'S RAISIN BRAN.

MAKES ONE 9-INCH LOAF

1. Preheat oven to 350°F.

2. Lightly coat a 9 x 5 x 3-inch loaf pan with nonstick cooking spray. Set aside.

3. Stir together flour, baking powder, and salt. Set aside.

4. Combine KELLOGG'S RAISIN BRAN and milk in a small mixing bowl, stirring to blend. Set aside for 2 minutes, or until the cereal has softened.

5. Combine the peanut butter and sugar in a large mixing bowl and beat until smooth. Add the egg and continue beating. Add the cereal mixture, beating to incorporate.

6. Stir in the flour mixture. Stir in the peanuts.

7. Scrape the batter into the prepared pan. Bake in the preheated oven for about 1 hour, or until a cake tester inserted into the center comes out clean.

8. Remove from oven and turn out the loaf onto a wire rack.

9. Cool completely before serving.

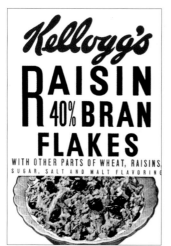

KELLOGG'S RAISIN BRAN was introduced in 1942 as the first fruit-added cereal in history. It remained the only fruit-added brand until the 1980s.

Double Apple Bread

2 cups KELLOGG'S APPLE JACKS

1 1/2 cups all-purpose flour

2 teaspoons baking powder

1/2 teaspoon baking soda

1 teaspoon ground cinnamon

1/2 teaspoon ground allspice

1/4 teaspoon salt

1/3 cup butter or margarine, softened

1/2 cup sugar

2 large eggs

1/2 teaspoon pure vanilla extract

1/2 cup fat-free milk

1 cup finely chopped, peeled tart apples

When first on the scene in 1965, APPLE JACKS were pale orange, O-shaped pieces. In the mid-1990s, green shapes were introduced to the mix.

Who would expect to find APPLE JACKS in a loaf of bread? The smart cooks in the KELLOGG KITCHENS thought that this kid-favorite cereal would be just the thing to make an apple bread stand out on the table.

MAKES ONE 9-INCH LOAF

1. Preheat oven to 350°F.

2. Lightly coat a 9 x 5 x 3-inch loaf pan with nonstick cooking spray. Set aside.

3. Place the APPLE JACKS in a resealable plastic bag. Seal the bag and, using a rolling pin, crush the cereal to a medium crumb. Open the bag and measure the crumbs; you should have 1 cup.

4. Combine the crumbs with the flour, baking powder, baking soda, cinnamon, allspice, and salt in a medium bowl. Set aside.

5. Place the butter in the bowl of a standing electric mixer, beating until light. Add the sugar and continue beating until light and fluffy. Beat in the eggs and vanilla. When well blended, alternately add the cereal mixture and the milk, beating until thoroughly incorporated.

6. Remove the bowl from the mixer and fold in the apples.

7. Scrape the batter into the prepared pan. Bake in the preheated oven for about 40 minutes, or until a cake tester inserted in the center comes out clean.

8. Remove from oven and place on a wire rack for 10 minutes.

9. Remove the bread from the pan and place on a wire rack to cool completely before slicing.

TOPPINGS AND STUFFINGS

Spoon-Ons: Sweet and Savory

1 cup KELLOGG'S ALL-BRAN

SAVORY

1 tablespoon Worcestershire sauce

1 tablespoon fresh lemon juice

½ teaspoon hot pepper sauce, or to taste

SWEET

¼ cup warm honey

½ teaspoon ground cinnamon

2 tablespoons warm water

If you keep both styles of Spoon-Ons on hand, you will have an instant garnish for both savory and sweet dishes. Savory Spoon-Ons work particularly well on salads, soups, and casseroles, while the sweet ones are the perfect topping for ice cream, frozen yogurt, and puddings or as the final flourish on an iced cake. MAKES 1 CUP

1. Preheat oven to 325°F.

2. Lightly coat a baking pan with nonstick cooking spray. Set aside.

3. Place the cereal in a mixing bowl.

4. *For the Savory Spoon-Ons,* combine the Worcestershire sauce, lemon juice, and hot pepper sauce, stirring to blend. *For the Sweet Spoon-Ons,* combine the honey and cinnamon with the water, stirring to blend well.

5. Pour seasoning mixture over the cereal and immediately toss to coat. Spread out the mixture in the prepared baking pan.

6. Bake in the preheated oven for about 15 minutes, or until dry and crisp.

7. Remove from oven and set aside to cool completely before serving or storing.

7. Store in an airtight container, at room temperature.

Salad Croutons

5 cups KELLOGG'S CORN FLAKES or SPECIAL K

3 tablespoons butter or margarine, melted

1 tablespoon Italian seasoning

1/2 teaspoon onion salt

1/4 teaspoon freshly ground pepper

3 tablespoons freshly grated Parmesan cheese

This Italian-flavored mix adds a nice crunch to salads—toss it in a mixed green salad or use it as a garnish on meat or fish salads. MAKES 4 1/2 CUPS

1. Preheat oven to 250°F.

2. Lightly coat a 13 x 9 x 2-inch baking pan with nonstick cooking spray. Set aside.

3. Place the cereal in a large mixing bowl.

4. Combine the butter with the seasoning, onion salt, and pepper in a small bowl, stirring to blend. Drizzle over the cereal, tossing to coat. Sprinkle on the cheese and again toss to coat evenly.

5. Transfer the mixture to the prepared pan. Bake in the preheated oven for about 10 minutes, or until the cereal begins to brown and crisp.

6. Remove from oven and set aside to cool completely before serving or storing.

7. Store in an airtight container, at room temperature.

NOTE: To make Mexican-Flavored Croutons, season the cereal with 1 tablespoon chili powder and 1 teaspoon onion powder in place of the Italian seasoning and onion salt. To make Lemon-Pepper Croutons, season the cereal with 1 1/2 teaspoons dried parsley flakes, 1 teaspoon lemon pepper, and 1/4 teaspoon garlic powder in place of the Italian seasoning and onion salt. You can use either olive oil or canola oil in both of these. Follow the same procedures as for the basic recipe.

Crunchy Ice Cream Topping

2 cups KELLOGG'S FROSTED FLAKES

1/2 cup chopped almonds or other nuts

3 tablespoons brown sugar

2 tablespoons butter or margarine, softened

This is a great pantry mix that, at the drop of a hat, turns a scoop of ice cream or frozen yogurt into a special dessert.
MAKES 1 1/2 CUPS

1. Place the FROSTED FLAKES in a resealable plastic bag. Seal the bag and, using a rolling pin, crush the cereal to fine crumbs.

2. Combine the crumbs with the nuts, sugar, and butter in a heavy frying pan over low heat. Cook, stirring constantly, for about 5 minutes, or until the sugar has melted and the mixture is crunchy.

3. Remove from heat and set aside to cool completely before serving or storing.

4. Store in an airtight container, refrigerated or frozen.

Stuffing Using KELLOGG'S® Stuffing Mix

1 package KELLOGG'S Stuffing Mix

1/2 cup finely chopped celery

1/4 cup chopped onion

1/2 cup butter or margarine, melted

1 1/2 cups hot water or chicken broth or vegetable broth

KELLOGG'S Stuffing Mix is the perfect base for any stuffing for meat or poultry. Since the mix is lightly seasoned, the cook can add whatever ingredients will give the stuffing a personal touch. One package of Stuffing Mix weighs 6 ounces and yields about 7 cups. This should make enough stuffing for one 6-pound bird. You will need 3 packages of KELLOGG'S Stuffing Mix moistened with about 1 1/2 cups butter and 3 cups liquid to stuff a large (20 pounds and over) holiday turkey.
ENOUGH FOR A 6-POUND BIRD

1. Pour KELLOGG'S Stuffing Mix into a large mixing bowl.

2. Cook celery and onions in butter until tender. Add to stuffing mix. Toss gently to combine. Add just enough of the water or broth to reach the consistency you prefer and stir lightly to blend. The full of amount of liquid will make a moist stuffing.

3. Stuff the bird (or other meat) as usual or transfer the stuffing to a 1½-quart casserole dish that has been lightly coated with nonstick cooking spray and bake, covered, in a preheated 350°F oven for about 30 minutes, or until heated through and lightly browned.

NOTE: If desired, omit celery and onions. Mix melted butter with Stuffing Mix before adding chicken broth.

KELLOGG'S® Stuffing Guide

Poultry Weight	6–8 lbs.	9–11 lbs.	12–15 lbs.	16–19 lbs.	20 lbs. & over
KELLOGG'S Stuffing Mix (6 oz. pkg.)	1 pkg.	1½ pkgs.	2 pkgs.	2½ pkgs.	3 pkgs.
Finely Chopped Celery	½ cup	1 cup	1 cup	1¼ cups	1½ cups
Chopped Onion	¼ cup	⅓ cup	½ cup	⅔ cup	¾ cup
Butter or Margarine	½ cup	¾ cup	1 cup	1¼ cups	1½ cups
Hot Chicken Broth	1 cup	1½ cups	2 cups	2½ cups	3 cups

Turkey Sausage Stuffing

1/2 pound lean turkey sausage

1 1/2 cups finely chopped celery

2/3 cup finely chopped onion

1 tablespoon chopped fresh parsley

2 teaspoons freshly grated lemon zest

1/4 teaspoon poultry seasoning

1 1/4 cups chicken broth

6 cups KELLOGG'S CORN FLAKES

Salt and freshly ground pepper to taste

This is a great dish to make when you are yearning for the warmth of the Thanksgiving table. All the flavors are here with none of the hard work of a big holiday meal. The casserole can be prepared early in the day and reheated for dinner. The mixture can also be used as a stuffing for turkey or chicken. SERVES 6

1. Preheat oven to 350°F.

2. Lightly coat a 1 1/2-quart casserole dish with nonstick cooking spray. Set aside.

3. Combine the sausage celery, and onions in a large sauté pan over medium heat. Cook, stirring frequently, for about 10 minutes, or until the meat is no longer pink and the vegetables are crisp-tender. Stir in the parsley, lemon zest, and poultry seasoning.

4. Add the broth followed by the cereal, tossing to just combine. Season with salt and pepper to taste.

5. Scrape the mixture into the prepared casserole. Cover and place in the preheated oven. Bake for 30 minutes. Remove the lid and bake for an additional 15 minutes, or until very hot and crisp on the top.

6. Remove from oven and serve.

NUTRITIONAL INFORMATION

Note: Nutrition facts reflect sodium levels based on original recipes provided by Kellogg Company. For the purposes of this cookbook, the editors have allowed for reader choice as to salt (and pepper) added to certain recipes, as reflected by the "to taste" notation. As such, values for sodium will serve as an estimate only and may not reflect the recipe as prepared in the individual home kitchen.

MASTER BREADS MIX (page 2)
Nutrition Facts: Serving size about 1/4 cup (59 grams) · Calories 195 · Fat cal 6 · **% Daily Value** Total fat 1% (0.7g) · Sat fat 1% (0.1g) · Cholest 0% (0mg) · Sodium 22% (524mg) · Total carb 15% (46g) · Fiber 19% (4.8g) · Sugars 15g · Protein 4.8g · Vitamin A 6% · Vitamin C 4% · Calcium 20% · Iron 20%

BREAKFAST QUESADILLA (page 3)
Nutrition Facts: Serving size 4 wedges (198 grams) · Calories 350 · Fat cal 120 · **% Daily Value** Total fat 12% (14g) · Sat fat 27% (5g) · Cholest 7% (20mg) · Sodium 31% (740mg) · Total carb 11% (34g) · Fiber 9% (2g) · Sugars 4g · Protein 24g · Vitamin A 20% · Vitamin C 4% · Calcium 20% · Iron 25%

BAKED FRENCH TOAST (page 4)
Nutrition Facts: Serving size 3 halves (136 grams) · Calories 310 · Fat cal 140 · **% Daily Value** Total fat 24% (16g) · Sat fat 21% (4g) · Cholest 37% (110mg) · Sodium 22% (540mg) · Total carb 11% (33g) · Fiber 0% (0g) · Sugars 6g · Protein 9g · Vitamin A 15% · Vitamin C 15% · Calcium 10% · Iron 30%

EASY FOUR-GRAIN PANCAKES (page 5)
Nutrition Facts: Serving size 1 pancake (76 grams) · Calories 123 · Fat cal 28 · **% Daily Value** Total fat 5% (3g) · Sat fat 6% (1g) · Cholest 14% (41mg) · Sodium 10% (238mg) · Total carb 7% (21g) · Fiber 6% (1g) · Sugars 5g · Protein 4g · Vitamin A 15% · Vitamin C 35% · Calcium 9% · Iron 40%

BRANCAKES (page 6)
Nutrition Facts: Serving size 1 pancake (63 grams) · Calories 103 · Fat cal 21 · **% Daily Value** Total fat 4% (21g) · Sat fat 5% (9g) · Cholest 7% (20mg) · Sodium 9% (205mg) · Total carb 6% (19g) · Fiber 11% (3g) · Sugars 5g · Protein 4g · Vitamin A 8% · Vitamin C 3% · Calcium 11% · Iron 11%

MEATLESS SAUSAGE-SPINACH QUICHE (page 7)
Nutrition Facts: Serving size 1/8 of quiche (181 grams) · Calories 304 · Fat cal 161 · **% Daily Value** Total fat 27% (18g) · Sat fat 30% (6g) · Cholest 7% (20mg) · Sodium 28% (676mg) · Total carb 6% (19g) · Fiber 11% (3g) · Sugars 1g · Protein 18g · Vitamin A 57% · Vitamin C 16% · Calcium 19% · Iron 16%

CHEEZ-IT SOUFFLÉ (page 8)
Nutrition Facts: Serving size 1/6 of souffle (156 grams) · Calories 380 · Fat cal 220 · **% Daily Value** Total fat 37% (24g) · Sat fat 48% (10g) · Cholest 71% (210mg) · Sodium 37% (880mg) · Total carb 9% (26g) · Fiber 3% (1g) · Sugars 4g · Protein 12g · Vitamin A 15% · Vitamin C 2% · Calcium 10% · Iron 4%

BANANA DROP BISCUITS (page 10)
Nutrition Facts: Serving size 1 biscuit (85 grams) · Calories 220 · Fat cal 80 · **% Daily Value** Total fat 13% (8g) · Sat fat 9% (1.5g) · Cholest 0% (0mg) · Sodium 15% (350mg) · Total carb 11% (34g) · Fiber 10% (2g) · Sugars 12g · Protein 4g · Vitamin A 15% · Vitamin C 10% · Calcium 2% · Iron 20%

BAKED BANANA DOUGHNUTS (page 11)
Nutrition Facts: Serving size 1 doughnut (60 grams) · Calories 172 · Fat cal 17 · **% Daily Value** Total fat 3% (2g) · Sat fat 1% (0.19g) · Cholest 0% (0mg) · Sodium 7% (172mg) · Total carb 12% (37g) · Fiber 4% (1g) · Sugars 18g · Protein 3g · Vitamin A 3% · Vitamin C 4% · Calcium 5% · Iron 8%

ORIGINAL **ALL-BRAN** MUFFINS (page 12)
Nutrition Facts: Serving size 1 regular muffin (57 grams) · Calories 170 · Fat cal 45 · **% Daily Value** Total fat 8% (5g) · Sat fat 4% (1g) · Cholest 6% (20mg) · Sodium 11% (270mg) · Total carb 9% (27g) · Fiber 15% (4g) · Sugars 12g · Protein 4g · Vitamin A 8% · Vitamin C 8% · Calcium 15% · Iron 15%

GLAZED PEACH MUFFINS (page 13)
Nutrition Facts: Serving size 1 muffin · Calories 180 · Fat cal 35 · **% Daily Value** Total fat 6% (4g) · Sat fat 0% (0g) · Cholest 0% (0g) · Sodium 14% (350mg) · Total carb 12% (36g) · Fiber 13% (3g) · Sugars 18g · Protein 3g · Vitamin A 6% · Vitamin C 10% · Calcium 10% · Iron 10%

BLUEBERRY LOVER'S MUFFINS (page 15)
Nutrition Facts: Serving size 1 muffin (98 grams) · Calories 180 · Fat cal 35 · **% Daily Value** Total fat 6% (4g) · Sat fat 0% (0g) · Cholest 0% (0g) · Sodium 10% (240mg) · Total carb 11% (34g) · Fiber 12% (3g) · Sugars 12g · Protein 5g · Vitamin A 10% · Vitamin C 15% · Calcium 6% · Iron 25%

ONION-DILL MUFFINS (page 16)

Nutrition Facts: Serving size 1 muffin (77 grams) · Calories 150 · Fat cal 35 · **% Daily Value** Total fat 6% (4g) · Sat fat 0% (0g) · Cholest 0% (0mg) · Sodium 11% (280mg) · Total carb 8% (25g) · Fiber 16% (4g) · Sugars 8g · Protein 5g · Vitamin A 6% · Vitamin C 8% · Calcium 8% · Iron 10%

COCOA-BANANA MUFFINS (page 17)

Nutrition Facts: Serving size 1 muffin · Calories 290 · Fat cal 50 · **% Daily Value** Total fat 9% (6g) · Sat fat 4% (1g) · Cholest 0% (0mg) · Sodium 24% (580mg) · Total carb 20% (59g) · Fiber 25% (6g) · Sugars 33g · Protein 8g · Vitamin A 10% · Vitamin C 15% · Calcium 20% · Iron 20%

APPLESAUCE-RAISIN MUFFINS (page 18)

Nutrition Facts: Serving size 1 muffin (80 grams) · Calories 130 · Fat cal 5 · **% Daily Value** Total fat 1% (0.5g) · Sat fat 0% (0g) · Cholest 0% (0mg) · Sodium 11% (260mg) · Total carb 10% (30g) · Fiber 19% (5g) · Sugars 9g · Protein 4g · Vitamin A 6% · Vitamin C 10% · Calcium 10% · Iron 15%

CORN FLAKE MUFFINS (page 18)

Nutrition Facts: Serving size 1 muffin (59 grams) · Calories 130 · Fat cal 35 · **% Daily Value** Total fat 6% (4g) · Sat fat 3% (0.5g) · Cholest 6% (20mg) · Sodium 10% (230mg) · Total carb 7% (22g) · Fiber 3% (1g) · Sugars 6g · Protein 3g · Vitamin A 15% · Vitamin C 10% · Calcium 10% · Iron 15%

SURPRISE MUFFINS (page 19)

Nutrition Facts: Serving size 1 muffin (63 grams) · Calories 160 · Fat cal 45 · **% Daily Value** Total fat 8% (5g) · Sat fat 4% (1g) · Cholest 6% (20mg) · Sodium 10% (230mg) · Total carb 9% (27g) · Fiber 3% (1g) · Sugars 6g · Protein 3g · Vitamin A 15% · Vitamin C 6% · Calcium 10% · Iron 15%

CHERRY-PEAR MUFFINS (page 20)

Nutrition Facts: Serving size 1 muffin (100 grams) · Calories 230 · Fat cal 25 · **% Daily Value** Total fat 4% (2.5g) · Sat fat 0% (0g) · Cholest 0% (0mg) · Sodium 12% (280mg) · Total carb 16% (49g) · Fiber 7% (2g) · Sugars 28g · Protein 3g · Vitamin A 8% · Vitamin C 10% · Calcium 2% · Iron 25%

CINNAMON-TOPPED DRIED PLUM MUFFINS (page 21)

Nutrition Facts: Serving size 1 muffin (71 grams) · Calories 170 · Fat cal 45 · **% Daily Value** Total fat 8% (5g) · Sat fat 0% (0g) · Cholest 6% (20mg) · Sodium 9% (220mg) · Total carb 10% (30g) · Fiber 6% (2g) · Sugars 9g · Protein 3g · Vitamin A 10% · Vitamin C 20% · Calcium 4% · Iron 20%

STREUSEL BRAN MUFFINS (page 22)

Nutrition Facts: Serving size 1 muffin (65 grams) · Calories 180 · Fat cal 55 · **% Daily Value** Total fat 9% (6g) · Sat fat 4% (1g) · Cholest 0% (0mg) · Sodium 11% (270mg) · Total carb 10% (29g) · Fiber 7% (2g) · Sugars 14g · Protein 3g · Vitamin A 6% · Vitamin C 4% · Calcium 10% · Iron 15%

PINEAPPLE UPSIDE-DOWN MUFFINS (page 24)

Nutrition Facts: Serving size 1 muffin (69 grams) · Calories 180 · Fat cal 60 · **% Daily Value** Total fat 10% (6g) · Sat fat 3% (0.5g) · Cholest 0% (0mg) · Sodium 13% (320mg) · Total carb 10% (29g) · Fiber 5% (1g) · Sugars 17g · Protein 3g · Vitamin A 6% · Vitamin C 6% · Calcium 2% · Iron 10%

BAKED CHEESE STICKS (page 26)

Nutrition Facts: Serving size 2 sticks (75 grams) · Calories 190 · Fat cal 50 · **% Daily Value** Total fat 9% (6g) · Sat fat 19% (4g) · Cholest 7% (20mg) · Sodium 25% (590mg) · Total carb 8% (23g) · Fiber 3% (1g) · Sugars 3g · Protein 12g · Vitamin A 60% · Vitamin C 15% · Calcium 25% · Iron 20%

CRUNCHY ZUCCHINI RINGS (page 28)

Nutrition Facts: Serving size ⅙ of recipe (79 grams) · Calories 79 · Fat cal 2 · **% Daily Value** Total fat 0% (0.26g) · Sat fat 0% (0.06g) · Cholest 0% (0mg) · Sodium 18% (441 mg) · Total carb 6% (18g) · Fiber 5% (1g) · Sugars 2g · Protein 3g · Vitamin A 12% · Vitamin C 22% · Calcium 1% · Iron 32%

TACO BITES (page 29)

Nutrition Facts: Serving size 4 waffle pieces (34 grams) · Calories 100 · Fat cal 30 · **% Daily Value** Total fat 5% (3g) · Sat fat 6% (1g) · Cholest 3% (10mg) · Sodium 14% (340mg) · Total carb 5% (15g) · Fiber 0% (0g) · Sugars 2g · Protein 3g · Vitamin A 10% · Vitamin C 4% · Calcium 2% · Iron 10%

CHEESY HAM SAVORIES (page 30)

Nutrition Facts: Serving size 1 ball (16g) · Calories 49 · Fat cal 20 · **% Daily Value** Total fat 3% (2g) · Sat fat 6% (1g) · Cholest 2% (7mg) · Sodium 4% (105mg) · Total carb 2% (6g) · Fiber 1% (0.23g) · Sugars 0.4g · Protein 2g · Vitamin A 5% · Vitamin C 2% · Calcium 2% · Iron 9%

ALL-BRAN CORN CAKES WITH PROSCIUTTO (page 31)

Nutrition Facts: Serving size 1 corn cake sandwich (260 grams) · Calories 364 · Fat cal 82 · **% Daily Value** Total fat 14% (9g) · Sat fat 12% (0.5g) · Cholest 23% (70mg) · Sodium 70% (1687mg) · Total carb 18% (55g) · Fiber 25% (6g) · Sugars 6g · Protein 21g · Vitamin A 15% · Vitamin C 38% · Calcium 26% · Iron 30%

CHICKEN FINGERS (page 32)

Nutrition Facts: Serving size 3–5 fingers (118 grams) · Calories 282 · Fat cal 94 · **% Daily Value** Total fat 16% (10g) · Sat fat 8% (2g) · Cholest 19% (58mg) · Sodium 35% (833mg) · Total carb 11% (32g) · Fiber 2% (0.45g) · Sugars 3g · Protein 14g · Vitamin A 3% · Vitamin C 1% · Calcium 1% · Iron 33%

SALMON AND LEMON PÂTÉ (page 33)

Nutrition Facts: Serving size about ¼ cup (64 grams) · Calories 173 · Fat cal 88 · **% Daily Value** Total fat 15% (10g) · Sat fat 22% (4g) · Cholest 13% (38mg) · Sodium 12% (287mg) · Total carb 4% (12g) · Fiber 2% (.44g) · Sugars 2g · Protein 10g · Vitamin A 19% · Vitamin C 22% · Calcium 8% · Iron 25%

CRAB AND SHRIMP APPETIZER BALLS (page 34)

Nutrition Facts: Serving size 3 balls + 1 tablespoon sauce (56 grams) · Calories 90 · Fat cal 35 · **% Daily Value** Total fat 6% (4g) · Sat fat 5% (1g) · Cholest 9% (25mg) · Sodium 13% (320mg) · Total carb 2% (7g) · Fiber 0% (0g) · Sugars 1g · Protein 6g · Vitamin A 6% · Vitamin C 8% · Calcium 4% · Iron 4%

CRISPIX MIX ORIGINAL (page 36)

Nutrition Facts: Serving size ¹/₂ cup (27 grams) · Calories 120 · Fat cal 60 · **% Daily Value** Total fat 11% (7g) · Sat fat 8% (1.5g) · Cholest 0% (0mg) · Sodium 9% (210mg) · Total carb 5% (14g) · Fiber 5% (1g) · Sugars 3g · Protein 2g · Vitamin A 8% · Vitamin C 10% · Calcium 2% · Iron 6%

MAPLE PRALINE MIX (page 37)

Nutrition Facts: Serving size ¹/₂ cup (40g) · Calories 170 · Fat cal 80 · **% Daily Value** Total fat 13% (9g) · Sat fat 8% (1.5g) · Cholest 0% (0mg) · Sodium 7% (170mg) · Total carb 8% (23g) · Fiber 5% (1g) · Sugars 9g · Protein 2g · Vitamin A 10% · Vitamin C 15% · Calcium 2% · Iron 8%

CEREAL SCRAMBLE (page 37)

Nutrition Facts: Serving size 1 cup (94 grams) · Calories 420 · Fat cal 150 · **% Daily Value** Total fat 26% (17g) · Sat fat 30% (6g) · Cholest 0% (0mg) · Sodium 3% (80mg) · Total carb 21% (63g) · Fiber 26% (7g) · Sugars 36g · Protein 8g · Vitamin A 6% · Vitamin C 45% · Calcium 4% · Iron 35%

SPICY MIX-UP (page 38)

Nutrition Facts: Serving size ¹/₂ cup (19 g) · Calories 80 · Fat cal 30 · **% Daily Value** Total fat 5% (3.5g) · Sat fat 8% (1.5g) · Cholest 2% (5mg) · Sodium 9% (220mg) · Total carb 4% (12g) · Fiber 3% (1g) · Sugars 1g · Protein 2g · Vitamin A 15% · Vitamin C 10% · Calcium 2% · Iron 4%

CORN POPS CRUNCH SNACK (page 39)

Nutrition Facts: Serving size about ¹/₂ cup (33 grams) · Calories 170 · Fat cal 110 · **% Daily Value** Total fat 18% (12g) · Sat fat 9% (1.5g) · Cholest 0% (0mg) · Sodium 11% (270 mg) · Total carb 5% (15g) · Fiber 3% (1g) · Sugars 7g · Protein 1g · Vitamin A 15% · Vitamin C 10% · Calcium 0% · Iron 6%

BARBECUED CORN DOGS (page 39)

Nutrition Facts: Serving size ¹/₂ cup (226 grams) · Calories 270 · Fat cal 35 · **% Daily Value** Total fat 6% (4g) · Sat fat 2% (0g) · Cholest 0% (0mg) · Sodium 35% (850 mg) · Total carb 15% (52g) · Fiber 10% (3g) · Sugars 21g · Protein 9g · Vitamin A 8% · Vitamin C 20% · Calcium 4% · Iron 8%

SPICY BEAN DIP (page 40)

Nutrition Facts: Serving size 2 tablespoons (40 grams) · Calories 30 · Fat cal 0 · **% Daily Value** Total fat 0% (0g) · Sat fat 0% (0g) · Cholest 0% (0mg) · Sodium 6% (160mg) · Total carb 2% (7g) · Fiber 8% (2g) · Sugars 1g · Protein 2g · Vitamin A 4% · Vitamin C 4% · Calcium 2% · Iron 4%

CRUMBLE-POTATO WONTONS (page 41)

Nutrition Facts: Serving size 2 wontons (71 grams) · Calories 110 · Fat cal 30 · **% Daily Value** Total fat 5% (3.5g) · Sat fat 4% (1g) · Cholest 0% (0mg) · Sodium 11% (260mg) · Total carb 4% (13g) · Fiber 7% (2g) · Sugars 1g · Protein 7g · Vitamin A 0% · Vitamin C 4% · Calcium 2% · Iron 10%

CHEESE WAFERS (page 42)

Nutrition Facts: Serving size 2 wafers (16 grams) · Calories 60 · Fat cal 35 · **% Daily Value** Total fat 6% (4g) · Sat fat 7% (1.5g) · Cholest 2% (5mg) · Sodium 6% (140mg) · Total carb 1% (3g) · Fiber 0% (0g) · Sugars 0g · Protein 3g · Vitamin A 6% · Vitamin C 2% · Calcium 6% · Iron 2%

FRESH TOMATO GAZPACHO (page 44)

Nutrition Facts: Serving size ¹/₆ recipe (326 grams) · Calories 190 · Fat cal 70 · **% Daily Value** Total fat 13% (8g) · Sat fat 8% (1.5g) · Cholest 12% (35mg) · Sodium 27% (660mg) · Total carb 9% (26g) · Fiber 15% (4g) · Sugars 10g · Protein 7g · Vitamin A 40% · Vitamin C 100% · Calcium 4% · Iron 15%

CHICKEN NOODLE SOUP (page 46)

Nutrition Facts: Serving size 2 cups (462 grams) · Calories 294 · Fat cal 72 · **% Daily Value** Total fat 12% (8g) · Sat fat 11% (2g) · Cholest 34% (101mg) · Sodium 89% (2129mg) · Total carb 10% (29g) · Fiber 22% (5g) · Sugars 4g · Protein 29g · Vitamin A 36% · Vitamin C 9% · Calcium 9% · Iron 25%

MINESTRONE (page 47)

Nutrition Facts: Serving size 1¹/₂ cups (399 grams) · Calories 170 · Fat cal 45 · **% Daily Value** Total fat 8% (5g) · Sat fat 4% (1g) · Cholest 0% (0mg) · Sodium 60% (1430mg) · Total carb 10% (29g) · Fiber 34% (9g) · Sugars 10g · Protein 9g · Vitamin A 120% · Vitamin C 50% · Calcium 15% · Iron 20%

TABBOULEH (page 48)

Nutrition Facts: Serving size 1 cup (160 grams) · Calories 180 · Fat cal 35 · **% Daily Value** Total fat 7% (4g) · Sat fat 3% (0.5g) · Cholest 0% (0mg) · Sodium 16% (380mg) · Total carb 10% (30g) · Fiber 39% (10g) · Sugars 6g · Protein 7g · Vitamin A 35% · Vitamin C 70% · Calcium 20% · Iron 100%

CATFISH SALAD SUPREME (page 49)

Nutrition Facts: Serving size 1 cup (373 grams) · Calories 150 · Fat cal 25 · **% Daily Value** Total fat 4% (3g) · Sat fat 3% (0.5g) · Cholest 15% (45mg) · Sodium 25% (600mg) · Total carb 6% (18g) · Fiber 28% (7g) · Sugars 6g · Protein 16g · Vitamin A 60% · Vitamin C 70% · Calcium 10% · Iron 20%

TURKEY-SPINACH SALAD (page 50)

Nutrition Facts: Serving size 1 salad (446 grams) · Calories 520 · Fat cal 90 · **% Daily Value** Total fat 15% (10g) · Sat fat 8% (1.5g) · Cholest 23% (70mg) · Sodium 31% (750mg) · Total carb 25% (74g) · Fiber 24% (6g) · Sugars 42g · Protein 39g · Vitamin A 15% · Vitamin C 90% · Calcium 15% · Iron 75%

LEMONY APPLE-BRAN SALAD (page 51)
Nutrition Facts: Serving size about 1/2 cup + lettuce (101 grams) · Calories 70 · Fat cal 5 · **% Daily Value** Total fat 1% (0.5g) · Sat fat 0% (0g) · Cholest 0% (0mg) · Sodium 3% (70mg) · Total carb 5% (15g) · Fiber 13% (3g) · Sugars 11g · Protein 2g · Vitamin A 6% · Vitamin C 15% · Calcium 6% · Iron 6%

WILTED LETTUCE SALAD (page 52)
Nutrition Facts: Serving size 1/2 cup (152 grams) · Calories 220 · Fat cal 170 · **% Daily Value** Total fat 28% (18g) · Sat fat 31% (6g) · Cholest 6% (20mg) · Sodium 18% (420mg) · Total carb 4% (13g) · Fiber 20% (5g) · Sugars 5g · Protein 6g · Vitamin A 20% · Vitamin C 20% · Calcium 10% · Iron 15%

DOUBLE-COATED CHICKEN (page 54)
Nutrition Facts: Serving size 1 piece without skin (332 grams) · Calories 510 · Fat cal 80 · **% Daily Value** Total fat 14% (9g) · Sat fat 11% (2g) · Cholest 56% (170mg) · Sodium 32% (780mg) · Total carb 15% (45g) · Fiber 7% (2g) · Sugars 5g · Protein 59g · Vitamin A 25% · Vitamin C 35% · Calcium 8% · Iron 70%

HOT AND SPICY CHICKEN QUESADILLAS (page 56)
Nutrition Facts: Serving size 1/8 of full quesadilla (234 grams) · Calories 620 · Fat cal 220 · **% Daily Value** Total fat 38% (25g) · Sat fat 53% (11g) · Cholest 39% (115mg) · Sodium 55% (1310mg) · Total carb 19% (56g) · Fiber 0% (0g) · Sugars 2g · Protein 43g · Vitamin A 6% · Vitamin C 30% · Calcium 30% · Iron 25%

CHICKEN ITALIENNE (page 57)
Nutrition Facts: Serving size 1/6 recipe (292 grams) · Calories 580 · Fat cal 310 · **% Daily Value** Total fat 53% (34g) · Sat fat 50% (10g) · Cholest 57% (170mg) · Sodium 34% (810mg) · Total carb 8% (23g) · Fiber 6% (1g) · Sugars 3g · Protein 44g · Vitamin A 25% · Vitamin C 35% · Calcium 4% · Iron 50%

CRISP ORANGE-BAKED CHICKEN (page 58)
Nutrition Facts: Serving size 1 piece (302 grams) · Calories 630 · Fat cal 330 · **% Daily Value** Total fat 56% (36g) · Sat fat 53% (11g) · Cholest 80% (240mg) · Sodium 24% (580mg) · Total carb 9% (27g) · Fiber 4% (1g) · Sugars 4g · Protein 47g · Vitamin A 20% · Vitamin C 40% · Calcium 40% · Iron 50%

LEMON-HERB CHICKEN (page 60)
Nutrition Facts: Serving size 1 piece (250 grams) · Calories 330 · Fat cal 110 · **% Daily Value** Total fat 18% (12g) · Sat fat 12% (2.5g) · Cholest 40% (115mg) · Sodium 30% (750mg) · Total carb 6% (19g) · Fiber 3% (1g) · Sugars 2g · Protein 38g · Vitamin A 50% · Vitamin C 25% · Calcium 2% · Iron 40%

CHICKEN KIEV (page 61)
Nutrition Facts: Serving size 1 breast (123 grams) · Calories 320 · Fat cal 197 · **% Daily Value** Total fat 34% (22g) · Sat fat 48% (10g) · Cholest 29% (87mg) · Sodium 28% (669mg) · Total carb 4% (13g) · Fiber 1% (0.13g) · Sugars 1.5g · Protein 18g · Vitamin A 18% · Vitamin C 2% · Calcium 2% · Iron 17%

CRUNCHY BAKED CHICKEN (page 62)
Nutrition Facts: Serving size 1/6 recipe (354 grams) · Calories 821 · Fat cal 576 · **% Daily Value** Total fat 99% (64g) · Sat fat 95% (19g) · Cholest 151% (454g) · Sodium 85% (2036mg) · Total carb 5% (16g) · Fiber 4% (1g) · Sugars 2g · Protein 37g · Vitamin A 64% · Vitamin C 46% · Calcium 7% · Iron 38%

DEEP-DISH CHICKEN PIE (page 64)
Nutrition Facts: Serving size 1/10 pie (254 grams) · Calories 335 · Fat cal 122 · **% Daily Value** Total fat 21% (14g) · Sat fat 19% (4g) · Cholest 8% (25mg) · Sodium 24% (578mg) · Total carb 13% (38g) · Fiber 13% (3g) · Sugars 5.6g · Protein 14g · Vitamin A 71% · Vitamin C 24% · Calcium 5% · Iron 18%

CHICKEN-VEGETABLE CRÊPES (page 66)
Nutrition Facts: Serving size 2 filled crêpes · Calories 144 · Fat cal 27 · **% Daily Value** Total fat 5% (3g) · Sat fat 5% (1g) · Cholest 8% (24mg) · Sodium 5% (129mg) · Total carb 6% (17g) · Fiber 11% (3g) · Sugars 7g · Protein 14g · Vitamin A 21% · Vitamin C 44% · Calcium 14% · Iron 10%

APRICOT-GLAZED CHICKEN (page 68)
Nutrition Facts: Serving size 1 chicken roll (364 grams) · Calories 440 · Fat cal 50 · **% Daily Value** Total fat 9% (6g) · Sat fat 7% (1.5g) · Cholest 46% (135mg) · Sodium 22% (520mg) · Total carb 14% (41g) · Fiber 20% (5g) · Sugars 18g · Protein 57g · Vitamin A 8% · Vitamin C 25% · Calcium 6% · Iron 60%

CHICKEN ENCHILADA CASSEROLE (page 69)
Nutrition Facts: Serving size about 2/3 cup (215 grams) · Calories 260 · Fat cal 80 · **% Daily Value** Total fat 14% (9g) · Sat fat 16% (3.5g) · Cholest 24% (70mg) · Sodium 20% (480mg) · Total carb 6% (17g) · Fiber 10% (2g) · Sugars 5g · Protein 27g · Vitamin A 20% · Vitamin C 15% · Calcium 20% · Iron 15%

BAKED CHICKEN SUPREME (page 70)
Nutrition Facts: Serving size 1 piece (307 grams) · Calories 670 · Fat cal 370 · **% Daily Value** Total fat 64% (42g) · Sat fat 60% (12g) · Cholest 70% (210mg) · Sodium 42% (1010mg) · Total carb 9% (28g) · Fiber 3% (1g) · Sugars 3g · Protein 47g · Vitamin A 25% · Vitamin C 20% · Calcium 8% · Iron 20%

NACHOS CASSEROLE (page 71)
Nutrition Facts: Serving size 1 cup (254 grams) · Calories 350 · Fat cal 120 · **% Daily Value** Total fat 21% (13g) · Sat fat 30% (6g) · Cholest 27% (80mg) · Sodium 35% (840mg) · Total carb 10% (30g) · Fiber 16% (4g) · Sugars 8g · Protein 27g · Vitamin A 25% · Vitamin C 35% · Calcium 25% · Iron 45%

GROUND TURKEY AND SPINACH ROLL (page 72)
Nutrition Facts: Serving size 1 slice (181 grams) · Calories 192 · Fat cal 79 · **% Daily Value** Total fat 13% (9g) · Sat fat 14% (3g) · Cholest 24% (71mg) · Sodium 20% (476mg) · Total carb 3% (10g) · Fiber 15% (4g) · Sugars 4g · Protein 40% (20g) · Vitamin A 35% · Vitamin C 21% · Calcium 13% · Iron 19%

CREOLE TURKEY ON A BUN (page 73)
Nutrition Facts: Serving size 1 sandwich (200 grams) · Calories 270 · Fat cal 80 · **% Daily Value** Total fat 14% (9g) · Sat fat 12% (2g) · Cholest 16% (46mg) · Sodium 26% (590mg) · Total carb 12% (34g) · Fiber 11% (2g) · Sugars 7g · Protein 15g · Vitamin A 20% · Vitamin C 30% · Calcium 10% · Iron 26%

BUSY-DAY TURKEY LOAF (page 74)
Nutrition Facts: Serving size 1 slice (133 grams) · Calories 170 · Fat cal 60 · **% Daily Value** Total fat 10% (6g) · Sat fat 9% (2g) · Cholest 20% (60mg) · Sodium 22% (520mg) · Total carb 4% (11g) · Fiber 0% (0g) · Sugars 4g · Protein 16g · Vitamin A 4% · Vitamin C 4% · Calcium 4% · Iron 8%

STIR-FRY BEEF AND VEGETABLES (page 75)
Nutrition Facts: Serving size 1/5 recipe · Calories 720 · Fat cal 28 · **% Daily Value** Total fat 28% (18g) · Sat fat 31% (4g) · Cholest 27% (80mg) · Sodium 28% (910mg) · Total carb 35% (105g) · Fiber 45% (11g) · Sugars 9g · Protein 38g · Vitamin A 35% · Vitamin C 20% · Calcium 10% · Iron 45%

MEAT 'N' TATER PIE (page 76)
Nutrition Facts: Serving size 1/6 pie (207 grams) · Calories 330 · Fat cal 160 · **% Daily Value** Total fat 27% (17g) · Sat fat 39% (8g) · Cholest 39% (115mg) · Sodium 33% (800mg) · Total carb 7% (20g) · Fiber 9% (2g) · Sugars 3g · Protein 22g · Vitamin A 15% · Vitamin C 20% · Calcium 15% · Iron 30%

TANGY MEATBALLS (page 77)
Nutrition Facts: Serving size 6 meatballs (236 grams) · Calories 375 · Fat cal 155 · **% Daily Value** Total fat 26% (17g) · Sat fat 33% (7g) · Cholest 32% (95mg) · Sodium 59% (1400mg) · Total carb 11% (34g) · Fiber 8% (2g) · Sugars 23g · Protein 21g · Vitamin A 15% · Vitamin C 30% · Calcium 20% · Iron 15%

HAMBURGER PIZZA PIE (page 78)
Nutrition Facts: Serving size 1/6 pie · Calories 280 · Fat cal 110 · **% Daily Value** Total fat 18% (12g) · Sat fat 29% (6g) · Cholest 14% (45mg) · Sodium 26% (610mg) · Total carb 6% (17g) · Fiber 7% (2g) · Sugars 6g · Protein 26g · Vitamin A 20% · Vitamin C 20% · Calcium 25% · Iron 30%

SPICY TOMATO MINI-LOAVES (page 79)
Nutrition Facts: Serving size 1 loaf (199 grams) · Calories 380 · Fat cal 190 · **% Daily Value** Total fat 33% (21g) · Sat fat 46% (9g) · Cholest 38% (115mg) · Sodium 22% (530mg) · Total carb 8% (24g) · Fiber 3% (1g) · Sugars 10g · Protein 24g · Vitamin A 15% · Vitamin C 60% · Calcium 2% · Iron 40%

STUFFED PEPPERS (page 80)
Nutrition Facts: Serving size 1 pepper (394 grams) · Calories 300 · Fat cal 100 · **% Daily Value** Total fat 18% (12g) · Sat fat 23% (4.5g) · Cholest 13% (40mg) · Sodium 36% (860mg) · Total carb 10% (30g) · Fiber 22% (6g) · Sugars 12g · Protein 23g · Vitamin A 50% · Vitamin C 270% · Calcium 10% · Iron 25%

SLOPPY JOES (page 81)
Nutrition Facts: Serving size 1/2 cup + 1 bun (160 grams) · Calories 310 · Fat cal 100 · **% Daily Value** Total fat 22% (14g) · Sat fat 26% (5g) · Cholest 14% (45mg) · Sodium 31% (750mg) · Total carb 11% (33g) · Fiber 8% (2g) · Sugars 6g · Protein 15g · Vitamin A 25% · Vitamin C 30% · Calcium 8% · Iron 30%

CORN FLAKE ENCHILADAS (page 82)
Nutrition Facts: Serving size 2 enchiladas (436 grams) · Calories 510 · Fat cal 200 · **% Daily Value** Total fat 35% (22g) · Sat fat 56% (11g) · Cholest 22% (65mg) · Sodium 42% (1020mg) · Total carb 16% (48g) · Fiber 27% (7g) · Sugars 5g · Protein 32g · Vitamin A 60% · Vitamin C 60% · Calcium 40% · Iron 35%

VEAL CORDON BLEU (page 83)
Nutrition Facts: Serving size 1 roll (198 grams) · Calories 407 · Fat cal 153 · **% Daily Value** Total fat 26% (17g) · Sat fat 40% (8g) · Cholest 43% (130mg) · Sodium 28% (674mg) · Total carb 9% (27g) · Fiber 1% (0.37g) · Sugars 3g · Protein 34g · Vitamin A 5% · Vitamin C 1% · Calcium 23% · Iron 30%

VEAL SCALOPPINI (page 84)
Nutrition Facts: Serving size 1 chop (283 grams) · Calories 388 · Fat cal 193 · **% Daily Value** Total fat 33% (21g) · Sat fat 31% (6g) · Cholest 33% (99mg) · Sodium 26% (623mg) · Total carb 6% (17g) · Fiber 5% (1g) · Sugars 4g · Protein 32g · Vitamin A 16% · Vitamin C 30% · Calcium 31% · Iron 38%

OVEN-CRISPED PORK CHOPS (page 86)
Nutrition Facts: Serving size 1 chop (149 grams) Calories 256 · Fat cal 105 · **% Daily Value** Total fat 18% (12g) · Sat fat 21% (4g) · Cholest 31% (94mg) · Sodium 39% (929mg) · Total carb 5% (14g) · Fiber 1% (0.16g) · Sugars 2g · Protein 23g · Vitamin A 1% · Vitamin C 6% · Calcium 3% · Iron 19%

GINGER PORK WITH APPLESAUCE (page 87)
Nutrition Facts: Serving size 1 pork filet (206 grams) · Calories 292 · Fat cal 37 · **% Daily Value** Total fat 6% (4g) · Sat fat 6% (1g) · Cholest 31% (94mg) · Sodium 36% (856mg) · Total carb 7% (21g) · Fiber 3% (0.79g) · Sugars 6g · Protein 41g · Vitamin A 11% · Vitamin C 7% · Calcium 2% · Iron 38%

JEWELER'S PURSE PORK LOIN (page 88)
Nutrition Facts: Serving size 5 ounces (140 grams) · Calories 560 · Fat cal 360 · **% Daily Value** Total fat 61% (40g) · Sat fat 75% (15g) · Cholest 47% (140mg) · Sodium 24% (560mg) · Total carb 4% (12g) · Fiber 4% (1g) · Sugars 2g · Protein 37g · Vitamin A 6% · Vitamin C 0% · Calcium 2% · Iron 40%

PORK STRIPS WITH SALSA (page 90)
Nutrition Facts: Serving size 4 strips + 1/4 cup salsa (182 grams) · Calories 270 · Fat cal 50 · **% Daily Value** Total fat 9% (6g) · Sat fat 10% (2g) · Cholest 26% (80mg) · Sodium 34% (810mg) · Total carb 9% (26g) · Fiber 3% (1g) · Sugars 6g · Protein 29g · Vitamin A 10% · Vitamin C 35% · Calcium 2% · Iron 40%

APPLE-GLAZED HAM LOAF (page 91)
Nutrition Facts: Serving size 1 slice (145 grams) · Calories 310 · Fat cal 100 · **% Daily Value** Total fat 17% (11g) · Sat fat 19% (4g) · Cholest 31% (90mg) · Sodium 27% (640mg) · Total carb 10% (31g) · Fiber 2% (1g) · Sugars 24g · Protein 22g · Vitamin A 20% · Vitamin C 10% · Calcium 4% · Iron 20%

HAM AND CHEESE MONTE CRISTOS (page 92)
Nutrition Facts: Serving size 1 sandwich (189 grams) · Calories 391 · Fat cal 127 · **% Daily Value** Total fat 22% (14g) · Sat fat 34% (7g) · Cholest 15% (45mg) · Sodium 54% (1293mg) · Total carb 16% (47g) · Fiber 9% (2g) · Sugars 6g · Protein 22g · Vitamin A 21% · Vitamin C 7% · Calcium 37% · Iron 21%

CATFISH SOUTHERN SHORES (page 94)
Nutrition Facts: Serving size 1/4 recipe (151 grams) · Calories 260 · Fat cal 80 · **% Daily Value** Total fat 14% (9g) · Sat fat 11% (2g) · Cholest 18% (55mg) · Sodium 16% (390mg) · Total carb 10% (29g) · Fiber 19% (5g) · Sugars 5g · Protein 21g · Vitamin A 25% · Vitamin C 25% · Calcium 4% · Iron 45%

PAN-ROASTED CRISP SEA BASS (page 95)
Nutrition Facts: Serving size 1/6 recipe (309 grams) · Calories 424 · Fat cal 225 · **% Daily Value** Total fat 38% (25g) · Sat fat 24% (5g) · Cholest 43% (130mg) · Sodium 28% (680mg) · Total carb 3% (10g) · Fiber 8% (2g) · Sugars 3g · Protein 39g · Vitamin A 19% · Vitamin C 6% · Calcium 5% · Iron 8%

FISH NUGGETS WITH CREOLE SAUCE (page 96)
Nutrition Facts: Serving size 6 nuggets + 1/4 cup sauce (209 grams) · Calories 220 · Fat cal 40 · **% Daily Value** Total fat 6% (4g) · Sat fat 20% (4g) · Cholest 19% (55mg) · Sodium 23% (560mg) · Total carb 10% (31g) · Fiber 10% (3g) · Sugars 8g · Protein 17g · Vitamin A 46% · Vitamin C 50% · Calcium 10% · Iron 40%

VEGETABLE-STUFFED FISH ROLLS (page 97)
Nutrition Facts: Serving size 1/6 recipe (227 grams) · Calories 437 · Fat cal 214 · **% Daily Value** Total fat 37% (24g) · Sat fat 31% (6g) · Cholest 29% (88mg) · Sodium 24% (571mg) · Total carb 9% (26g) · Fiber 6% (1.5g) · Sugars 5g · Protein 31g · Vitamin A 54% · Vitamin C 43% · Calcium 6% · Iron 50%

TUNA CROQUETTES WITH DILL-MUSTARD SAUCE (page 99)
Nutrition Facts: Serving size 1 croquette + 1/4 cup sauce · Calories 150 · Fat cal 20 · **% Daily Value** Total fat 4% (2.5g) · Sat fat 0% (0g) · Cholest 4% (15mg) · Sodium 22% (530 mg) · Total carb 7% (20g) · Fiber 22% (6g) · Sugars 7g · Protein 14g · Vitamin A 15% · Vitamin C 30% · Calcium 15% · Iron 20%

SHRIMP WITH BLACK PEPPER–SEASONED **CORN POPS** (page 100)
Nutrition Facts: Serving size 1/10 recipe (179g) · Calories 163 · Fat cal 98 · **% Daily Value** Total fat 17% (11g) · Sat fat 16% (3g) · Cholest 17% (50mg) · Sodium 9% (222mg) · Total carb 3% (10g) · Fiber 3% (0.77g) · Sugars 4g · Protein 8g · Vitamin A 14% · Vitamin C 23% · Calcium 4% · Iron 12%

SEAFOOD FONDUE (page 102)
Nutrition Facts: Serving size 1/9 recipe serving without sauce (157 grams) · Calories 310 · Fat cal 141 · **% Daily Value** Total fat 24% (16g) · Sat fat 7% (1g) · Cholest 31% (93mg) · Sodium 21% (502mg) · Total carb 6% (17g) · Fiber 1% (0.22g) · Sugars 1.3g · Protein 24g · Vitamin A 4% · Vitamin C 3% · Calcium 4% · Iron 19%

CRISPY LEMON-DILL FISH FILLETS (page 104)
Nutrition Facts: Serving size 1 fillet (180 grams) · Calories 250 · Fat cal 70 · **% Daily Value** Total fat 12% (8g) · Sat fat 8% (1.5g) · Cholest 19% (55mg) · Sodium 24% (570mg) · Total carb 5% (16g) · Fiber 3% (1g) · Sugars 1g · Protein 28g · Vitamin A 20% · Vitamin C 25% · Calcium 2% · Iron 35%

GARDEN-FRESH LASAGNA (page 105)
Nutrition Facts: Serving size 1 piece (217 grams) · Calories 210 · Fat cal 65 · **% Daily Value** Total fat 10% (7g) · Sat fat 20% (4g) · Cholest 10% (30mg) · Sodium 25% (600mg) · Total carb 8% (25g) · Fiber 30% (6g) · Sugars 8g · Protein 16g · Vitamin A 82% · Vitamin C 42% · Calcium 48% · Iron 24%

"SPROUTING OUT" CUSTARD PIE (page 106)
Nutrition Facts: Serving size 1 slice (214g) · Calories 230 · Fat cal 80 · **% Daily Value** Total fat 14% (9g) · Sat fat 15% (3g) · Cholest 5% (15mg) · Sodium 22% (540mg) · Total carb 9% (26g) · Fiber 19% (5g) · Sugars 11g · Protein 15g · Vitamin A 20% · Vitamin C 30% · Calcium 25% · Iron 25%

EGGS CHIMAY (page 107)
Nutrition Facts: Serving size 1 filled egg · Calories 205 · Fat cal 99 · **% Daily Value** Total fat 17% (11g) · Sat fat 13% (3g) · Cholest 83% (248mg) · Sodium 15% (361mg) · Total carb 5% (16g) · Fiber 1% (0.3g) · Sugars 2g · Protein 9g · Vitamin A 11% · Vitamin C 1% · Calcium 3% · Iron 19%

SUMMER SQUASH AND CHILIES BAKE (page 110)
Nutrition Facts: Serving size 1/2 cup · Calories 210 · Fat cal 110 · **% Daily Value** Total fat 19% (12g) · Sat fat 28% (6g) · Cholest 14% (40mg) · Sodium 27% (640mg) · Total carb 4% (13g) · Fiber 7% (2g) · Sugars 4g · Protein 12g · Vitamin A 20% · Vitamin C 35% · Calcium 25% · Iron 6%

VANILLA-SCENTED BAKED WINTER SQUASH AND APPLES (page 111)
Nutrition Facts: Serving size about 2/3 cup (148 grams) · Calories 169 · Fat cal 64 · **% Daily Value** Total fat 11% (7g) · Sat fat 11% (2g) · Cholest 3% (10mg) · Sodium 11% (261mg) · Total carb 9% (27g) · Fiber 14% (4g) · Sugars 13g · Protein 2g · Vitamin A 71% · Vitamin C 52% · Calcium 5% · Iron 38%

ZUCCHINI AND TOMATOES (page 112)
Nutrition Facts: Serving size 1/2 cup (165 grams) · Calories 80 · Fat cal 45 · **% Daily Value** Total fat 7% (5g) · Sat fat 5% (1g) · Cholest 0% (0mg) · Sodium 8% (190mg) · Total carb 3% (10g) · Fiber 8% (2g) · Sugars 3g · Protein 2g · Vitamin A 20% · Vitamin C 40% · Calcium 2% · Iron 10%

OVEN-FRIED ONION RINGS (page 113)
Nutrition Facts: Serving size 4 rings (188 grams) · Calories 150 · Fat cal 0 · **% Daily Value** Total fat 0% (0g) · Sat fat 0% (0g) · Cholest 0% (0mg) · Sodium 22% (520mg) · Total carb 11% (33g) · Fiber 14% (4g) · Sugars 11g · Protein 5g · Vitamin A 10% · Vitamin C 35% · Calcium 4% · Iron 35%

STUFFED ZUCCHINI BOATS (page 114)
Nutrition Facts: Serving size 1 stuffed zucchini half · Calories 50 · Fat cal 10 · **% Daily Value** Total fat 1% (1g) · Sat fat 0% (0g) · Cholest 0% (0mg) · Sodium 11% (260mg) · Total carb 4% (11g) · Fiber 17% (4g) · Sugars 4g · Protein 3g · Vitamin A 15% · Vitamin C 30% · Calcium 6% · Iron 10%

WINTER VEGETABLES AU GRATIN (page 116)
Nutrition Facts: Serving size ³/4 cup (206 grams) · Calories 260 · Fat cal 120 · **% Daily Value** Total fat 20% (13g) · Sat fat 20% (4g) · Cholest 7% (20mg) · Sodium 35% (840mg) · Total carb 8% (23g) · Fiber 12% (3g) · Sugars 6g · Protein 12g · Vitamin A 150% · Vitamin C 90% · Calcium 30% · Iron 15%

TURNIP-APPLE BAKE (page 118)
Nutrition Facts: Serving size ¹/2 cup (130 grams) · Calories 113 · Fat cal 47 · **% Daily Value** Total fat 8% (5g) · Sat fat 13% (3g) · Cholest 5% (14mg) · Sodium 18% (434mg) · Total carb 4% (13g) · Fiber 6% (2g) · Sugars 6g · Protein 4g · Vitamin A 6% · Vitamin C 16% · Calcium 6% · Iron 8%

CORN FRITTERS (page 119)
Nutrition Facts: Serving size ¹/2 cup (116 grams) · Calories 193 · Fat cal 60 · **% Daily Value** Total fat 10% (7g) · Sat fat 3% (0.5g) · Cholest 0% (1mg) · Sodium 28% (676mg) · Total carb 9% (28g) · Fiber 14% (4g) · Sugars 5g · Protein 5g · Vitamin A 1% · Vitamin C 47% · Calcium 3% · Iron 48%

BACON-SPINACH STUFFED TOMATOES (page 120)
Nutrition Facts: Serving size 1 stuffed tomato (133 grams) · Calories 170 · Fat cal 69 · **% Daily Value** Total fat 12% (8g) · Sat fat 20% (4g) · Cholest 8% (24g) · Sodium 24% (581mg) · Total carb 4% (12g) · Fiber 6% (1.5g) · Sugars 4g · Protein 13g · Vitamin A 32% · Vitamin C 33% · Calcium 24% · Iron 20%

OVEN-FRIED GREEN TOMATOES (page 121)
Nutrition Facts: Serving size 2 slices (78 grams) · Calories 110 · Fat cal 0 · **% Daily Value** Total fat 0% (0g) · Sat fat 0% (0g) · Cholest 0% (0mg) · Sodium 18% (420mg) · Total carb 8% (24g) · Fiber 6% (1g) · Sugars 3g · Protein 4g · Vitamin A 50% · Vitamin C 35% · Calcium 0% · Iron 35%

MALLOW-WHIPPED SWEET POTATOES (page 122)
Nutrition Facts: Serving size ¹/2 cup (194 grams) · Calories 290 · Fat cal 55 · **% Daily Value** Total fat 8% (6g) · Sat fat 5% (1g) · Cholest 0% (0mg) · Sodium 18% (400mg) · Total carb 20% (57g) · Fiber 12% (2.5g) · Sugars 40g · Protein 4g · Vitamin A 300% · Vitamin C 16% · Calcium 8% · Iron 16%

CHEESE POTATO CRISPS (page 123)
Nutrition Facts: Serving size 1 cup (120 grams) · Calories 170 · Fat cal 40 · **% Daily Value** Total fat 6% (4g) · Sat fat 14% (2.5g) · Cholest 2% (5mg) · Sodium 28% (660mg) · Total carb 9% (28g) · Fiber 8% (2g) · Sugars 5g · Protein 5g · Vitamin A 8% · Vitamin C 40% · Calcium 10% · Iron 20%

POTATO-ONION CASSEROLE (page 124)
Nutrition Facts: Serving size ¹/2 cup (209 grams) · Calories 160 · Fat cal 50 · **% Daily Value** Total fat 9% (6g) · Sat fat 6% (1g) · Cholest 0% (0mg) · Sodium 23% (560mg) · Total carb 7% (21g) · Fiber 8% (2g) · Sugars 5g · Protein 5g · Vitamin A 10% · Vitamin C 8% · Calcium 8% · Iron 10%

STUFFED POTATOES (page 126)
Nutrition Facts: Serving size 1 stuffed potato shell (190 grams) · Calories 245 · Fat cal 45 · **% Daily Value** Total fat 8% (5g) · Sat fat 12% (2g) · Cholest 4% (13mg) · Sodium 28% (678mg) · Total carb 13% (39g) · Fiber 14% (4g) · Sugars 3g · Protein 11g · Vitamin A 3% · Vitamin C 33% · Calcium 11% · Iron 17%

SAVORY BRAN-RICE PILAF (page 127)
Nutrition Facts: Serving size ¹/2 cup (76 grams) · Calories 130 · Fat cal 35 · **% Daily Value** Total fat 6% (4g) · Sat fat 4% (1g) · Cholest 0% (0mg) · Sodium 12% (290mg) · Total carb 8% (23g) · Fiber 19% (5g) · Sugars 3g · Protein 3g · Vitamin A 10% · Vitamin C 15% · Calcium 6% · Iron 25%

GRITS CASSEROLE (page 128)
Nutrition Facts: Serving size 1 cup (292 grams) · Calories 550 · Fat cal 310 · **% Daily Value** Total fat 54% (35g) · Sat fat 73% (15g) · Cholest 49% (145mg) · Sodium 71% (1710mg) · Total carb 11% (33g) · Fiber 0% (0g) · Sugars 3g · Protein 26g · Vitamin A 15% · Vitamin C 8% · Calcium 25% · Iron 25%

PARMESAN NOODLES (page 129)
Nutrition Facts: Serving size 1 cup (72 grams) · Calories 190 · Fat cal 90 · **% Daily Value** Total fat 16% (10g) · Sat fat 21% (4g) · Cholest 10% (30mg) · Sodium 16% (390mg) · Total carb 6% (17g) · Fiber 3% (1g) · Sugars 1g · Protein 9g · Vitamin A 10% · Vitamin C 8% · Calcium 20% · Iron 15%

SHRIMP STUFFING (page 130)
Nutrition Facts: Serving size ¹/2 cup (158 grams) · Calories 200 · Fat cal 65 · **% Daily Value** Total fat 11% (7g) · Sat fat 8% (2g) · Cholest 7% (20mg) · Sodium 44% (1070mg) · Total carb 7% (20g) · Fiber 4% (1g) · Sugars 2g · Protein 15g · Vitamin A 20% · Vitamin C 45% · Calcium 20% · Iron 6%

RICE KRISPIES TREATS (page 132)
Nutrition Facts: Serving size 2 squares (40 grams) · Calories 150 · Fat cal 25 · **% Daily Value** Total fat 5% (3g) · Sat fat 3% (0.5g) · Cholest 0% (0g) · Sodium 8% (200mg) · Total carb 10% (30g) · Fiber 0% (0g) · Sugars 20g · Protein 1g · Vitamin A 8% · Vitamin C 10% · Calcium 0% · Iron 4%

CHOCOLATE WAFER STACK-UPS (page 134)

Nutrition Facts: Serving size 1 cookie (21 grams) · Calories 90 · Fat cal 45 · **% Daily Value** Total fat 7% (5g) · Sat fat 6% (1g) · Cholest 2% (5mg) · Sodium 4% (90mg) · Total carb 4% (11g) · Fiber 2% (1g) · Sugars 6g · Protein 2g · Vitamin A 4% · Vitamin C 2% · Calcium 0% · Iron 2%

CHOCOLATE SCOTCHEROOS (page 135)

Nutrition Facts: Serving size 2 bars (53 grams) · Calories 230 · Fat cal 80 · **% Daily Value** Total fat 15% (9g) · Sat fat 21% (4g) · Cholest 0% (0mg) · Sodium 6% (140mg) · Total carb 12% (35g) · Fiber 5% (1g) · Sugars 24g · Protein 3g · Vitamin A 4% · Vitamin C 6% · Calcium 0% · Iron 4%

RICE KRISPIES COOKIES (page 136)

Nutrition Facts: Serving size 1 cookie (18 grams) · Calories 70 · Fat cal 30 · **% Daily Value** Total fat 5% (3.5g) · Sat fat 10% (2g) · Cholest 6% (15mg) · Sodium 4% (90mg) · Total carb 3% (10g) · Fiber 0% (0g) · Sugars 5g · Protein 1g · Vitamin A 2% · Vitamin C 0% · Calcium 2% · Iron 2%

GINGER DISKS (page 138)

Nutrition Facts: Serving size 2 cookies (37 grams) · Calories 130 · Fat cal 20 · **% Daily Value** Total fat 3% (2g) · Sat fat 0% (0g) · Cholest 0% (0mg) · Sodium 5% (115mg) · Total carb 8% (25g) · Fiber 3% (1g) · Sugars 12g · Protein 2g · Vitamin A 4% · Vitamin C 2% · Calcium 0% · Iron 6%

CREAM CHEESE COOKIES (page 139)

Nutrition Facts: Serving size 2 cookies (46 grams) · Calories 170 · Fat cal 50 · **% Daily Value** Total fat 9% (6g) · Sat fat 10% (2g) · Cholest 2% (5mg) · Sodium 8% (190mg) · Total carb 9% (27g) · Fiber 0% (0g) · Sugars 17g · Protein 2g · Vitamin A 6% · Vitamin C 4% · Calcium 6% · Iron 4%

JUMBO **KELLOGG'S CORN FLAKES** COOKIES (page 140)

Nutrition Facts: Serving size 1 cookie (69 grams) · Calories 310 · Fat cal 140 · **% Daily Value** Total fat 23% (15g) · Sat fat 20% (4g) · Cholest 9% (25mg) · Sodium 14% (340mg) · Total carb 13% (39g) · Fiber 4% (1g) · Sugars 14g · Protein 4g · Vitamin A 45% · Vitamin C 10% · Calcium 4% · Iron 20%

ALMOND MACAROONS (page 142)

Nutrition Facts: Serving size 2 cookies (23 grams) · Calories 90 · Fat cal 35 · **% Daily Value** Total fat 6% (4g) · Sat fat 0% (0g) · Cholest 0% (0g) · Sodium 2% (40mg) · Total carb 4% (13g) · Fiber 4% (1g) · Sugars 9g · Protein 2g · Vitamin A 2% · Vitamin C 2% · Calcium 2% · Iron 6%

CHERRY DOT COOKIES (page 143)

Nutrition Facts: Serving size 2 cookies (44 grams) · Calories 160 · Fat cal 60 · **% Daily Value** Total fat 11% (7g) · Sat fat 6% (1g) · Cholest 4% (10mg) · Sodium 6% (130mg) · Total carb 8% (22g) · Fiber 4% (1g) · Sugars 12g · Protein 2g · Vitamin A 8% · Vitamin C 4% · Calcium 0% · Iron 8%

FROSTED LEMON BARS (page 144)

Nutrition Facts: Serving size 1 bar (28 grams) · Calories 120 · Fat cal 50 · **% Daily Value** Total fat 8% (5g) · Sat fat 12% (2.5g) · Cholest 6% (15g) · Sodium 6% (155mg) · Total carb 6% (17g) · Fiber 0% (0g) · Sugars 12g · Protein 2g · Vitamin A 2% · Vitamin C 2% · Calcium 2% · Iron 6%

WHOLE WHEAT APPLE BARS (page 146)

Nutrition Facts: Serving size 1 bar (32 grams) · Calories 90 · Fat cal 15 · **% Daily Value** Total fat 2% (1.5g) · Sat fat 0% (0g) · Cholest 3% (10mg) · Sodium 5% (110mg) · Total carb 7% (20g) · Fiber 4% · Sugars 11g · Protein 1g · Vitamin A 2% · Vitamin C 6% · Calcium 2% · Iron 10%

HOLIDAY WREATHS (page 147)

Nutrition Facts: Serving size 1 small wreath (38 grams) · Calories 160 · Fat cal 50 · **% Daily Value** Total fat 9% (6g) · Sat fat 6% (1g) · Cholest 2% (5mg) · Sodium 8% (190mg) · Total carb 9% (26g) · Fiber 0% (0g) · Sugars 17g · Protein 1g · Vitamin A 35% · Vitamin C 10% · Calcium 0% · Iron 15%

RASPBERRY STREUSEL BARS (page 148)

Nutrition Facts: Serving size 1 serving · Calories 90 · Fat cal 20 · **% Daily Value** Total fat 3% (2g) · Sat fat 0% (0g) · Cholest 0% (0mg) · Sodium 4% (100mg) · Total carb 6% (19g) · Fiber 6% (1g) · Sugars 10g · Protein 1g · Vitamin A 2% · Vitamin C 2% · Calcium 2% · Iron 4%

BROWNIES (page 149)

Nutrition Facts: Serving size 1 brownie (40 grams) · Calories 160 · Fat cal 60 · **% Daily Value** Total fat 11% (7g) · Sat fat 6% (1g) · Cholest 9% (25mg) · Sodium 3% (65mg) · Total carb 8% (23g) · Fiber 4% (1g) · Sugars 17g · Protein 2g · Vitamin A 2% · Vitamin C 2% · Calcium 0% · Iron 4%

ALL-BRAN ICEBOX COOKIES (page 150)

Nutrition Facts: Serving size 2 cookies (34 grams) · Calories 130 · Fat cal 45 · **% Daily Value** Total fat 8% (5g) · Sat fat 5% (1g) · Cholest 3% (10mg) · Sodium 2% (55mg) · Total carb 7% (21g) · Fiber 5% (1g) · Sugars 14g · Protein 2g · Vitamin A 4% · Vitamin C 2% · Calcium 2% · Iron 4%

KELLOGG'S CRACKLIN' OAT BRAN RAISIN SPICE COOKIES (page 152)

Nutrition Facts: Serving size 2 cookies (42 grams) · Calories 160 · Fat cal 50 · **% Daily Value** Total fat 9% (6g) · Sat fat 7% (1.5g) · Cholest 8% (25mg) · Sodium 9% (220mg) · Total carb 8% (24g) · Fiber 6% (1g) · Sugars 12g · Protein 3g · Vitamin A 8% · Vitamin C 4% · Calcium 2% · Iron 6%

LEMON CRUNCH COOKIES (page 153)

Nutrition Facts: Serving size 1 cookie (20 grams) · Calories 70 · Fat cal 20 · **% Daily Value** Total fat 4% (2.5g) · Sat fat 3% (0.5g) · Cholest 2% (5mg) · Sodium 4% (90mg) · Total carb 4% (12g) · Fiber 0% (0g) · Sugars 6g · Protein 1g · Vitamin A 4% · Vitamin C 2% · Calcium 0% · Iron 4%

PEANUT BUTTER COOKIES (page 154)

Nutrition Facts: Serving size 2 cookies (45 grams) · Calories 180 · Fat cal 65 · **% Daily Value** Total fat 10% (7g) · Sat fat 6% (1.5g) · Cholest 0% (0mg) · Sodium 9% (220mg) · Total carb 9% (27g) · Fiber 6% (2g) · Sugars 15g · Protein 4g · Vitamin A 8% · Vitamin C 4% · Calcium 2% · Iron 10%

MERINGUES (page 155)

Nutrition Facts: Serving size 3 meringues (22 grams) · Calories 70 · Fat cal 0 · **% Daily Value** Total fat 0% (0g) · Sat fat 0% (0g) · Cholest 0% (0mg) · Sodium 1% (35mg) · Total carb 6% (17g) · Fiber 0% (0g) · Sugars 14g · Protein 1g · Vitamin A 4% · Vitamin C 6% · Calcium 0% · Iron 2%

FIESTA COOKIES (page 155)

Nutrition Facts: Serving size 2 cookies (23 grams) · Calories 110 · Fat cal 50 · **% Daily Value** Total fat 9% (6g) · Sat fat 6% (1g) · Cholest 0% (0mg) · Sodium 4% (100mg) · Total carb 4% (12g) · Fiber 0% (0g) · Sugars 5g · Protein 1g · Vitamin A 8% · Vitamin C 2% · Calcium 0% · Iron 4%

CIRCUS COOKIES (page 157)

Nutrition Facts: Serving size 2 cookies (49 grams) · Calories 150 · Fat cal 55 · **% Daily Value** Total fat 9% (6g) · Sat fat 4% (1g) · Cholest 6% (18mg) · Sodium 4% (108mg) · Total carb 8% (24g) · Fiber 3% (0.5g) · Sugars 13g · Protein 2g · Vitamin A 20% · Vitamin C 8% · Calcium 0% · Iron 6%

WALNUT DROP COOKIES (page 158)

Nutrition Facts: Serving size 2 cookies (32 grams) · Calories 140 · Fat cal 70 · **% Daily Value** Total fat 12% (8g) · Sat fat 6% (1.5g) · Cholest 2% (5mg) · Sodium 7% (180mg) · Total carb 6% (17g) · Fiber 0% (0g) · Sugars 11g · Protein 2g · Vitamin A 6% · Vitamin C 6% · Calcium 0% · Iron 10%

TONY THE TIGER COOKIES (page 159)

Nutrition Facts: Serving size 1 cookie (16 grams) · Calories 70 · Fat cal 40 · **% Daily Value** Total fat 7% (4.5g) · Sat fat 7% (1.5g) · Cholest 2% (5mg) · Sodium 4% (95mg) · Total carb 3% (8g) · Fiber 0% (0g) · Sugars 3g · Protein 1g · Vitamin A 4% · Vitamin C 2% · Calcium 0% · Iron 4%

SOUR CREAM CRUNCHIES (page 160)

Nutrition Facts: Serving size 2 cookies (33 grams) · Calories 120 · Fat cal 35 · **% Daily Value** Total fat 6% (4g) · Sat fat 6% (1.5g) · Cholest 4% (10mg) · Sodium 4% (100mg) · Total carb 7% (20g) · Fiber 0% (0g) · Sugars 10g · Protein 1g · Vitamin A 6% · Vitamin C 4% · Calcium 0% · Iron 8%

LEMON CAKE (page 161)

Nutrition Facts: Serving size 1/16 cake with glaze (74 grams) · Calories 217 · Fat cal 71 · **% Daily Value** Total fat 12% (8g) · Sat fat 4% (1g) · Cholest 9% (27mg) · Sodium 11% (265mg) · Total carb 11% (34g) · Fiber 1% (0.32g) · Sugars 21g · Protein 3g · Vitamin A 1% · Vitamin C 5% · Calcium 6% · Iron 9%

FAVORITE CHOCOLATE CAKE (page 162)

Nutrition Facts: Serving size 1/15 cake · Calories 450 · Fat cal 240 · **% Daily Value** Total fat 42% (27g) · Sat fat 22% (4.5g) · Cholest 4% (15mg) · Sodium 26% (620mg) · Total carb 17% (51g) · Fiber 4% (1g) · Sugars 32g · Protein 4g · Vitamin A 10% · Vitamin C 4% · Calcium 2% · Iron 15%

APPLESAUCE CAKE (page 164)

Nutrition Facts: Serving size 1/15 cake (80 grams) · Calories 270 · Fat cal 110 · **% Daily Value** Total fat 19% (13g) · Sat fat 12% (2.5g) · Cholest 9% (30mg) · Sodium 5% (115mg) · Total carb 13% (38g) · Fiber 10% (3g) · Sugars 24g · Protein 5g · Vitamin A 2% · Vitamin C 4% · Calcium 2% · Iron 10%

COFFEE COCONUT CAKE (page 165)

Nutrition Facts: Serving size 1/12 cake (60 grams) · Calories 170 · Fat cal 60 · **% Daily Value** Total fat 9% (6g) · Sat fat 8% (1.5g) · Cholest 0% (0mg) · Sodium 6% (150mg) · Total carb 9% (28g) · Fiber 6% (1g) · Sugars 15g · Protein 2g · Vitamin A 2% · Vitamin C 2% · Calcium 2% · Iron 6%

RAISIN PUMPKIN CAKE (page 166)

Nutrition Facts: Serving size 1/16 cake (104 grams) · Calories 250 · Fat cal 70 · **% Daily Value** Total fat 13% (8g) · Sat fat 10% (2g) · Cholest 16% (45mg) · Sodium 15% (350mg) · Total carb 15% (44g) · Fiber 19% (5g) · Sugars 17g · Protein 5g · Vitamin A 150% · Vitamin C 10% · Calcium 10% · Iron 15%

MANGO-PANGO CHEESECAKE (page 167)

Nutrition Facts: Serving size 1/8 cake (118g) · Calories 320 · Fat cal 140 · **% Daily Value** Total fat 24% (15g) · Sat fat 35% (7g) · Cholest 17% (50mg) · Sodium 12% (300mg) · Total carb 12% (36g) · Fiber 3% (1g) · Sugars 22g · Protein 7g · Vitamin A 30% · Vitamin C 15% · Calcium 6% · Iron 6%

SWEET CHOCOLATE CAKE (page 168)

Nutrition Facts: Serving size 1 slice (233 grams) · Calories 810 · Fat cal 380 · **% Daily Value** Total fat 66% (43g) · Sat fat 58% (12g) · Cholest 50% (150mg) · Sodium 27% (650mg) · Total carb 33% (100g) · Fiber 22% (6g) · Sugars 76g · Protein 11g · Vitamin A 35% · Vitamin C 6% · Calcium 15% · Iron 20%

GOLDEN CARROT CAKE (page 170)

Nutrition Facts: Serving size 1/12 cake (94 grams) · Calories 250 · Fat cal 70 · **% Daily Value** Total fat 11% (7g) · Sat fat 4% (0.5g) · Cholest 12% (35mg) · Sodium 10% (250mg) · Total carb 15% (46g) · Fiber 9% (2g) · Sugars 33g · Protein 3g · Vitamin A 80% · Vitamin C 6% · Calcium 4% · Iron 10%

RED BERRY ANGEL FOOD CAKE (page 172)

Nutrition Facts: Serving size 1/12 cake (149 grams) · Calories 333 · Fat cal 135 · **% Daily Value** Total fat 23% (15g) · Sat fat 46% (9g) · Cholest 18% (54mg) · Sodium 7% (179mg) · Total carb 15% (44g) · Fiber 4% (1g) · Sugars 29g · Protein 7g · Vitamin A 20% · Vitamin C 36% · Calcium 4% · Iron 17%

KELLOGG'S CORN FLAKES PIE CRUST (page 174)
Nutrition Facts: Serving size 1/8 pie crust (27 grams) · Calories 110 · Fat cal 25 · **% Daily Value** Total fat 4% (3g) · Sat fat 3% (0.5g) · Cholest 1% (5mg) · Sodium 8% (200mg) · Total carb 7% (20g) · Fiber 0% (0g) · Sugars 8g · Protein 1g · Vitamin A 40% · Vitamin C 15% · Calcium 0% · Iron 25%

EASY BRAN PIE CRUST (page 175)
Nutrition Facts: Serving size 1/8 pie crust (39 grams) · Calories 173 · Fat cal 105 · **% Daily Value** Total fat 18% (12g) · Sat fat 29% (6g) · Cholest 10% (30mg) · Sodium 4% (97 mg) · Total carb 5% (16g) · Fiber 9% (2g) · Sugars 1g · Protein 3g · Vitamin A 13% · Vitamin C 2% · Calcium 3% · Iron 9%

FRUIT PIZZA (page 176)
Nutrition Facts: Serving size 1/12 pizza (111 grams) · Calories 250 · Fat cal 100 · **% Daily Value** Total fat 17% (8g) · Sat fat 30% (8g) · Cholest 10% (30 mg) · Sodium 12% (300 mg) · Total carb 11% (34g) · Fiber 5% (1g) · Sugars 24g · Protein 5g · Vitamin A 40% · Vitamin C 25% · Calcium 4% · Iron 15%

RUSTIC RHUBARB TART WITH VANILLA ALMOND CRUST (page 178)
Nutrition Facts: Serving size 1/8 tart (237 grams) · Calories 610 · Fat cal 300 · **% Daily Value** Total fat 51% (33g) · Sat fat 91% (18g) · Cholest 34% (101mg) · Sodium 15% (351mg) · Total carb 23% (70g) · Fiber 15% (4g) · Sugars 38g · Protein 10g · Vitamin A 29% · Vitamin C 54% · Calcium 15% · Iron 63%

CREAMY PINEAPPLE PIE WITH BLUEBERRY SAUCE (page 181)
Nutrition Facts: Serving size 1/8 pie (147 grams) · Calories 370 · Fat cal 190 · **% Daily Value** Total fat 32% (21g) · Sat fat 40% (8g) · Cholest 10% (30mg) · Sodium 9% (210mg) · Total carb 14% (43g) · Fiber 13% (3g) · Sugars 28g · Protein 4g · Vitamin A 15% · Vitamin C 15% · Calcium 2% · Iron 6%

COCOA KRISPIES FROZEN PEANUT BUTTER PIE (page 182)
Nutrition Facts: Serving size 1/8 pie (119 grams) · Calories 470 · Fat cal 270 · **% Daily Value** Total fat 47% (30g) · Sat fat 71% (14g) · Cholest 4% (10mg) · Sodium 10% (250mg) · Total carb 13% (40g) · Fiber 11% (3g) · Sugars 31g · Protein 13g · Vitamin A 10% · Vitamin C 8% · Calcium 2% · Iron 10%

OATMEAL RAISIN COOKIE PIE (page 183)
Nutrition Facts: Serving size 1/8 pie (124 grams) · Calories 430 · Fat cal 110 · **% Daily Value** Total fat 19% (12g) · Sat fat 13% (2.5g) · Cholest 32% (95mg) · Sodium 14% (340mg) · Total carb 26% (77g) · Fiber 8% (2g) · Sugars 51g · Protein 5g · Vitamin A 6% · Vitamin C 0% · Calcium 4% · Iron 8%

BUTTERY APPLE TART (page 184)
Nutrition Facts: Serving size 1/8 tart (148 grams) · Calories 350 · Fat cal 130 · **% Daily Value** Total fat 22% (14g) · Sat fat 15% (370mg) · Cholest 0% (0mg) · Sodium 15% (370mg) · Total carb 19% (56g) · Fiber 8% (2g) · Sugars 35g · Protein 3g · Vitamin A 15% · Vitamin C 10% · Calcium 2% · Iron 8%

BRAN-APPLE CRISP (page 185)
Nutrition Facts: Serving size 1/8 crisp (118 grams) · Calories 200 · Fat cal 60 · **% Daily Value** Total fat 10% (6g) · Sat fat 6% (1g) · Cholest 0% (0mg) · Sodium 6% (140mg) · Total carb 12% (37g) · Fiber 23% (6g) · Sugars 25g · Protein 2g · Vitamin A 10% · Vitamin C 15% · Calcium 4% · Iron 10%

PEACH CRISP (page 187)
Nutrition Facts: Serving size 1/2 cup (221 grams) · Calories 510 · Fat cal 230 · **% Daily Value** Total fat 40% (26g) · Sat fat 28% (6g) · Cholest 36% (105mg) · Sodium 20% (480 mg) · Total carb 22% (67g) · Fiber 8% (2g) · Sugars 48g · Protein 6g · Vitamin A 70% · Vitamin C 20% · Calcium 4% · Iron 30%

PEAR DUMPLINGS (page 188)
Nutrition Facts: Serving size 1 dumpling · Calories 470 · Fat cal 160 · **% Daily Value** Total fat 27% (17g) · Sat fat 15% (3g) · Cholest 0% (0mg) · Sodium 39% (930mg) · Total carb 26% (78g) · Fiber 26% (6g) · Sugars 46g · Protein 6g · Vitamin A 20% · Vitamin C 15% · Calcium 20% · Iron 15%

KELLOGG'S SUMMER STRAWBERRY DELIGHT (page 189)
Nutrition Facts: Serving size 1/16 of recipe (148 grams) · Calories 234 · Fat cal 109 · **% Daily Value** Total fat 19% (12g) · Sat fat 33% (7g) · Cholest 11% (33mg) · Sodium 2% (39mg) · Total carb 10% (30g) · Fiber 11% (3g) · Sugars 21g · Protein 3g · Vitamin A 13% · Vitamin C 88% · Calcium 4% · Iron 8%

BAKED PANCAKE WITH APPLES (page 191)
Nutrition Facts: Serving size 1/6 pancake + 1/3 cup fruit (155 grams) · Calories 240 · Fat cal 55 · **% Daily Value** Total fat 9% (6g) · Sat fat 5% (1g) · Cholest 0% (0g) · Sodium 5% (125mg) · Total carb 14% (43g) · Fiber 11% (2g) · Sugars 27g · Protein 4g · Vitamin A 10% · Vitamin C 12% · Calcium 8% · Iron 6%

ALL-AMERICAN PARTY PUDDING (page 192)
Nutrition Facts: Serving size about 1/2 cup (172 grams) · Calories 320 · Fat cal 80 · **% Daily Value** Total fat 14% (9g) · Sat fat 16% (3.5g) · Cholest 39% (115mg) · Sodium 13% (300mg) · Total carb 18% (55g) · Fiber 15% (4g) · Sugars 34g · Protein 10g · Vitamin A 8% · Vitamin C 2% · Calcium 10% · Iron 60%

PENNSYLVANIA FALL HARVEST (page 193)
Nutrition Facts: Serving size 1/3 cup (163 grams) · Calories 410 · Fat cal 160 · **% Daily Value** Total fat 28% (18g) · Sat fat 30% (6g) · Cholest 1% (20mg) · Sodium 1% (240mg) · Total carb 20% (60g) · Fiber 12% (3g) · Sugars 30g · Protein 3g · Vitamin A 35% · Vitamin C 20% · Calcium 4% · Iron 10%

FRUIT SHORTCAKES (page 195)
Nutrition Facts: Serving size 1 shortcake wedge (269 grams) · Calories 411 · Fat cal 155 · **% Daily Value** Total fat 26% (17g) · Sat fat 21% (4g) · Cholest 0% (1.2mg) · Sodium 19% (460mg) · Total carb 20% (60g) · Fiber 21% (5g) · Sugars 27g · Protein 6g · Vitamin A 6% · Vitamin C 185% · Calcium 12% · Iron 35%

KAREN'S SUNDAE CUPS (page 196)
Nutrition Facts: Serving size 1 filled cup sundae (118 grams) · Calories 365 · Fat cal 208 · **% Daily Value** Total fat 36% (23g) · Sat fat 47% (9g) · Cholest 11% (33mg) · Sodium 7% (173mg) · Total carb 12% (37g) · Fiber 10% (2.5g) · Sugars 22g · Protein 8g · Vitamin A 12% · Vitamin C 5% · Calcium 7% · Iron 6%

CARAMEL NUT BITES (page 197)
Nutrition Facts: Serving size 2 bites (44 grams) · Calories 190 · Fat cal 90 · **% Daily Value** Total fat 15% (10g) · Sat fat 18% (4g) · Cholest 0% (0mg) · Sodium 8% (190mg) · Total carb 8% (25g) · Fiber 4% (1g) · Sugars 17g · Protein 2g · Vitamin A 25% · Vitamin C 8% · Calcium 4% · Iron 15%

CHOCOLATE PECAN CLUSTERS (page 198)
Nutrition Facts: Serving size 2 clusters (28 grams) · Calories 150 · Fat cal 100 · **% Daily Value** Total fat 17% (11g) · Sat fat 19% (4g) · Cholest 1% (5mg) · Sodium 2% (45mg) · Total carb 5% (15g) · Fiber 5% (1g) · Sugars 10g · Protein 2g · Vitamin A 2% · Vitamin C 2% · Calcium 4% · Iron 4%

HONEY SMACKS BRITTLE (page 199)
Nutrition Facts: Serving size 1 piece brittle (40 grams) · Calories 160 · Fat cal 40 · **% Daily Value** Total fat 6% (4g) · Sat fat 6% (1g) · Cholest 1% (5mg) · Sodium 2% (45mg) · Total carb 10% (30g) · Fiber 4% (1g) · Sugars 24g · Protein 3g · Vitamin A 8% · Vitamin C 10% · Calcium 2% · Iron 8%

TIGER PAWS (page 200)
Nutrition Facts: Serving size 1 candy (19 grams) · Calories 75 · Fat cal 26 · **% Daily Value** Total fat 4% (3g) · Sat fat 9% (2g) · Cholest 1% (2g) · Sodium 1% (35mg) · Total carb 4% (12g) · Fiber 2% (0.6g) · Sugars 7g · Protein 1g · Vitamin A 0% · Vitamin C 1% · Calcium 2% · Iron 2%

FRUITY SNOWBALLS (page 201)
Nutrition Facts: Serving size 1 ball · Calories 150 · Fat cal 5 · **% Daily Value** Total fat 1% (0.5g) · Sat fat 0% (0g) · Cholest 0% (0mg) · Sodium 1% (35mg) · Total carb 13% (39g) · Fiber 12% (3g) · Sugars 17g · Protein 2g · Vitamin A 8% · Vitamin C 8% · Calcium 4% · Iron 8%

CRISPIX MIX SWEET MINGLERS (page 202)
Nutrition Facts: Serving size 1/2 cup (36g) · Calories 170 · Fat cal 70 · **% Daily Value** Total fat 12% (8g) · Sat fat 14% (2.5g) · Cholest 0% (0mg) · Sodium 5% (110mg) · Total carb 8% (24g) · Fiber 7% (2g) · Sugars 13g · Protein 3g · Vitamin A 6% · Vitamin C 10% · Calcium 0% · Iron 8%

POLLY-POPS (page 203)
Nutrition Facts: Serving size 1 polly-pop (24 grams) · Calories 100 · Fat cal 30 · **% Daily Value** Total fat 5% (3g) · Sat fat 6% (1g) · Cholest 0% (0mg) · Sodium 2% (45 mg) · Total carb 6% (17g) · Fiber 0% (0g) · Sugars 11g · Protein 2g · Vitamin A 2% · Vitamin C 4% · Calcium 0% · Iron 2%

MILK CHOCOLATE **RICE KRISPIES** CRUNCHIES (page 204)
Nutrition Facts: Serving size 1 candy (5 grams) · Calories 24 · Fat cal 11 · **% Daily Value** Total fat 2% (1g) · Sat fat 4% (0.7g) · Cholest 0% (0.9mg) · Sodium 0% (11mg) · Total carb 1% (4g) · Fiber 0% (0g) · Sugars 2g · Protein 0.4g · Vitamin A 1% · Vitamin C 0% · Calcium 0% · Iron 0%

CINNAMON COFFEE CAKE (page 206)
Nutrition Facts: Serving size 1/8 cake (99 grams) · Calories 320 · Fat cal 110 · **% Daily Value** Total fat 20% (13g) · Sat fat 13% (2.5g) · Cholest 18% (55mg) · Sodium 16% (390mg) · Total carb 15% (46g) · Fiber 4% (1g) · Sugars 27g · Protein 5g · Vitamin A 15% · Vitamin C 4% · Calcium 4% · Iron 15%

BLUEBERRY KUCHEN (page 207)
Nutrition Facts: Serving size 1/12 cake (108 grams) · Calories 300 · Fat cal 80 · **% Daily Value** Total fat 14% (9g) · Sat fat 8% (1.5g) · Cholest 3% (10mg) · Sodium 17% (410mg) · Total carb 18% (53g) · Fiber 9% (2g) · Sugars 40g · Protein 3g · Vitamin A 35% · Vitamin C 10% · Calcium 10% · Iron 25%

PLUM-MARMALADE COFFEE CAKE (page 208)
Nutrition Facts: Serving size 1/8 cake · Calories 330 · Fat cal 60 · **% Daily Value** Total fat 11% (7g) · Sat fat 6% (1.5g) · Cholest 9% (25mg) · Sodium 16% (390mg) · Total carb 23% (68g) · Fiber 16% (4g) · Sugars 50g · Protein 5g · Vitamin A 15% · Vitamin C 10% · Calcium 10% · Iron 10%

ORANGE JUICE COFFEE CAKE (page 209)
Nutrition Facts: Serving size 1/9 cake (70 grams) · Calories 250 · Fat cal 80 · **% Daily Value** Total fat 14% (9g) · Sat fat 25% (5g) · Cholest 15% (45mg) · Sodium 5% (130mg) · Total carb 14% (40g) · Fiber 4% (1g) · Sugars 20g · Protein 4g · Vitamin A 16% · Vitamin C 12% · Calcium 2% · Iron 32%

ALMOND TEA RING (page 210)
Nutrition Facts: Serving size 1/9 ring (101 grams) · Calories 329 · Fat cal 92 · **% Daily Value** Total fat 16% (10g) · Sat fat 16% (3.2g) · Cholest 12% (36mg) · Sodium 8% (195mg) · Total carb 18% (53g) · Fiber 11% (3g) · Sugars 20g · Protein 7g · Vitamin A 7% · Vitamin C 2% · Calcium 4% · Iron 15%

CORN FLAKE–BANANA BREAD (page 212)
Nutrition Facts: Serving size 1/16 loaf (67 grams) · Calories 200 · Fat cal 70 · **% Daily Value** Total fat 12% (8g) · Sat fat 7% (1.5g) · Cholest 9% (25mg) · Sodium 10% (240mg) · Total carb 10% (30g) · Fiber 5% (1g) · Sugars 14g · Protein 4g · Vitamin A 8% · Vitamin C 8% · Calcium 0% · Iron 15%

ANADAMA BREAD (page 214)
Nutrition Facts: Serving size 1/15 loaf (30 grams) · Calories 110 · Fat cal 30 · **% Daily Value** Total fat 5% (3.5g) · Sat fat 4% (1g) · Cholest 2% (5mg) · Sodium 12% (280mg) · Total carb 6% (18g) · Fiber 2% (1g) · Sugars 4g · Protein 2g · Vitamin A 0% · Vitamin C 2% · Calcium 2% · Iron 10%

LEMON POPPY SEED BREAD (page 216)
Nutrition Facts: Serving size ¹/₁₆ loaf (60 grams) · Calories 160 · Fat cal 30 · **% Daily Value** Total fat 5% (3g) · Sat fat 0% (0g) · Cholest 0% (0mg) · Sodium 8% (190mg) · Total carb 10% (30g) · Fiber 3% (1g) · Sugars 14g · Protein 3g · Vitamin A 4% · Vitamin C 10% · Calcium 4% · Iron 15%

GRANDMA'S MOLASSES BROWN BREAD (page 217)
Nutrition Facts: Serving size ¹/₁₄ loaf (35 grams) · Calories 100 · Fat cal 20 · **% Daily Value** Total fat 3% (2g) · Sat fat 0% (0g) · Cholest 0% (0mg) · Sodium 8% (200mg) · Total carb 7% (20g) · Fiber 15% (3g) · Sugars 10g · Protein 2.5g · Vitamin A 10% · Vitamin C 6% · Calcium 4% · Iron 12%

ALL-BRAN CORN BREAD WITH BACON (page 218)
Nutrition Facts: Serving size ¹/₁₂ bread (69g) · Calories 180 · Fat cal 80 · **% Daily Value** Total fat 13% (9g) · Sat fat 18% (3.5g) · Cholest 11% (35mg) · Sodium 12% (300mg) · Total carb 7% (21g) · Fiber 7% (2g) · Sugars 4g · Protein 6g · Vitamin A 4% · Vitamin C 10% · Calcium 4% · Iron 8%

HEARTY BRAN ROLLS (page 220)
Nutrition Facts: Serving size 1 roll (52g) · Calories 100 · Fat cal 15 · **% Daily Value** Total fat 3% (2g) · Sat fat 0% (0g) · Cholest 0% (0mg) · Sodium 12% (290mg) · Total carb 6% (18g) · Fiber 11% (3g) · Sugars 3g · Protein 4g · Vitamin A 4% · Vitamin C 4% · Calcium 4% · Iron 8%

BRAN PITA BREAD (page 221)
Nutrition Facts: Serving size 1 bread · Calories 150 · Fat cal 45 · **% Daily Value** Total fat 8% (5g) · Sat fat 0% (0g) · Cholest 0% (0mg) · Sodium 7% (170mg) · Total carb 8% (25g) · Fiber 17% (4g) · Sugars 2g · Protein 4g · Vitamin A 4% · Vitamin C 6% · Calcium 4% · Iron 15%

BRAN ENGLISH MUFFINS (page 222)
Nutrition Facts: Serving size 1 muffin (54 grams) · Calories 140 · Fat cal 25 · **% Daily Value** Total fat 4% (3g) · Sat fat 4% (1g) · Cholest 1% (5mg) · Sodium 11% (260mg) · Total carb 8% (24g) · Fiber 8% (2g) · Sugars 2g · Protein 4g · Vitamin A 4% · Vitamin C 4% · Calcium 4% · Iron 10%

BRAN-CHERRY BREAD (page 224)
Nutrition Facts: Serving size ¹/₁₆ loaf (68 grams) · Calories 220 · Fat cal 70 · **% Daily Value** Total fat 12% (8g) · Sat fat 5% (1g) · Cholest 5% (15mg) · Sodium 11% (270mg) · Total carb 11% (33g) · Fiber 7% (2g) · Sugars 12g · Protein 10g · Vitamin A 8% · Vitamin C 6% · Calcium 8% · Iron 8%

PEANUT BUTTER BREAD (page 225)
Nutrition Facts: Serving size ¹/₁₅ loaf (60 grams) · Calories 160 · Fat cal 50 · **% Daily Value** Total fat 8% (5g) · Sat fat 7% (1.5g) · Cholest 6% (15mg) · Sodium 9% (220mg) · Total carb 8% (24g) · Fiber 8% (2g) · Sugars 11g · Protein 5g · Vitamin A 2% · Vitamin C 0% · Calcium 4% · Iron 8%

DOUBLE APPLE BREAD (page 226)
Nutrition Facts: Serving size ¹/₁₅ loaf (50 grams) · Calories 140 · Fat cal 40 · **% Daily Value** Total fat 7% (4.5g) · Sat fat 5% (1g) · Cholest 10% (30mg) · Sodium 8% (180mg) · Total carb 7% (21g) · Fiber 3% (1g) · Sugars 10g · Protein 3g · Vitamin A 8% · Vitamin C 4% · Calcium 2% · Iron 8%

SPOON-ONS: SWEET AND SAVORY (page 228)
Nutrition Facts: Serving size 1 tablespoon Sweet (4 grams) · Calories 15 · Fat cal 0 · **% Daily Value** Total fat 0% (0g) · Sat fat 0% (0g) · Cholest 0% (0mg) · Sodium 1% (30mg) · Total carb 1% (3g) · Fiber 8% (2g) · Sugars 1g · Protein 1g · Vitamin A 8% · Vitamin C 4% · Calcium 0% · Iron 0%

Nutrition Facts: Serving size 1 tablespoon Savory (7 grams) · Calories 15 · Fat cal 0 · **% Daily Value** Total fat 0% (0g) · Sat fat 0% (0g) · Cholest 0% (0mg) · Sodium 3% (70mg) · Total carb 1% (3g) · Fiber 8% (2g) · Sugars 1g · Protein 1g · Vitamin A 2% · Vitamin C 8% · Calcium 0% · Iron 6%

SALAD CROUTONS (page 229)
Nutrition Facts: Serving size 2 tablespoons (6 grams) · Calories 25 · Fat cal 10 · **% Daily Value** Total fat 2% (1g) · Sat fat 0% (0g) · Cholest 0% (0mg) · Sodium 4% (85mg) · Total carb 1% (3g) · Fiber 0% (0g) · Sugars 0g · Protein 0g · Vitamin A 4% · Vitamin C 4% · Calcium 0% · Iron 6%

CRUNCHY ICE CREAM TOPPING (page 230)
Nutrition Facts: Serving size 2 tablespoons (17 grams) · Calories 80 · Fat cal 35 · **% Daily Value** Total fat 6% (3.5g) · Sat fat 3% (0.5g) · Cholest 0% (0mg) · Sodium 3% (65mg) · Total carb 3% (10g) · Fiber 2% (1g) · Sugars 6g · Protein 1g · Vitamin A 4% · Vitamin C 6% · Calcium 2% · Iron 6%

STUFFING USING **KELLOGG'S** STUFFING MIX (page 230)
Nutrition Facts: Serving size 1 cup (100 grams) · Calories 230 · Fat cal 130 · **% Daily Value** Total fat 23% (15g) · Sat fat 12% (2.5g) · Cholest 0% (0mg) · Sodium 27% (660mg) · Total carb 7% (21g) · Fiber 0% (0g) · Sugars 1g · Protein 5g · Vitamin A 15% · Vitamin C 2% · Calcium 4% · Iron 8%

TURKEY SAUSAGE STUFFING (page 232)
Nutrition Facts: Serving size 1 cup (169 grams) · Calories 220 · Fat cal 60 · **% Daily Value** Total fat 10% (7g) · Sat fat 11% (2g) · Cholest 10% (30mg) · Sodium 47% (1130mg) · Total carb 10% (29g) · Fiber 8% (2g) · Sugars 4g · Protein 12g · Vitamin A 40% · Vitamin C 35% · Calcium 4% · Iron 20%

ACKNOWLEDGMENTS

Thanks to Kellogg Company; everyone at Bulfinch Press—Betty Wong, Denise LaCongo, Jill Cohen, Karen Murgolo, and Jennifer Panicali; book designers Joel Avirom, Jason Snyder, and Meghan Day Healey for their amazing work; photographer Ben Fink; and food stylist Roscoe Betsill.

Many special thanks go to the wonderful restaurants and chefs who contributed their recipes: '21' Club, David Burke, John Doherty, Andrew Dornenburg, Charlie Palmer, Jean-Georges Vongerichten, and Kate Zuckerman.

CREDITS

Photographs by Ben Fink appear on pages ii–iii, vi, xv, 5, 9, 11, 23, 26, 31, 34, 45, 50, 55, 58, 65, 66, 84, 89, 93, 98, 101, 103, 108, 112, 115, 119, 125, 133, 137, 148, 156, 170, 177, 179, 186, 192, 194, 198, 213, 219.

All other images and photographs appear under license and with permission of the Kellogg North American Co.

The following trademarks and characters are used with permission of the Kellogg Company:
ALL-BRAN® BRAN BUDS®, APPLE JACKS®, BETTER'N EGGS®, CHEEZ-IT®, COCOA KRISPIES®, COMPLETE® Oat Bran Flake Cereal, COMPLETE® Wheat Bran Flakes, KELLOGG'S® Corn Flake Crumbs, CORN POPS®, CRACKLIN' OAT BRAN®, CRISPIX®, CRUNCHY BLENDS™ JUST RIGHT® Fruit & Nut, CRUNCHY BLENDS™ Low Fat Granola, DIG 'EM®, EGGO®, FROOT LOOPS®, KASHI®, KATY THE KANGAROO™, KEEBLER® Foods, KEEBLER® READY CRUST®, KELLOGG KITCHENS™, KELLOGG'S® MINI-WHEATS®, KELLOGG'S® ALL-BRAN®, KELLOGG'S CORN FLAKES®, KELLOGG'S FROSTED FLAKES®, KELLOGG'S® HONEY SMACKS®, KELLOGG'S® Stuffing Mix, MORNINGSTAR FARMS® GRILLERS® Burger Style Veggie RECIPE CRUMBLES®, MORNINGSTAR FARMS® Mini Corn Dogs, MORNINGSTAR FARMS® Sausage Style RECIPE CRUMBLES®, MORNINGSTAR FARMS® SCRAMBLERS®, MORNINGSTAR FARMS® Veggie Breakfast Sausage Patties, MUESLIX®, NEWT THE GNU™, NUTRI-GRAIN®, PRODUCT 19®, KELLOGG'S RAISIN BRAN®, RICE KRISPIES®, RICE KRISPIES TREATS®, SNAP!™ CRACKLE!™ POP!™, SPECIAL K®, SPECIAL K® Red Berries, SPECIAL K® Vanilla Almond, SMACKS®, SWEETHEART OF THE CORN™, TIGER POWER™, TONY THE TIGER™, TOUCAN SAM®, ZEK THE ZEBRA™

INDEX (Page references in *italic* refer to captions and illustrations.)

KELLOGG is the world's number one producer of cereal and a leading producer of convenience foods. KELLOGG'S products are manufactured in seventeen countries and marketed in more than 180 countries around the world.

Judith Choate is a writer, chef, and pioneer in the promotion of American food. She has written and coauthored more than twenty cookbooks, including *The Great American Pie Book, The Art of Aureole, Great American Food,* and *Homemade.* She lives in New York City.